Alcoholism/Chemical Dependency and the College Student

Alcoholism/Chemical Dependency and the College Student

Timothy M. Rivinus
Editor

The Haworth Press
New York • London

Alcoholism/Chemical Dependency and the College Student has also been published as *Journal of College Student Psychotherapy*, Volume 2, Numbers 3/4 1988.

The Haworth Press, Inc., 12 West 32 Street, New York, NY 10001
EUROSPAN/Haworth, 3 Henrietta Street, London WC2E 8LU England

Cover design by Mary Madeira. Art by Marshall Andrews.

LIBRARY OF CONGRESS
Library of Congress Cataloging-in-Publication Data

Alcoholism/chemical dependency and the college student / Timothy M. Rivinus, editor.
p. cm.
Published also as v. 2, no. 3/4 of the Journal of college student psychotherapy.
Includes bibliographies and index.
ISBN 0-86656-734-8. ISBN 0-86656-812-3 (pbk.)
1. College students – United States – Alcohol use. 2. College students – United States – Drug use. 3. Alcoholism – Treatment – United States. 4. Drug Abuse – Treatment – United States. 5. Alcoholism Counseling – United States. 6. Drug abuse counseling – United States. I. Rivinus, Timothy M.
HV5135.A42 1988
362.2'9'088375 – dc19 88-9443
CIP

Alcoholism/Chemical Dependency and the College Student

CONTENTS

ABOUT THE EDITOR

Timothy M. Rivinus, MD, is a trained and certified physician in the specialties of pediatrics, general psychiatry and neurology, and child psychiatry. During his nearly 10 years in the field of chemical dependency, he has served as director of a chemical dependency treatment program for veterans and their families and has treated college students with problems of chemical dependency.

Dr. Rivinus is currently Assistant Professor of Psychiatry and Human Behavior at Brown University, Coordinator of Chemical Dependency Treatment Services at Bradley Hospital in East Providence, Rhode Island, and consultant to a halfway house for young women with chemical abuse problems. He has published in the areas of chemical dependency and college students, eating disorders, post-traumatic stress disorder, and psychopharmacology.

Preface

Alcohol and other substance abuse in college and university students is easily one of the most difficult and important problems for psychotherapists and counselors. Seldom do substance abusing students present themselves directly for help with their substance abuse. More often, the abuse itself and myriad associated problems are denied. As a result, many of the students who most need help for themselves and whose problems cause great distress to others are never seen except by disciplinary authorities.

This special thematic issue of the *Journal of College Student Psychotherapy* and the hardcover book edition represent ways that the counselor, psychotherapist, dean, professor and parent as well as student can grasp the nature of these problems and be of significant help. The chapter authors are forthright and clear in their descriptions, explanations and suggestions. They observe that these problems actually grow rather than diminish during what is supposed to be the prime period of growth into adulthood, the college years. That is, these problems tend to grow considerably unless we – all of us concerned with college life actively do something about them. Left alone, substance abuse problems proliferate during college and on into adult life when they then affect the next generation. At present, colleges and universities actually advance the "drugging of America."

Psychiatrist Timothy Rivinus and the other professionals and students who have written this book have all demonstrated that they can be of help and that they are not mere passive observers of the "drug scene" that so often leads to despair rather than effective action. Counselors and psychotherapists, already familiar with the helpful methods of empathy, support and interpretation, will be enabled to combine these skills with caring forms of confrontation which must be developed to help the substance abuser and all those who collude with substance abuse. As Guest Editor for this *Journal* issue, Dr. Rivinus has assembled an outstanding group of contributors who take us a long way on the road to solving rather than denying and avoiding one of our society's great dilemmas.

Leighton C. Whitaker, PhD
Editor

Foreword

Ernest L. Boyer

All human communities have their dark side, and college communities are no exception. As the papers in this issue of the *Journal of College Student Psychotherapy* remind us, the same environments that foster personal growth, learning, and commitment to others, may also intensify the dangers of drug and alcohol abuse. College environments encourage curiosity and collegiality. Yet, while a young person's eagerness to try new things is essential to growth and learning, it is also a source of vulnerability. And, while a young person's desire to form close ties can lead to lasting friendships, it can also lead to substance use and abuse.

Alcohol, especially, has long had a place in campus life. From faculty sherry hours to fraternity parties, alcohol is publicly accepted and publicly consumed. For young people on campus, the risks are large. We recently visited a university where we were told that drinking is probably the most popular "unofficial student activity." A dean estimated that between 6 and 10 percent of the undergraduates at this prestigious southern campus were alcoholics in need of serious help; another 30 to 40 percent were serious weekend abusers of alcohol. Nationwide, over 75 percent of college students drink. Marijuana and hallucinogens may be used less widely now than in the 1960s, but with their decline, cocaine's popularity rose.

While the pleasures students derive from drinking and drugs are public, the pain has been privately suffered in lost days, lost selves and, tragically, lost lives. Colleges long have been reluctant to take responsibility for these casualties of campus life. As one chaplain

---

Ernest L. Boyer is President of the Carnegie Foundation for the Advancement of Teaching.

told us, alcohol abuse among undergraduates often has been simply "hushed up." Today, however, there is a growing acceptance of the idea that something constructive can and should be done. On campuses around the country, urgent discussions are taking place on how to lessen the dangers and on what to do about students with alcohol and drug related problems.

College counselors are playing a vital role in these discussions. As the essays collected here will show, important questions are being raised about diagnosis; about methods of treatment; and about the design of prevention programs. Easy answers will not be found. But understanding that the whole community is implicated in the issue of alcohol and drug abuse is an essential fact that counselors are helping administrators, faculty, and students to see. Some of the most innovative programs involve many campus groups working together to educate the community about substance use and abuse, and to provide help to those in need.

Making the campus a safer and healthier environment should be a top priority for colleges today. Yet it is crucially important to keep the broader issue of community in sight. A feeling of anomie is not unusual among college students today, especially in the critical first year when attitudes towards college life are formed. Many areas of renewal and reform are relevant. For example, orientation programs could do much better at helping new students feel they are joining a community with a history, a structure, traditions and ideals. Academic advising could more effectively involve faculty with students. Coherent curricula could help students make connections between the different departments and fields of academic life. And, by fostering a sense of social responsibility, service programs could diminish students' suspicions that college life is not life in the "real world."

In our report, *College – The Undergraduate Experience in America* (Harper & Row, 1987), we wrote that "the challenge, in the building of community, is to extend the resources for learning on the campus and to see academic and nonacademic life as interlocked." As long as alcohol and drugs are used and abused in the larger society, they will remain a problem for young people. Professional college student counselors are uniquely situated to help the larger college community understand the depth of the problem on campus, and to envision the breadth of appropriate response.

Acknowledgements

As Guest Editor for this issue of the *Journal of College Student Psychotherapy* and the hardcover book edition, I wish to thank all of the chapter authors and those other colleagues as well who helped me to prepare this work and to gain understanding of substance abuse. Having had no formal education in the substance abuse field I learned from talking with many professionals and students. In particular, I wish to note, with gratitude, the staff of the ADTP, Northampton (Massachusetts) Veterans Administration Hospital, George Vaillant, MD and Steven Dashef, MD, Susan Raesner, MSW, and Robert May, PhD. My attempt to convince Dr. May of the importance of this project resulted in his helping give early direction to it.

I thank Marguerite Chadwick, MSW, and Marge Corvese for editorial suggestions and help with the transcript, and Leighton Whitaker, PhD for overall sponsorship and assistance as Editor of the *Journal*. May our interest and work in the substance abuse field go on to help solve one of the most important problems of our day.

Timothy M. Rivinus, MD
Guest Editor

Introduction

Timothy M. Rivinus

I'm a sonofagun for beer,
I like my whiskey clear,
And if I had a son, sir,
I'll Tell you what he'd do,
He'd yell, "To Hell
With Harvard!"
Like his Daddy used to do.

—A College Drinking Song

Though times have changed—drugs are stronger and their availability easier—I would consider myself to be prototypical of a college student and university graduate student. In the '50s and '60s I had my brush with alcohol and drug abuse in college and in medical school. I suspect that many others, perhaps readers of this book, like me have and will.

I was a callow youth. I'd never used drugs in high school. Yet when I reached college, a wide variety of alcoholic possibilities were made available to me. They were used freely and widely by my peers. Some of those peers have gone on to develop full-blown substance use disorder, alcoholism, in later life. I feel it is in many ways just a matter of chance and luck that I did not follow a similar course.

In college I was bewildered, depressed, and overwhelmed by the number of choices available to me. I chose friends who appeared to be successful: successful both in making it through the system and in having fun at the same time. Having fun, in those days, as well as these days, was to attend functions in which a large amount and wide variety of alcoholic beverages were available. Many of my friends became intoxicated on these beverages. Mostly, I chose not to drink to intoxicate (I didn't like how it felt) but found myself being affected by alcohol, nevertheless. I found myself forced to choose between the academic life and the social life. My motivation deteriorated. My grades deteriorated. I left college to join the army.

When I returned to college, I no longer associated with peers who drank. I worked and did not drink, even in "moderation." I experienced greater success academically in these years than I ever had while trying to "socialize" in the accepted ways, which is today the ways of that peer group which I accepted as "the norm."

Later in medical school I had my personal denouement with biochemistry. A biochemistry mid-term exam was coming up. Shortly before it, I was offered my first "toke" of a marijuana cigarette. The medical school classmate who offered me this toke was, to my mind, the most interesting man in the class. He read Jean Paul Sartre. He was a connoisseur of the Beatles. As I first experienced marijuana (and loved it) he played a Beatles' song whose refrain went ". . . I'd love to turn you on . . ."

I had discovered my "drug of choice," marijuana. It beckoned me into the world of self-preoccupation and pleasure, a world of personal biochemistry in direct opposition to the biochemistry of medical school and the memory required to remember its equations. The pleasure principle, as Freud (1911) has described, was victorious over the reality principle. The next day, or maybe it was the day after that (I can't remember), I failed my mid-term biochemistry examination.

It was either me, my medical school career, and the mastery of biochemistry or it was "pot," the mastery of biochemistry over me. To remember biochemistry required a clear memory incompatible with the one in which I would float out into the boundaryless, shimmering and dream-like state of perceived ecstasy that I felt at the moment of first using marijuana.

I was only to discover later, on further attempts to try marijuana at less demanding stages of my life, that marijuana could not only make me feel intense pleasure but could make me experience intense fear and depression. How lucky and grateful I am to whatever intuition I had within myself which commanded me to *stop*, to survive at medical school, and to relinquish pleasure for reality.

My parents, forbearers, teachers and mentors taught me nothing of the dangers of substance use. Substance use was "a given" in the family and culture in which I grew up. It was also a given in college and medical school, a social and accepted course of pleasure. No strings attached. In college I learned that drinking was "a thing to do." In medical school I learned from my peers that drugs could produce ecstasy and nothing else. In hospitals where I trained, alcoholics and users of substances were treated with contempt and therapeutic nihilism. That situation, gratefully, has changed in the last 20 years.

SCOPE OF THE PROBLEM

Evidence suggests that today's college student differs little from the student that I was thirty years ago. Only the number of drugs and their capability for producing dependence (not problem use, however) is greater.

One study notes that 55% of undergraduates have driven after drinking and 41% have driven knowing that they have had too much to drink. Twenty percent of that same sample have come to class after drinking and 25% have missed classes because of hangovers. Twenty-two percent of seniors feel that at one time of their relatively short lives they may have had a drinking problem. Sixty-four percent of fraternity and sorority house undergraduates drink in a moderately heavy to heavy manner. Less than 9% of freshmen feel that they may have had a drug or alcohol problem while yet 18% of seniors feel that they may have had a substance use problem, demonstrating that drug and alcohol use (and the perception that it is abusive) probably increases during college years (Bloch and Ungerleider, 1986).

The best predictor of a level of substance use is peer pressure. Students use substances "to cheer up, to forget worries, to socialize, to relieve tension" and "to combat boredom" (see also Chapter 3). This finding parallels that found by researchers who have studied the expectations about substances of students who go on to develop Substance Use Disorder (SUD) (Brown, 1985).

A recent survey of the reasons why drinking and other drug use come to the attention of college authorities lists the following as major reasons: driving while under the influence of drugs or alcohol; destruction of property; fighting; disturbance of the peace; overdoses; suicide attempts; reports of forced sex by male students upon females, and academic problems (Woodruff, 1987). One study found that over 45% of students reported being sexually active after drinking or drug use when they might not otherwise have so desired. Over 20% engaged in unprotected intercourse while under the influence of drugs (Bloch and Ungerleider, 1986).

There's a higher incidence of alcohol use on college and university campuses than in the U.S. population at large. Eighty-five percent of college students drink beverage alcohol compared with 70% of the general population. Surveys of college student populations find that heavy drinkers range between 21 and 27% of the college student population surveyed (Bloch and Ungerleider, 1986; Engs, 1977; Engs and Hanson, 1985 a & b; Gonzalez, 1981). It may be a sign of the "invulnerability" of youth that more casualties are not associated with this high rate of alcohol use. However, it still is overlooked that the highest source of mortality in the late adolescent and young adult population is alcohol and drug related motor vehicle fatalities.

The colleges and universities all over the United States are playing a larger role in guarding the lives of students. Colleges and universities substantially increased their programming for students regarding drugs and alcohol. This effort comes from a motivation both to protect students and to avoid liability. The increasing recognition of the cause of alcohol and drugs in accidental deaths, suicides and their roles in rapes and other acts of violence and vandalism in colleges and universities spurred this direct connection. James Read, Dean of Rutgers University has stated, "tragedies began taking place, and we couldn't claim anymore that students are adults and are not our responsibility. We have a moral imperative to reassert authority" (Fiske, 1987).

THE RESPONSE TO THE PROBLEM

In response to this there has been a gratifying increase in services offered by colleges and universities in the United States, related to substance use. The significant increases in these services between the years of 1979 and 1985, as recorded by Anderson and Gadaleto (1985), are outlined in Table I.

Evidence of this growth of services at colleges and universities shines through the collection of chapters of this book, especially in Chapters 3, 4, and 6 through 10.

As the chapters unfold the field is covered: the drugs themselves,

TABLE I*

Comparison of Alcohol and Drug Service Policies at Colleges and Universities 1979 to 1985*

	1979	1985
Education and Prevention Projects	69%	88%
Groups for Problem Drinkers	33%	50%
Groups for Childdren of Alcoholics	21%	53%
Substance Use Specialist at the Institution	14	48
Substance Use Task Forces and Committees	37	64
Substance Awareness Programs	13	63
Publications on SUD	52	76
Non-alcoholic Beverage Requests at Functions	54	86
Food Offered with Alcohol at Funtions	24	71
Alcohol not Advertised as Primary Focus of Functions	51	87

* Adapted from Anderson and Gadaleto, 1985.

the ethical and clinical challenges, primary prevention, secondary and tertiary care, and university policy issues.

Radcliffe and Rush are authors of the most comprehensible book on the pharmacology of abused chemicals available, *The Pharmer's Almanac* (Radcliffe et al., 1985). In their chapter, Chapter 1, they make clear the importance of the biological and toxicological basis of chemical abuse. These authors clarify this disease as one which has a progression and whose key concepts of compulsion, loss of control and continued use despite adverse consequences has its roots in the biology of pleasure production and pain reduction within the human organism. Illustrating with the drugs of abuse popular in the college population, they trace the biologic process from ingestion of the drug to the production of psychiatric and behavioral symptoms. They remind us of the powerful effects the marketplace has on the potency of drugs available and the danger of drug and adulterant effects on the human organism. Contrary to popular notions, adolescence is not a cause of the malaise that had led to a rising suicide rate in that group, particularly in males. Increasing abuse of substances in adolescents most certainly is the prime cause of this tragic trend. Biological bases of this trend are made clear here.

Dr. Robert DuPont's chapter (Chapter 2) entitled, "The Counselor's Dilemma" lays out a challenge to counselors. He is a psychiatrist and physician who is at the forefront of both the substance abuse field and the movement of positive health and lifestyle promotion. The challenge, as he describes it, is not for the counselor alone. The dilemma, and the challenge, are for the counselors, college and university deans, administrators, and all concerned for the university.

Dr. DuPont describes the process of individual and group "denial" and "enabling." These phenomena are rooted both in biology and in the structure of our society and are major blocks in our ability to confront the problems of substance abuse (Tarter et al., 1984). He shows how denial and enabling can permeate a counseling service and college community. If his chapter is read, there should be no excuse for lack of cognitive understanding of this process. And yet, its social and emotional roots are deep.

DuPont discusses the legal liabilities and responsibilities of substance use disorder, and notes also the often necessary use of urine testing. Specifically, he advocates psychotherapy for the substance abuser; but only after he/she is drug free. He touches on and makes important points about confidentiality of family involvement in the treatment of the substance abusing student.

The chapter by John Brooklyn and Harry Duran (Chapter 3) is a response to the invitation of a dialogue with students about substance abuse on campuses. It provides a critique, from the students' point of view, of substance abuse education both during undergraduate years and during the graduate experience of medical school. They describe how deeply ingrained drinking and other drugging patterns are at a university. They also describe the painful facts of the university's role as a potential "enabler" in this process. They voice the wish on the part of many students for guidelines and limits to help them when it comes to violation of the rights of others related to substance use. They also provide a critique of "quickie" solutions to the drug and alcohol experience on campus. Brooklyn and Duran call for the institution of adequate role models within the university; they ask that the self-help movements (AA, NA and Alanon) be even more closely embraced on campus as a part of a learning experience. Their major contribution is in describing *the problem* of using substances to deal with developmental issues and in their providing a summary of "educative" suggestions which would make alternatives both more attractive and growth promoting for students.

Gerardo Gonzalez' chapter (Chapter 4) speaks for itself when he says "alcohol and drug education is . . . something . . . colleges cannot afford to be without." Dr. Gonzalez, the founder of the BACCHUS (Boost Alcohol Consciousness Concerning the Health of the University Students), is a national figure who has a specific appointment at a university for the teaching of alcohol and drug education. He has long and broad experience. Dr. Gonzalez has taken his experience one step further by writing an academic review of prevention programs. The field is now old enough to deserve such a review. He rightly points out that not only does alcohol and drug education include prevention efforts but "discontinuation" efforts. He gives attention to future directions in alcohol and drug education services. He suggests long-term programs built into the university structure with extensive peer involvement and research.

The present author (Chapter 5) covers the topic of diagnosis when the question of substance use disorder is involved. Numerous diagnoses can disguise substance use disorder or coexist with substance use disorder. Whether a masquerade or a simultaneous "dual diagnosis," little treatment progress can be expected if substance use disorder, per se, is not identified and treated. The plight of the child of the alcoholic or substance abusing parent (COA) is also identified as a diagnosis "not to be missed."

Careful scrutiny of the diagnostic criteria for substance use disorder would classify many college students as having this disorder. How many such students go on to develop dependence on substances during college or university life is an important research question. The fact that many students qualify as abusers suggests the magnitude of the problem itself. Frankel and Whitehead (1966) suggested over two decades ago that *the degree of exposure to substances of potential abuse is directly proportional to the number of individuals who will abuse and be injured by those substances; the more substances used and experimented with in colleges and universities, the higher the likelihood of abuse as a problem.*

Chapter 6, by Suchman and Broughton, presents a "state of the art" integration of a counseling service within the university community where substance abuse problems are concerned. The University of Florida offers a wide range of services for the substance user and abuser (see also Chapter 10). They understand the university as a community and attempt to set an atmosphere for students which would "raise the bottom" so that a student at every turn has an opportunity to question his or her use of substances in the mode of an educational experience. Others may wish to base an assessment or development of their services on this chapter. They give important suggestions on the assessment and clarification of students. In their framework, the student who uses substances but is not yet abusing them is just as important in terms of service as others with more serious problems. Triage and the matching of their various offerings to students' case examples provide the capstone of the chapter.

Chapter 7, by Elena Gonzales, PhD, "Integrated Treatment Approach with the Chemically Dependent Young Adult," is in many ways a centerpiece chapter of this collection. It represents a working model for the psychotherapist working with college students with SUD. Dr. Gonzales shares valuable experience with addicted students in specific case material. She integrates the cases into a framework which draws from widely varied sources including the steps of recovery developed by the self-help movements (such as AA and NA), psychoanalytic, cognitive, environmental, behavioral, and relapse-prevention models. Furthermore, she integrates this material into the developmental matrix of late adolescence and the specific problems of the college and university student. Her model makes it clear that the therapist does not work alone, but works as a part of a larger team within the university.

Dr. Gonzales makes the point that insight is always possible in the psychotherapy of the substance dependent patient. In the early stages of recovery the insight must be into the SUD itself – not into the origins of neurotic or obsessive-compulsive behavior in early childhood. Psychodynamic insight only becomes possible at later stages of treatment once mastery of chemical abuse has been achieved and the patient is "sober and clean."

She gives an excellent example of the danger of a premature diagnosis which omits SUD by labeling a patient "borderline." Dr. Gonzales makes references to the special problems encountered by women who abuse substances, and demonstrates how a referral to a drug and alcohol rehabilitation program may be integrated into the course of therapy with a student.

Chapter 8 by William White and David Mee-Lee introduces us to the student with a serious substance use disorder. They offer us an introduction to the tools for his/her effective identification and introduce us to a time-proven method of intervention, namely treatment in a specialized substance abuse program. They describe the components of an inpatient program, demystifying such programs for those counselors, students and their families who may know little about such programs and their formulas for success. By introducing us to the RAATE (a severity and prognostic rating scale), they give us the means for assessing a student's needs for inpatient intervention which implies temporary separation from the college community. They correctly point out that the number of students seriously involved with substance abuse and requiring hospitalization is unknown. Yet, most of us have encountered such students in our work or heard them spoken of by college administrators and deans. They are the students who take a sudden turn in their life course, change friends, run into financial difficulties, have repeated accidents, legal or medical problems, or public intoxication. Separation and total intervention are needed to emphasize to the student and his/her family the problem of substance abuse as a serious disorder, diagnosis, or disease. After treatment, White and Mee-Lee offer guidelines by which the student may be either reintegrated into college life with an ongoing treatment program or be urged to interrupt college plans for a time to pursue continued intensive outpatient rehabilitation.

Any impediment to necessary referral to a rehabilitation unit or to a substance abuse specialist may signal the problem of *denial*. A therapist's denial is the countertransference malady that impedes substance abuse diagnosis. It springs from a lack of knowledge and a breakdown, at some level, in boundaries between a therapist and patient. Referral for more intensive treatment implies the relative helplessness of the therapist. Yet substance use disorder represents a similar loss of control for the patient, one which is readily denied by the patient, family and peers. To make a referral to an inpatient service implies use of a power and authority which is unfamiliar to many therapists. Yet such a recommendation, especially in the face of life-threatening problems, is the life-blood of good therapy.

All of the chapters highlight that accurate empathy and understanding of the substance abuse is the key to identifying the substance use disorder. The earlier this diagnosis is made, the stronger the therapeutic alliance. The longer it is deferred for both patient and therapist, the greater the possibility for loss of trust.

David Landers and Linda Hollingdale present us with pioneering group work in Chapter 9. The rapidly growing movement of Children of Alcoholics has probably done more to help people and raise the level of consciousness of this problem than many schools of therapy combined. Landers and Hollingdale apply their knowledge to students who volunteer to join groups for Children of Alcoholics at a college. Basing their work on the distinguished work of Claudia Black and Sharon Wegscheider-Cruse and others, they offer their program to show how such groups can be run; they include innovative developments from the self-help movements such as specific group exercises and psychodrama.

College after all is a group experience in its major aspects. Major choices and affiliations are made during college, and yet, many students, such as children of alcoholics or other groups who have had similarly painful family experiences, bring basic anxiety and depression to college. If all colleges and universities offered these groups of college students course credit for their work on their emotional problems, a significant impact on mental health could be made. Landers and Hollingdale point out that their college *nurtures their idea* by public recognition of the problem. It is the objective of this collection of Chapters to urge other colleges and universities to do the same.

In "Alcohol and Other Drug Issues at Brown University: Two Administrative Perspectives on a Common Problem," (Chapter 10), Deans Bruce Donovan and Toby Simon cover the evolution of 10 years of policy change at a major university in regard to chemical use and abuse. Their presentation is a tribute to dialectical and evolutionary change. Vigorous prohibitions, which characterize certain approaches toward the problem of psychoactive substances, are not present here. Yet, Deans Donovan and Simon's presentation is punctuated with bold developments. The appointment of a dean of chemical dependency at a major university is one. The choice of a recovering person to fill the appointment is another. Our experience is that credibility in this field is buttressed by those "who have been there." Its symbolism within a university may be misinterpreted but cannot be misunderstood.

Deans Donovan and Simon offer many suggestions and programs for students, faculty and administrators. They seem, always, to arrive at a collaborative effort between administration and students. A dramatic step in their approach was to form a weekly senior administration meeting to review alcohol and drug related incidents within the university. This provided an internal monitoring system which goes far beyond any "snapshot" of the problem or its incidence at any one place and time. It makes the problem of chemical use "our problem" as opposed to "their problem."

SPECIAL PROBLEMS

Counselor as Enabler

This introduction is directed both to those who have had experience with substance use disordered patients in their practice and those who have not. Counseling becomes harmful, whether one is well or poorly informed, when the counselor becomes an "enabler." The cardinal rule of SUD counseling is "never allow continued experimentation or use of a drug in the face of deleterious effects." To do so would be, first, to deny the basic diagnostic criteria for drug abuse, namely continued experimentation or use of the drug in the face of deleterious effects. Second, and by proxy, it includes the counselor as part of the problem since the counselor tacitly permits experimentation of a drug in the face of deleterious effects (DSM III-R, p. 169). Once counseling begins, drug or alcohol use ceases to be "somebody else's problem." It becomes the shared problem of both the student and the counselor.

The Student Who Appears to Refuse Help

A difficult question for colleges and counseling services is, "What about the student who refuses to go to an educational or counseling program?" Some of the answer to this question comes from the student him/herself since the student must have some willingness for help to be received. However, the larger role of the university, including its policies, atmosphere and interaction between administrators and substance abuse educators and counseling service, cannot be overlooked. If a student, for example, apprehended for vandalism while under the influence of a substance, is allowed to "choose," he or she often will not accept help. However, if there is a policy and a triage continuum which offers a student a number of alternatives including education, a prolonged set of counseling meetings and placement on a probationary status within the college or university, that student can often be helped. The chapters by Donovan and Simon, Suchman and Broughton,

Elena Gonzales and Gerardo Gonzalez suggest ways in which this can be done. The literature shows substance users referred by courts to counseling programs have equal success rates when compared to those who are not "legally referred" or "compelled" to enter rehabilitation (Friedman et al., 1986).

An open and informed atmosphere within the college or university and a receptive atmosphere in the counseling office are essential first ingredients for success. Of equal importance is an attitude of firmness, both on the part of administration and within counseling. There is considerable controversy, both philosophically and within clinical circles, about the need for confrontation and limit-setting in therapy (Hellman, 1981; Gordon and Beresin, 1983; Smith et al., 1984). Yet, clinical experience shows that where a substance use problem or substance use disorder is in question, there is little doubt that confrontation and limit-setting within the context of therapy are absolutely necessary. Administrators and deans as well as counselors may learn from this clinical experience; little clinical progress is possible in the area of substance use disorder where there is no firm clinical contract.

The contract with a student with substance use disorder begins something like this: "I'm very concerned about your problem with the abuse of (the substance or substances of abuse); I personally think that there's a good chance that you're having the problems you've described as a result of (the substance or substances). You'll need special help to stop. Treatment is available. It works. And here's how it works. . . ."

The troubled student may refuse the diagnosis and assert that the counselor or professional who has identified this as a problem is simply launching a moralistic attack on the substance user's values and pattern of living. Denial is often sine qua non evidence that the substance use disorder is a major problem.

The student is allowed to refuse acceptance of the diagnosis and the treatment but must, nevertheless, be reminded that she/he will need to accept all administrative and academic consequences of his/her behavior. This is where firmly in-place policies are essential. If vandalism or the rights of others have been abused as a result of alcohol or drug use then there are certain administrative, educational and counseling consequences that are "fixed." If a student refuses help, then he or she will be governed by the administrative policies which govern "refusal" of help.

Within the clinical context, the therapist or counselor may say: "It seems to me as if you have a substance abuse problem. If you choose to accept help, I think the plan we outline can be of important help to you. If you refuse, it's okay to try it your own way but, of course, you have to deal with any consequences of continuing to use the drug(s) without help. If you find that 'trying it your own way' is not working, you know that you always can and should return for help before anything serious occurs again."

Whether to involve the family or peers in confrontation of a student's behavior resulting from substance abuse must be answered in terms of the seriousness of the problem. The question of family involvement is touched on in Chapter 2 by Dr. DuPont. A large body of experience with persons with substance use disorder has demonstrated that a gathering of concerned family, friends and professionals may, in some cases, be the only way "to help someone who doesn't want help" (Johnson, 1986).

The Student Who Admits Abuse in the Course of Therapy

Sandra, a 24-year-old student, had returned to college after a four year interval and had begun counseling. She had dropped out of college at the end of her freshman year because of, as she described it, "anxiety and exhaustion." She described chronic problems dating from childhood in an extremely chaotic family. She had been hospitalized after leaving college and stated she "did not remember" her diagnosis except to describe it as a "nervous breakdown." She acknowledged that she'd had a problem with "alcohol at the time." Therapy began and she began to relate her still current chaotic lifestyle and impulsive behavior to her early childhood and family disturbance.

When records of her hospitalization were obtained, a diagnoses of "borderline personality disorder and alcohol abuse" were described. She acknowledged at this point in therapy that others had described her as an alcoholic. She stated that she was no longer using alcohol. Therapy proceeded but her progress appeared to be slow.

During her 15th counseling session, she announced to her counselor, "Oh, by the way, I'm using Ecstasy. It's the most amazing drug. It really lives up to its name." At that point she attempted to shift the topic and again began to talk about the fights that her mother and her father had had shortly prior to their divorce when she was nine.

The therapist attempted to ask her more about her use of "Ecstasy," to which Sandra replied, "What's wrong with using a drug? Have you got something against drugs? I bet you use them yourself. Don't you ever take a drink? Just don't give me any more of those Gestapo cross-examinations the way they did in the hospital, please!"

Gentle pursuance over the next session was needed to review Sandra's drug use history. It was related to alcoholism in both parents and her "relapse" in which the student, after being "dry" from drugs and alcohol for a number of years, had relapsed without definitive treatment or ongoing support into temptation to use a seductively named "designer" drug, "Ecstasy." Therapy at this point included referral to a drug-free group, referral to Alcoholics Anonymous and a new and more productive period of individual therapy began.

The Student Who Abuses Prescribed Medication

Problems of polysubstance abuse, cross tolerance (substitution of *one drug of abuse with another*) and the dangers of prescribing substances of potential abuse to those who have a problem with substance abuse disorder are referred to in Chapter 4. Yet it is a problem which will be especially noted here, first, because many prescribed drugs are potential substances of abuse, especially those prescribed for anxiety, sleep disorder and pain; and second, because counselors and others overlook prescribed medicines of abuse because they consider them to be "medical" (prescribed by doctor and therefore beyond reproach or therapeutic examination).

Any prescription used for anxiety, sleep disorder or pain that is used for longer than one week is a potential substance of abuse. Many prescribing doctors are uninformed about substance use disorder and may prescribe to relieve symptoms but without considering the consequences. Many abusers of substances seek doctors who willingly prescribe. They may change doctors so that they may obtain more prescriptions (Hollister, 1981; Straw, 1983).

The following are some guidelines that may be of use to the counselor who finds him/herself encountering a student who takes prescribed substances with abuse potential:

1. Any prescribed substance of potential abuse should be of concern to *any* therapist working with a student, whether the therapist has medical training or not;
2. Any prescribed substance that is used for more than a few days has abuse potential. There are exceptions which can be discussed with qualified physicians, e.g., the chronic pain of cancer or serious injury; the use of stimulants for attention deficit disorder or narcolepsy, etc.;
3. When a student receives a prescription from a source other than the therapist (or a multidisciplinary team working with the therapist), the therapist needs to gain a concrete understanding of why the medication is used. Permission from the patient may be sought to call the prescribing doctor to get a better understanding and to include that doctor and his/her prescriptions in the program of treatment;
4. If the student obtains a prescription or a substance of abuse without informing the therapist, this should be considered "acting out" in the context of therapy;
5. Any prescribing, for problems that are undergoing diagnosis and treatment by a counselor, requires a careful history taking and liaison with a prescribing psychiatrist;
6. If the prescription is a potential substance of abuse, the prescribing psychiatrist should first be well-versed in the diagnosis and treatment of substance use disorder.

CONCLUSION

It's a myth that we, as administrators and counselors, have nothing to teach students about how to live. The last 50 years taught us a great deal about what a threat psychoactive substances and their abuse may be to the human condition. Adolescents are not beyond our responsibility to influence or teach. If we neglect to teach them the lessons that we have learned, we allow them to act out our own unresolved personal and social conflicts and permit them to repeat the mistakes of our own previous generations. Isn't this the effort, the challenge of the university in our day (Boyer, 1987, p. 203)?

If this volume provides any stepping-stone, it will be to help to reverse the trend of ambivalence and confusion of administrators and college counselors regarding the area of substance use disorder. It does not mean or imply a "taking control" of students' lives. If students wish more control, they should have it, together with demonstrated responsibility. Many of the services described in these chapters have been developed with the advice and consent and creative force of the students themselves. The chapter by John Brooklyn and Harry Duran suggests that students not only have important concerns to bring to this evolution in education but also important corrective suggestions to make. The chapters by Brooklyn and Duran (Chapter 3), by Landers and Hollingdale (Chapter 9) and Donovan and Simon (Chapter 10), suggest how willingly students respond to the call for dialogue. The objective of this volume will be met if it urges the dialogue to continue in many new places.

REFERENCES

Anderson, P. S., Gadaleto, A. F. *Results of the 1979, 1982 and 1985 College Alcohol Survey*. Dept. of Residence Life, Ohio Univ., Athens, OH, 1985.

Blane, H. T. and Hewitt, L. E. *Alcohol and Youth: An Analysis of the Literature*. Report No. PB-268-698, NIAAA, Rockville, MD, 1977.

Bloch, S. A., Ungerleider, S. *The Brown University Chemical Dependency Project*. Integrated Research Services, Eugene, OR, 1986, pp. 29-65.

Boyer, E. L. *College: The Undergraduate Experience in America*. Harper & Row, NY, 1987.

Brown, S. Expectancies versus background in the prediction of college drinking patterns. *J. Consult. Clin. Psychol.*, 53: 123-130, 1985.

DSM III-R. *Diagnostic and Statistical Manual of Mental Disorders (Third Ed. Revised)*. American Psychiatric Association, Washington, DC, 1987, pp. 165-186.

Engs, R. C. Drinking patterns and drinking problems of college students. *J. Stud. Alcohol*, 39: 2144-56, 1977.

Engs, R. C. & Hanson, D. J. (a) *Drinking related problems of college students: Comparison over two years between over and under 21 year old legal drinking age*. Indiana Univ., Bloomington, IN 1985.

Engs, R. C. & Hanson, J. D. (b) The drinking patterns and problems of college students: 1983. *J. Alcohol and Drug Ed.*, 31: 65-83, 1985.

Fiske, E. B. Colleges Playing Large Role in Guiding Lives of Students. *NY Times*, Sunday, Feb. 22, 1987, pp. 1 & 28.

Frankel, G., Whitehead, P. *Drinking and Damage: Theoretical Advances and Implications for Prevention*. Rutgers Centre for Alcohol Studies, New Brunswick, NJ, 1966.

Freud, S. Formations on the two principles of mental functioning, *Standard Edition of the Work of Sigmund Freud*, Vol. XII. Hogarth Press, London, 1958 (1911), pp. 218-226.

Friedman, A. S., Utada, A., Glickman, N. W. Outcome for Court-referred drug-abusing male adolescents. *J. Nerv. Ment. Dis.*, 174: 680-688, 1986.

Gonzalez, G. M., *Alcohol Use and Level of Knowledge About Alcohol Among Students Who Visited Datona Beach, FL, During Their Spring Break, 1981*. University of Florida, Gainesville, FL, 1981.

Gordon, C., Beresin, G. Conflicting treatment models for inpatient management of the borderline patient. *Am. J. Psychiat.*, 140: 979-983, 1983.

Helman, J. M. Alcohol abuse and the borderline patient. *Psychiatry*, 44: 307-317, 1981.

Hollister, L. E. Management of the anxious patient prone to drug abuse. *J. Clin. Psychiat.*, 42: 35-39, 1981.

Johnson, V. E. *Intervention, How to Help Someone Who Doesn't Want Help*, Johnson Institute Bks., Minneapolis, MN, 1986.

Radcliffe, A., Rush, D., Sites, C. F., Cruse, J. *The Pharmer's Almanac*. M. A. C., Denver, CO, 1985.

Smith, D. E., Milkman, H. B., Sonderwirth, S. G. Addictive disease: concept and controversy. In *The Addictions: Multidisciplinary Perspective and Treatment*, Milkman, H. B., Shaffer, H. J. (Eds.), Heath, Lexington MA, 1985.

Straw, R. N., Implications of benzodiazepine prescribing. In *Benzodiazepines Divided*, Trimble, M. R. (Ed.) Wiley, NY, 1983, pp. 67-77.

Tarter, R. E., Alterman, A. I., Edwards, K. Alcoholic denial: A biopsychosocial interpretation. *J. Study on Alcohol*, 45: 214-218, 1984.

Woodruff, J. Personal Communication from Roger Williams College, Bristol, R.I., June, 1987.

Chapter 1

Physical Effects and Consequences of Mind Altering Drugs Used by College Students

Anthony B. Radcliffe
Peter A. Rush

SUMMARY. The effects of mind altering drugs are reviewed, with careful attention to use in the college aged population. Chemical dependency is a disease process. This means that it takes place over time. Use of mind altering drugs is fairly common among college students and it is the time when this disease process often begins. Loss of self-esteem, family, and jobs occur later in this disease process. In addition to observation of the effects of mind altering drugs on the body (Pharmacology) the actions of the body on the drug (Biopharmaceutics) are reviewed, with close attention to the primary substances used on college campuses in the 1980s: alcohol, cocaine, and marijuana.

BACKGROUND

Through the 1980s, Americans' attention to the national problem of mind altering drug usage has increased greatly due to heightened awareness by the media, notable celebrities seeking treatment for

---

Anthony B. Radcliffe, MD, and Peter A. Rush, PharmD, Chemical Dependency Recovery Services, Kaiser Foundation Hospital, Fontana, CA.

Send requests for reprints to: Peter A. Rush, PharmD, Kaiser Foundation Hospital, Chemical Dependency Recovery Services, 17046 Marygold Avenue, Fontana, CA 92335.

chemical dependency, and athletes dying of overdoses. Federal and state governments, as well as industry, have begun to consider initiating mandatory drug testing programs for employees. Alarm continues to grow as the extent of mind altering drug use among American adolescents and young adults is recognized.

This article will focus on the physical effects and consequences of mind altering drugs used on college campuses. The social, legal, emotional, and spiritual consequences of this drug usage, although difficult to measure, may be equally grave.

THE PROCESS OF DEPENDENCY

Dependency as described by the World Health Organization (WHO) is a "compulsion that requires periodic or continuous administration of a drug to produce pleasure or avoid discomfort." The chemically dependent person is no longer considered a "recreational" (infrequent) user. As dependency progresses to a more severe and debilitating state, it is termed addiction. Addiction is described by the WHO as, "a state of periodic or chronic intoxication, detrimental to the individual and society, produced by repeated consumption of the drug, and characterized by a compulsion to take the drug, a tendency to increase the amount consumed," and withdrawal upon cessation of drug use (Pradhan & Dutta, 1977). Once a person has become dependent on or addicted to a chemical, returning to recreational use is usually impossible. Attempts to do so from a state of abstinence (which is the only recommended treatment) may be extremely hazardous.

DISEASE CONCEPT OF DEPENDENCY

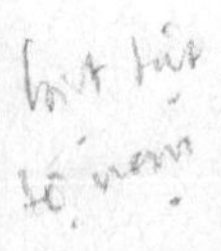

In spite of the public perception of chemical dependency as a psychological malady, more and more evidence is surfacing that chemical dependency is a disease process with not only psychological, but sociocultural and biologic components as well. A disease is defined by McCarthy (1985) as "a definite morbid process having a characteristic train of symptoms; affecting the whole body or any of its parts, and its etiology, pathology and prognosis may be known or unknown." The "morbid process" is the regular or periodic use of mind altering drugs in a habitual manner.

There are predictable symptoms of chemical dependency involving physical, social, mental, and/or financial markers. Use of mind altering drugs that lead to chemical dependency is marked by characteristics of: *denial, compulsion, loss of control*, and *continued use in spite of adverse consequences*. Washton (1985) described these markers in cocaine dependent persons. *Denial* is when the person denies the existence of their drug usage, down-plays the seriousness of adverse effects, or acts defensively in response to questions about drug use. A simple example of denial would be a student who senses he has just failed an exam who says to a fellow student, "I think I just 'aced' the biology exam, lets go celebrate." *Compulsion* is marked by persistent or episodic cravings even when drug-induced euphoria no longer occurs. Sometimes the compulsion drives the user to take other drugs in lieu of the drug of choice. There can be fears of being without the drug, and desire to use which overrides the desire to stop. *Loss of control* can be viewed as being unsuccessful in quitting for significant periods of time, inability to refuse when offered the drug, unable to limit quantity of use, and bingeing. *Continued use* transpires in spite of adverse medical, psychiatric, and social consequences.

Remembering these criteria, we can begin to try and separate persons who develop dependency from those who do not become dependent. Evidence is mounting that biochemical differences, based on genetic predisposition, exist between users who become chemically dependent and users that do not.

DEFINITION OF TERMS

Some background knowledge of certain pharmacologic concepts is important in gaining an understanding of the powerful effects of drugs on the college student who abuses or becomes dependent on them. *Pharmacology* describes the actions of a drug on the living organism (i.e., using cocaine produces a high). *Biopharmaceutics* describes the actions of the organism on the drug (i.e., the liver degrades one-half of the alcohol consumed and directed there for metabolism). How a drug affects the body is determined to a great extent on how the body processes the drug. The four main biopharmaceutical effects are: *absorption*, *distribution*, *metabolism*, and *elimination*.

Absorption describes how a drug enters the main circulation. Drugs may be absorbed from the stomach or intestine, the rectum, through the skin, from the muscle, or via the lungs. Phencyclidine (PCP) is rapidly absorbed by all routes, even skin exposure can cause intoxication. Smoking cocaine has a much more rapid onset of action than cocaine absorbed through the blood vessels of the nose.

Distribution of the drug occurs from the main circulation to various organs and tissues of the body. Most drugs are not distributed uniformly, but have greater affinity for some organs or tissues than for others. For example PCP and delta-9-tetrahydrocannabinol (THC, the active ingredient in marijuana) are both stored in fat tissue for long periods of time and may remain in body fluids long after the drugs have been used. Some tissues have barriers to distribution of a drug. The brain, for example, has a series of membranes which reduce the distribution of certain substances from the blood to the brain. This "blood brain barrier" is a membranous lining around the blood vessels in the brain which impedes most drugs from gaining access to the brain. There are also membranes which prevent certain drugs from crossing the placenta. This "placental barrier" sometimes serves as a protective barrier for the fetus.

Drug *metabolism*, a third aspect of biopharmaceutics, is the various chemical reactions involved in the transformation of a drug within the body. Usually metabolism converts drugs from an active to an inactive or less active form. Some drugs undergo extensive metabolism, producing many different "metabolites," others undergo little or no metabolism. Endogenous chemicals called enzymes are the catalysts involved in the changing of a drug molecule. The greatest concentration of enzymes exists in the liver which is the principle organ involved in drug metabolism. Enzymes are essential for the termination of drug action. Amounts and types of drug metabolizing enzymes vary from person to person, depending largely on inherited characteristics. A person who is deficient in one type of drug metabolizing enzyme may incur a greater drug effect than a person with normal enzyme levels. A person with excessive enzymes may experience less of an effect from a drug. One major role of drug metabolism is the preparation of a drug for elimination from the body.

Elimination deals with the excretion of drugs and metabolites from the body. Urine is the most common route of elimination of a drug, however drugs may also be excreted via feces, sweat, tears, and expired air. Drug elimination in the urine requires that a drug be water soluble. Some drugs have a high degree of water solubility, others must be converted by metabolic processes from fat soluble to water soluble chemicals before they can be excreted in urine. Water soluble drugs are usually excreted more rapidly than fat soluble drugs. Because drugs are usually excreted via urine, it becomes a convenient body fluid for toxicological testing (drug screens) for drugs of abuse and their metabolites. The rate of drug elimination from the body is measured in terms of biologic half-life of the drug.

The *biologic half-life* of a drug (abbreviated T½) is the length of time required to eliminate half of the drug molecules from the body. Drugs with long half-lives, such as methadone, may appear in urine long after they have been used and the physical effects have disappeared. Small quantities of drug remain available to influence effects in subsequent use or interact with other drugs. For any given drug, half-life may vary from individual to individual depending on physiologic factors, genetic factors, disease states, and extent and quantity of drug use.

Neurons are nerve cells. They are the individual units of the nervous system. In order for a drug to have an effect on the body, it must first react with the cells of the body. For many drugs, this is by means of chemical attachment to specific receptor sites on the cells. Upon binding to a cell, a drug can cause or inhibit a cellular response. Mind altering chemicals exert their actions by causing alterations in the normal function of the neurons of the brain. Drug binding to cell receptor sites is reversible, and since metabolism and elimination remove a drug from the circulation, drug effect eventually ceases. How any particular drug exerts its effects varies with many factors including a person's nutritional status, age, dose taken, other drugs in the system, amount of drug ingested, duration of drug use, effect of drugs on detoxifying organs such as liver or target organs such as the brain, and genetic influences.

CLASSIFICATION OF MIND ALTERING DRUGS

Mind altering drugs that cause dependency are classified according to the various effects they have on the central nervous system. Cocaine use can cause a high. Heroin use can cause nodding off and tiredness. The five following classifications will be used to present physical effects of commonly abused substances in this discussion: *psychomotor stimulants*, *sedative-hypnotic drugs*, *narcotic analgesics*, *cannabinoids*, and *perceptual distorters*.

Psychomotor Stimulants

One of the major trends of drug use in young adults during the 1980s has been a sharp increase in the use of potent psychomotor stimulants, particularly cocaine and the amphetamines. The psychomotor stimulants are drugs that increase electrical activity and excite the central nervous system and therefore the person. Use of two milder stimulants, nicotine and caffeine, is also common in our society, and there is growing evidence that regular use over time can lead to heart, vascular, lung, and pancreas damage.

Cocaine

Beginning in the mid-1970s, the prevalence of cocaine use in the United States began to increase dramatically. Clayton (1985) discusses several myths regarding cocaine that have contributed to this current cocaine epidemic including: (a) cocaine is not physically addicting, (b) cocaine improves a person's sex life, (c) "everybody" is using it, (d) cocaine use symbolizes success. In addition to these myths aiding the rise in cocaine use among college students, some circumstances have added fuel to the cocaine fire, including: (a) a declining cost of purchasing street cocaine, (b) the increasingly prevalent use of highly addictive cocaine freebase via smoking, (c) greater availability of cocaine.

The main active ingredient of the coca plant, cocaine, was isolated and named in 1859. Cocaine has been controlled as a dangerous drug in the U.S. since the Harrison Act of 1914 which prohibited all nonmedical use. Since that time, the predominant form of cocaine available both for medicinal and illicit use has been cocaine hydrochloride. Beginning in the early 1970s, cocaine dealers from California began to promote smoking cocaine in various forms, eventually leading to the heavy use of the form known as cocaine base. Freebase cocaine, as it is called, also carries the street names "rock," "crack," and "base." Cocaine hydrochloride (the powdered form) and cocaine freebase (the rock form) are the same drug, the only chemical difference being the inactive "hydrochloride" salt on cocaine hydrochloride. This salt causes cocaine to melt at a much higher temperature which results in destruction of a large portion of the drug when heat is applied for smoking. On the other hand, freebase cocaine has a much lower melting point, with the result that it vaporizes before the molecule is destroyed by heat and therefore can be smoked.

Biopharmaceutics of Cocaine. Cocaine hydrochloride, which dissolves in water, is the form of cocaine which is "snorted," or placed in the nose by inhaling through a straw. Cocaine hydrochloride can be absorbed from other membranes, including those in the mouth, intestines, genitals, or rectum (Gold, 1984). Because it dissolves in water, cocaine hydrochloride is also the form of cocaine which is abused by intravenous injection. One common way of injecting cocaine is by using it intravenously with heroin in a combination known as a "speedball."

Freebase cocaine is not water soluble, and therefore is not used by intravenous injection. Cocaine freebase is most often used by smoking, through a glass pipe or other paraphernalia, resulting in an onset of effects in the brain and cardiovascular system within seconds. Once cocaine enters the blood, it is distributed throughout the body, with high concentrations in the liver, kidney, heart, and brain. Cocaine (both hydrochloride and freebase) is detoxified by enzymes in the blood and the liver called "cholinesterases." Cocaine is detectable in the blood only for a relatively short period of time, since its half-life is around 1.5 hours. It is broken down and metabolites which have longer half-lives are eliminated through the urine. This is why urine and not blood is used by laboratories to analyze for the presence of cocaine. When cocaine is snorted, cocaine metabolites may be detected for a longer period of time. It is unlikely that cocaine will be detected in urine much longer than 48 to 72 hours after use, no matter how a person uses it.

Pharmacology of Cocaine. Cocaine has two unrelated modes of action. It is a local anesthetic (pain numbing) agent and a powerful central nervous system (CNS) stimulant. Cocaine is unique in this respect in that other CNS stimulants, such as amphetamine, lack local anesthetic characteristics and other local anesthetic agents, such as procaine and lidocaine, lack the ability to be CNS stimulants. Because of its activity as a local anesthetic and vasoconstrictor, which decreases bleeding, cocaine is still used in ocular and nasal surgery. Cocaine's stimulant action is attributed to its actions on a group of nerves collectively called the sympathetic nervous system (SNS).

The SNS is also commonly called the "fight or flight" nervous system. It is the system of nerves which dominates during stressful situations, preparing the body for some type of physical action. For example, when a boxer is fighting in the ring, a number of changes occur automatically which establish a fight or flight response. The body is ready to do battle.

The neurotransmitter that causes these effects in the brain is norepinephrine. When people become excited, frightened or under the influence of cocaine, more norepinephrine is released in the CNS, resulting in a more rapid heart rate, higher blood pressure, pupil dilation, sweating, and tremor. Understanding the reaction of the body under this type of stressful situation contributes to an understanding of the body's response to cocaine.

Another neurotransmitter, dopamine, also is important in the actions of cocaine. By increasing the amount of dopamine in key parts of the brain cocaine causes euphoria, decreased appetite, hyperactivity, and sexual excitement (Gold, Washton, & Dackis, 1985).

These effects of cocaine may be fairly consistent in the occasional user. However, as use becomes more frequent, norepinephrine and dopamine supplies may become depleted, resulting in hunger, depression (the "cocaine blues"), exhaustion (or "crashing"), and lack of sexual interest.

Adverse Reactions to Cocaine. Case histories of patients and studies with animals have demonstrated cocaine to be one of the most highly addicting of mind altering drugs. This means that using small amounts of cocaine can result in the need to continue using.

Cocaine dependent animals will choose to undergo painful experiences, such as electric shock, in order to obtain cocaine. The search for and use of cocaine becomes the central motivating force in one's life, replacing studying or even going to classes. Hungry animals prefer cocaine to food, and male animals prefer cocaine to a receptive female. Cocaine is a powerful reinforcing agent. When a user has access to large amounts of cocaine his/her response resembles that of laboratory animals. Cocaine-dependent humans prefer it to all other activities, and unless recovery occurs, they will continue to use the drug until supplies are depleted or the user is exhausted or dies (Cohen, 1985).

In order, the most popular ways in which cocaine is used are intranasally (snorting), by smoking (freebasing), and by injecting into the vein (slamming). Some of the medical consequences of cocaine use vary according to the route of administration. Snorting cocaine can result in runny nose, bleeding, and erosion of the nasal mucosal lining leading to septum perforation. (The septum is the cartilaginous structure separating the two nostrils.) Smoking of cocaine can cause different complications, including hoarseness, bronchitis, and in long-term use, lung damage. Intravenous drug users run risks of forming blood clots, and if needles are shared, risk infections including hepatitis and AIDS.

Cocaine use has potential for a variety of toxic effects. Most prominent of these are the effects on the heart and blood pressure. By constricting blood vessels which carry oxygen to the heart muscle, cocaine can cause chest pain (angina) or a heart attack. This effect can be especially dangerous because cocaine causes the heart rate to increase, which increases the demand for oxygen to the heart muscle. Persons with pre-existing heart disease, such as occluded arteries, are at greatest risk for angina or heart attack. The occurrence of a heart attack in a young patient without other risk factors normally seen should raise suspicions of cocaine (or other psychomotor stimulants) in any person under the age of forty in treatment for a heart attack.

Another of the potentially toxic effects of cocaine on the heart is an irregular heart beat (arrhythmia), particularly a rapid heart beat. Some of these arrhythmias may be life threatening and require prompt medical treatment. Sudden deaths in young people with normal hearts at autopsies may well be due to this phenomenon.

Toxic effects of cocaine on the central nervous system (CNS) are ordinarily only seen when very high blood levels of cocaine are achieved. The rapidity by which cocaine rises in the brain can produce seizures. The most common CNS toxic effects are high fever (hyperpyrexia) and seizures. Strokes from cocaine use have also been reported in adults, and one newborn whose mother had used several hours prior to delivery (Cregler & Mark, 1986).

Several other complications to pregnancy can occur with cocaine use, including premature delivery or spontaneous abortion, and decreased blood flow to the unborn child. There is recent data suggesting that infants whose mothers used cocaine run greater risks of physical deformities, behavioral impairment, and death shortly after delivery.

Cocaine also can cause severe psychiatric complications including paranoid psychosis and profound depression. Impairment of sexual function and periods of complete sexual disinterest can occur with chronic cocaine use.

Often to modify the overexcited feeling that cocaine creates, students use "downer" drugs, such as marijuana, alcohol, or other sedatives. This attempt to chemically balance the CNS, a downer balancing an upper, may lead to dependency on the downer as well.

One further complication of chronic cocaine use is the signs and symptoms of withdrawal. After discontinuing heavy use because of inability to obtain the drug or sheer exhaustion, moderate to severe depression occurs. This depression may last for weeks and be so profound that students commit suicide. In most cases however, cocaine withdrawal does not require treatment with medications. Students who withdraw from a more mild cocaine dependency, although rarely experiencing depression, may temporarily lose the ability to enjoy ordinary pleasure until the body is able to replace depleted dopamine supplies. They are seen as more irritable, restless and difficult to get close to.

Cocaine dependency has become a serious problem in this country, affecting all social classes and major ethnic groups. It may impair students lives in many ways: decreasing class attendance and motivation to study, breaking up friendships and causing isolation in personal relationships. Often the first sign is financial irresponsibility, students having no money left after buying cocaine, and relying on family members to unknowingly support their habit. At a time in life where one is most intellectually vital and at a threshold to make major decisions in one's life, use of cocaine should be viewed as a dangerous matter. The intense craving to use cocaine complicates treatment and makes relapse a problem even when students know that it is ruining their college lives.

Amphetamines

The amphetamines are centrally active stimulants commonly called "speed," or "uppers." The two most potent amphetamines are dextro-amphetamine (Dexedrine® or "dexies"), and methamphetamine (also known as "crank" or "crystal meth"). Many street speed samples also include over-the-counter relatives of the amphetamines, such as the decongestants phenylpropanolamine (PPA) or ephedrine, and caffeine. These drugs are more mild central stimulants – however, tolerance, dependency, and withdrawal can occur with these substances. Tolerance results in decreased effectiveness of a drug at a particular dose and a requirement to increase amount consumed or frequency of use in order to receive equal results. Commonly, drugs like PPA and caffeine are packaged in capsules or tablets that look like prescription amphetamines. These "look-a-like" drugs, as they are called, are marketed through mail-order drug houses and some diet clinics as legal stimulants. When large doses of PPA or other legal stimulants are ingested, toxic effects similar to amphetamines may occur.

Biopharmaceutics of Amphetamines. The stimulant effects of the amphetamines, although similar to cocaine in type, are much longer in duration. The half-life of amphetamines ranges from 5 to 20 hours. Amphetamines have such large ranges in half-life and duration of action because their excretion is largely dependent on acidity of urine. Amphetamines are more water soluble in an acid urine than in an alkaline urine and under acidic conditions, will be excreted more rapidly. Sometimes people take advantage of this property by taking alkaline substances, such as baking soda, to prolong the effects of amphetamine. Also sometimes urine is acidified to cause rapid excretion and to clean the body out several days prior to drug testing.

Amphetamines are mainly used in three ways: by mouth, by snorting, and by intravenous (IV) injection. A common use on college campuses of these stimulants is to stay awake to study longer. The awareness of the potential harm plus the problem of crashing (i.e., falling asleep during the actual exam) should be considered before attempting this practice. The adverse consequences to snorting and IV use are similar to those of cocaine.

Pharmacology of Amphetamines. Amphetamine causes a fight or flight response similar to cocaine except that it lasts longer. Very rapid tolerance to the effects of amphetamine occurs. This means that using a few "whites" or "mini bennies" at age 18 to get high might require 20 pills with the same amount of amphetamine two years later to get the same "high" when tolerance has occurred.

Chronic use of amphetamines in high doses can result in paranoia. As paranoia progresses, psychosis results, and the person is no longer able to differentiate between reality and delusion. The psychosis usually clears when drug use is discontinued, however, amphetamines can worsen existing psychotic tendencies, in which case permanent psychosis may occur. The loss of friends and relationships during this time is not always recoverable as distrust can lead to isolation.

Sedative-Hypnotic Drugs

The best known and most widely used of sedative hypnotic drugs (SHDs) is alcohol. Alcohol is still the most popular of all mind altering drugs used by college students. It is legal and most available. Other SHDs used on campuses are prescription tranquilizers and sleeping pills obtained either from physicians or illicitly. Anesthetic agents, such as laughing gas, which were once used on college campuses have become more of a historical curiosity. Their actions are similar to alcohol in many ways.

Alcohol

The active ingredient in alcoholic beverages is ethanol. There is less alcohol by volume in beer than in distilled liquor such as vodka or whiskey. However, a 12 ounce beer, a 4 ounce glass of wine, and a 1 ounce shot of whiskey all contain about the same total amount of alcohol by weight. The form that alcohol comes in is immaterial, the effect from ethanol is what students seek when they drink.

Most college students drink safely and sanely but alcoholism does exist among college students. Those at greatest risk are students who are raised in dysfunctional families where one or both parents are alcoholic. Repeated use of alcohol can lead to problems in relationships, school work, legal difficulties and a greater risk for serious accidents. Since the average age of first drink for boys is 11.9 years and for girls is 12.7 years (Rogers, Harris, & Jarmuskewicz, 1987) it is possible to see college aged alcoholics with drinking histories of 10 years or more of regular drinking.

Students ascribe many powers to alcohol. Students believe it can make shy people talkative, inhibited people uninhibited, and wallflowers glamorous. There is little truth to these magical thoughts. In reality, regular use (two to three times a week for a prolonged time) can cause isolation, lack of sexual interest, and depression. While alcohol remains the social lubricant on most college campuses, students need to learn when too much is enough and how to drink safely. Many deaths or accidents occur with students under the influence.

Biopharmaceutics of Alcohol. Alcohol is rapidly absorbed from an empty stomach and intestine into the blood, and distributes to all organs of the body. Absorption is slowed and therefore effects delayed when food is present, particularly fatty food. Alcohol is broken down by enzymes in the liver, first to acetaldehyde, which causes toxic effects, and eventually to water and other nontoxic byproducts which are eliminated mainly in urine. The rate at which alcohol is eliminated from the body varies from person to person. This is because of individual differences in the activity of liver enzymes which break down alcohol. Persons who drink alcohol regularly stimulate these same enzymes to become more active, which causes alcohol to be broken down more rapidly. The result is physiologic tolerance. Therefore, one has to drink more to get a given effect. Usually, people break down one-half to one ounce of pure alcohol per hour (equal to around one 12 ounce beer).

Pharmacology of Alcohol. College students who drink alcohol rarely have the serious physical effects seen in older adults who have been drinking for many years. The most significant effects on young adults are those of alcohol on the central nervous system (CNS). Ethanol is a CNS depressant, and generally slows down mental processes. In low doses of around 100mg/dl or less (100 milligrams per deciliter of blood), alcohol acts to block inhibitions, making the drinking person appear to be stimulated. The result is that the person's behavior is acted out without the usual inhibitions. They may become more talkative, combative, or aggressive. Many altercations and aggressive acts are carried out under the influence of alcohol. Also, low blood ethanol levels may cause impaired judgment. This impaired judgment may result in motor vehicle, boating, and work related accidents. With increasing blood alcohol levels of 150 to 250mg/dl, judgment becomes more impaired and slurred speech and staggering occur. Levels of around 250 to 350mg/dl produce lethargy and stupor. The lethal level in most people is around 500mg/dl. With heavy drinking, people may experience a phenomenon known as blackout. Blackouts are periods of amnesia, where a person is unable to recall recent events while under the influence, even though conscious during the experience.

One of the tragic effects of alcoholism in infants is fetal alcohol syndrome (FAS). FAS is marked by mental retardation, low birth weight, height, and head size, and characteristic structural abnormalities of the face. It is not known at what maternal blood alcohol level FAS occurs, therefore women are best advised to abstain from drinking alcoholic beverages during pregnancy (Rogers et al., 1987).

Alcohol interacts with most prescription medications and many non-prescription drugs. These interactions may impair the ability of the drug to work, or may make the drug more potent or toxic. An especially dangerous practice is that of combining alcohol with tranquilizers and sleeping pills. The result is a greatly enhanced sedative effects which may prove to be lethal. This is called synergism, the unexpected greater effect of two chemicals when taken together than should occur (i.e., 2 + 2 = 20 in a synergistic combination).

Tranquilizers and Sleeping Pills

Today the most commonly used sedative hypnotic drugs (other than alcohol) are benzodiazepines drugs, such as Valium®, Ativan®, and Xanax®. These drugs have replaced the tranquilizers and sleepers such as the barbiturates ("reds," "yellows," and "rainbows"). Students obtain benzodiazepines either from physicians by prescription or illicitly in order to cope with stress, nervousness, or insomnia. Combining drugs like Valium® with alcohol can be an especially dangerous practice and has resulted in many deaths, both accidental and intentional. Tranquilizer or sleeping pill use is combined at times with stimulant use to counteract some of the troublesome physical effects of the uppers.

One other sedative hypnotic drug that should be mentioned is methaqualone (Quaalude® or "ludes"). Quaalude® produces very rapid effects including loss of inhibitions. This may be the reason for its acquired reputation of being an aphrodisiac. Methaqualone is no longer produced legally in this country, but has become a major illegal import. In some places methaqualone has replaced marijuana as the recreational drug of choice (Kulberg, 1986).

Narcotic Analgesics

The narcotic analgesics are powerful drugs which imitate the actions of the body's own natural pain relievers, the endorphins. Endorphins are not only involved in natural relief of pain, they are suspected to play a part in pleasurable sensations associated with eating, sex, and exercise.

Narcotic analgesic drugs are obtained either illicitly or by prescription. Examples of prescription narcotic analgesics are morphine, codeine, Demerol®, and Darvon®. The best known illicit narcotic analgesic is heroin. The prescription narcotic analgesics are also sold on the street in illicit fashion. On the West Coast, a number of "synthetic" heroin substitutes have surfaced in street samples sold as heroin. Many of these were synthesized in clandestine laboratories by graduate chemists. These synthetic heroins have been called "Designer Drugs" by law enforcement and the media. The use of a synthetic Demerol® (MPTP) sold as "new heroin" has caused chronic illnesses of the nervous system similar in appearance to Parkinson's disease.

Besides causing analgesia (pain relief), the narcotics cause some drowsiness in normal doses. They are sometimes used together with stimulants in much the same way as other downer drugs to counteract some of the unpleasant effects of uppers. The most serious complication of narcotic analgesic use is respiratory depression (slowing or cessation of breathing), which may cause death. This occurs most often when high doses (overdoses) are taken or when narcotics are used together with sedative hypnotics. A complication of intravenous drug use which is seen in heroin users who share needles is contracting infectious diseases, such as AIDS, or hepatitis. The narcotic analgesics are usually not first choice drugs on college campuses, but are often used for recreation in combinations with other mind altering drugs.

Cannabinoids

The most commonly used sources of the drugs called cannabinoids are marijuana ("pot" or "weed") and hashish ("hash" or "hash oil"). Marijuana comes from the leaves and flowering parts of the plant *cannabis sativa*. There are many cannabinoid compounds in marijuana, delta-9-tetrahydrocannabinol (delta-9-THC or just THC) is the predominant form and responsible for most effects.

From 1962 through 1980 there was a striking increase in reported marijuana use by persons between the ages of 18 and 25 years from 4% to 68%. From 1980 through 1984 the number of people in the 18-25-year-old group who had tried marijuana declined to around 40% (Millman & Sbriglio, 1986). In a survey of graduating seniors in 1985, it was revealed that 5% use marijuana on a daily basis, down from 10% of the class of 1979.

The potency of marijuana has increased almost tenfold over the last 20 years. Marijuana samples in 1975 contained 1.2% active ingredients (i.e., delta-9-THC) on the average. By 1985, concentrations as high as 14% had been noted, with average concentrations of 4.1% (Schwartz, 1987).

The physical and emotional consequences of marijuana use today are different than they were 20 years ago because: the THC content of marijuana is greater now, more people are using, and users in general start at younger ages. For a long time and for debatable reasons marijuana use was not associated with dependency or addiction. This is simply not borne out by the reports of clinicians who work in this field. Though less potent than cocaine, regular use of pot can lead to dependency and in even more cases continued use of pot does not allow chemically dependent people to recover from other mind altering drugs.

Biopharmaceutics of delta-9-THC. THC is very fat soluble, and when smoked crosses rapidly from the lungs into the bloodstream. Effects begin as soon as two to three minutes after use and subside in around three to six hours (Schwartz, 1987). It is also well absorbed from the gastrointestinal tract, although use by mouth results in delayed onset of effects. Delta-9-THC is well distributed throughout the body and may be stored for long periods of time in fatty tissues such as the brain and reproductive organs. THC is completely metabolized by the liver to a number of products and excreted mainly in feces and also in urine. The half-life of THC in fat is approximately 7 to 8 days. (Millman & Sbriglio, 1986). Repeated use of marijuana at intervals of less than one week results in accumulation of delta-9-THC and its metabolites in fat. These chemicals are released gradually and unevenly into the bloodstream. Cannabinoid metabolites are detectable in urine for 2 or 3 days following single use and may be detected for four weeks to several months after cessation of use in daily users. This underscores the current reality of urine testing which finds a positive THC result when a person has not used for a month.

Effects of delta-9-THC.

(1) *Heart and Lung.* The most notable effect of smoking marijuana on the heart is an increase in heart rate. The reason for this cardiac effect is unknown and may be due to smoke. Marijuana has a broad range of effects on the lungs. It acts as an irritant on airways and with heavy use, may cause long-term dry, hacking cough, con-

gestion, and bronchitis. The long-term effect of pot smoking on the lungs is not yet known.

(2) *Reproductive System*. There are some reports that chronic regular use of THC can suppress testicular function. It can cause decreased blood levels of testosterone (male hormone) and decrease sperm count and motility. The permanence of effect of marijuana on male fertility is still inconclusive but warning should be given to developing adolescent users about the potential for impaired maturation and fertility. Heavy use of marijuana has been associated with disrupted menstrual cycle in some women, and may have an effect on female fertility. The placental barrier reduces amount of transfer of delta-9-THC into an unborn child's circulation. However, some studies have demonstrated reduced fetal growth with regular prolonged maternal exposure to marijuana, and an increased number of premature births (Tennes, Avitable, Blackard, Boyles, Hassun, Holmes, & Kreye, 1985). It is not yet clear if these effects are due to THC, or other factors such as nutrition or other drug use.

(3) *Central Nervous System Effects*. Usually, the immediate effects of marijuana are pleasant ones with altered perceptions of the senses, relaxation, and passivity. Hence its associated use to come down from a cocaine high. However, the effects of marijuana may be unpredictable at times, even in experienced users and can result in panic reactions and toxic psychosis (commonly called a "bad trip" or "bummer"). THC impairs coordination and reaction time, compromising safe operation of a motor vehicle or other machinery. Coordination and reaction time is impaired up to 12 to 24 hours following use, long after euphoric effects have dissipated. Making this effect more dangerous is the fact that users are unaware that performance is impaired. With longer term use students may develop the so called "amotivational syndrome." This condition is characterized by passivity, slothfulness, and lack of ambition. While there is conjecture over whether such a syndrome exists and is caused by use of pot, there is little question that chronic use of pot can be associated with all these characteristics. The result is inevitably poor school performance and personality deterioration. Heavy use of marijuana during adolescence may result in emotional imma-

turity and inability to utilize effective coping skills in adulthood. This lack of maturation can lead to 22-year-olds who act like 10-year-olds.

Other effects. Marijuana users often have irritated eyes and commonly use eye drops to get rid of tell-tale redness. Chronic, frequent marijuana smoking causes damage to the immune system and may result in an impaired ability to fight off infections. Tolerance to marijuana can also be demonstrated in long-term users, resulting in increasing frequency of use. Withdrawal from THC is characterized by irritability, drowsiness, and increased appetite, especially for "sweets."

Marijuana use is not as benign as previously thought. It can prevent persons dependent on other chemicals from recovering. The excuse being, "why go to an Alcoholics Anonymous, Narcotics Anonymous, or Cocaine Anonymous meeting when you can relax with a joint of marijuana." There are a variety of detrimental physical and emotional effects including dependence and withdrawal. Though college students work in laboratories, it is a new twist to consider that they might be the mice in an experiment to find out the harmful effects of a drug.

Perceptual Distorters

Phencyclidine (PCP) and lysergic acid diethylamide (LSD or "acid") have been the most notable of perceptual distorters in recent years. Although the overall effects of these two drugs differ greatly and will be discussed independently of one another, they are both used for their ability to "scramble" the senses. Users report distortions of imagery, vision with vibrant colors, and the ability to hear colors and see smells. For this reason at times people have called perceptual distorters "hallucinogens" or "psychedelic" drugs.

Phencyclidine

PCP is a veterinary anesthetic (used to make animals unconscious for surgical procedures) which is commonly called "angel dust," "animal tranquilizer," or "hog" by illicit users. The person under the influence is said to be "dusted" (from angel dust). PCP can act as a stimulant, depressant, or perceptual distorter, based on route of use and dose taken. In street form it is sold as a liquid, powder, capsule, or tablet and often placed on a tobacco cigarette (called "super cools") or a marijuana joint (called a "Sherman" or "Sherm"). Phencyclidine is most often taken by college students by smoking, but may also be used by snorting, smoking, and very rarely by intravenous injection (Brown & Braden, 1987).

Phencyclidine is a drug with some very interesting chemical properties. It is very fat soluble and can stay in fatty tissues for a very long period of time (up to months in some individuals). PCP also is attracted to acidic fluids such as the cerebral spinal fluid which bathes the brain. In the body PCP can transfer from the blood to the stomach (which is very acidic), then from the intestine (which is less acidic) back to the blood. The result is that PCP is recycled in the body and effects may reoccur or continue long after the drug has been used.

The effects of PCP are at times bizarre and unpredictable. Behavior can be extremely violent and may lead to death from trauma or accidents, including drowning. Fortunately PCP is not frequently used on college campuses.

Lysergic Acid Di-ethylamide (LSD)

LSD is an extremely potent drug. The usual dose is 60 to 300 micrograms, meaning that a one gram paper clip would contain about the same as 3300 or more doses of LSD. Like PCP, use of LSD is not as prevalent on most college campuses today as it was in the 1960s. In the rare instance when students do use it, it is taken by mouth. With LSD use there is risk of extreme paranoia, permanent personality changes, and "flashbacks." Flashbacks are reoccurrences of a previous drug experience which take place long after the substance was ingested. These flashbacks may occur at very inopportune times (such as during class!). An LSD experience is referred to as a "trip." The trip may be emotionally positive (a good trip) or negative (a bad trip). It is impossible to predict in whom or at what time a bad trip will occur, that is, previous good trips do not always predict future good trips.

CONCLUSION

College students are uniquely suited to use mind altering drugs. They are curious and eager to try new things. Many college students experiment with mind altering drugs and never use again. With more public awareness many are just saying no. Alcohol remains the most widely used and accessible drug taken by college students. Roughly only 10% or less of college students become dependent or addicted to alcohol. However many of its deleterious effects occur in students who become intoxicated and die in accidents or suicides. Cocaine is widely gaining in popularity and because of its greater potency the potential for addiction is much greater. Informal studies show that most college students who use do not become dependent or addicted. Marijuana use continues at low levels but often masks other problems such as loneliness and depression. It is fitting that we present relevant material to college students who are our future leaders. How future generations use mind altering drugs depends on the legacy of real information and experiences shared openly with them.

REFERENCES

Adams, E. H., & Kozel, N. J. (1985). Cocaine use in America: Introduction and overview. In J. K. Nicholas, & E. H. Adams, (Eds.), *Cocaine use in America: Epidemiologic and clinical perspectives* (Research Monograph No. 61, pp. 1-7). Rockville, MD: National Institute on Drug Abuse.

Ambre, J. (1985). The urinary excretion of cocaine and metabolites in humans: A kinetic analysis of published data. *Journal of Analytical Toxicology*, *9*(6), 241-245.

Brown, R. T., & Braden, N. J. (1987). Hallucinogens. *The Pediatric Clinics of North America, 34*(2), 341-347.

Clayton, R. R. (1985). Cocaine use in the United States: In a blizzard or just being snowed. In J. K. Nicholas, & E. H. Adams (Eds.), *Cocaine use in America: Epidemiologic and clinical perspectives*. (Research Monograph No. 61 pp. 8-33). Rockville, MD: National Institute on Drug Abuse.

Cohen, S. (1985). Reinforcement and rapid delivery system: Understanding adverse consequences of cocaine. In J. K. Nicholas, & E. H. Adams (Eds.), *Cocaine use in America: Epidemiologic and clinical perspectives.* (Research Monograph No. 61, pp. 151-157). Rockville, MD: National Institute on Drug Abuse.

Cregler, L. L., & Mark, H. (1986). Medical complications of cocaine abuse. *New England Journal of Medicine*, *315*(23), 1495-1500.

Furnham, A., & Lowick, V. (1984). Lay theories of the causes of alcoholism. *British Journal of Medical Psychology*, *57*, 319-332.

Gold, M. S. (1984). *800-Cocaine*. New York: Bantam Books.

Gold, M. S., Washton, A.M., & Dackis, C.A. (1985). Cocaine abuse: Neurochemistry, phenomenology, and treatment. In J. K. Nicholas, & E. H. Adams, (Eds.), *Cocaine use in America: Epidemiologic and clinical perspectives*. (Research Monograph No. 61, pp. 130-150). Rockville, MD: National Institute on Drug Abuse.

Kuhlberg, A. (1986). Substance abuse: Clinical identification and management. *Pediatric Clinics of North America, 33*(2), 325-361.

McCarthy, J. C. (1985). The concept of addictive disease. In D. E. Smith, & D. R. Wesson (Eds.), *Treating the cocaine abuser* (pp. 21-30). Center City, MN: Hazelden Foundation.

Millman, R. B., & Sbriglio, R. (1986). Patterns of use and psychopathology in chronic marijuana users. *Psychiatric Clinics of North America*, *9*(3), 533-545.

Pradhan, S. N., & Dutta, S. N. (Eds.). (1977). *Drug abuse: Clinical and basic aspects*. St. Louis: C. V. Mosby.

Rogers, P. D., Harris, J., & Jarmuskewicz, J. (1987). Alcohol and adolescence. *Pediatric Clinics of North America, 34*(2), 289-303.

Schwartz, R. H. (1987). Marijuana: An overview. *Pediatric Clinics of North America*, *34*(2), 305-317.

Siegal, R. K. (1982). History of cocaine smoking: Part 1. *Journal of Psychoactive Drugs*, *14*(4), 277-299.

Smith, H. M. (1983). Marijuana and public health. *MD,* (2), 137-152.

Tennes, K., Avitable, M. A., Blackard, C., Boyles, C., Hassun, B., Holmes, L., & Kreye, M. (1985). Marijuana: Prenatal and postnatal exposure in the human. In Pinkert, T. M., (Ed.), *Consequences of maternal drug abuse* (Research Monograph No. 59, pp. 48-60). Rockville, MD: National Institute on Drug Abuse.

Washton, A. M. (1985). Cocaine abuse treatment. *Psychiatry Letter*, *3*(9), 51-56.

Chapter 2

The Counselor's Dilemma: Treating Chemical Dependence at College

Robert L. DuPont

SUMMARY. The college counselor faces a troubling dilemma when dealing with student chemical dependence. A non-directive approach to student drug and alcohol use will not only miss most chemical dependence problems, but will all but doom the counseling process itself for many students. On the other hand, a strong no-drugs-or-alcohol stand by the counselor flies in the face of the contemporary value systems of both counseling and college.

A solution to this dilemma requires an understanding of the chemical dependence syndrome and the purposes of the college experience. With this perspective it is usually possible to form a powerful therapeutic alliance around the student's best interests while at college, which includes a rejection of the "chemical high" as either a way to cope with stress or a way to have fun.

INTRODUCTION

If I were going to create an environment that encouraged chemical dependence I could hardly improve on the contemporary American college. There are four elements that perpetuate the connection between drugs and campuses – a connection which has been unmistakable since Timothy Leary, the "Harvard professor," began his

Robert L. DuPont, MD, is Chairman, Center for Behavioral Medicine, 6191 Executive Boulevard, Rockville, MD 20852; and Clinical Professor of Psychiatry, Georgetown University Medical School, Washington, DC.

career as the Pied Piper of chemical "mind expansion" twenty-five years ago, before today's college students were born.

Chemical dependence starts primarily between the ages of 12 and 21. Drug use, both legal and illegal, peaks in the 18-25 age group. These are the peak ages for consumption of beer and cigarettes as well as for marijuana and cocaine. College students are potential drug abusers, many of whom began use prior to coming to college, while others start or accelerate use at college. Thus, colleges contain people at peak ages for both incidence and prevalence of chemical dependence.

Drug use costs money and consumes time. Colleges have many vulnerable young people who have more discretionary income and more discretionary time than is typical of either younger or older ages.

Social control is a powerful barrier to chemical dependence. For children, social control is exerted primarily in the family and in the school. For older adults, it is often exerted by the spouse and the employer. Social control over drug and alcohol use is at its lowest point in the modern American human life cycle during the college years. Authorities and family are simply not likely to say no to drug and alcohol use at college. Being close to teachers, administrators, parents, and other adults is commonly seen as evidence of immaturity and insecurity among college students.

The values at college, especially at the most prestigious colleges, encourage drug use. College youth are encouraged to throw off older, traditional values and identifications and to experiment with life to find new, independent, personal identities. College values typically glorify the image of assertive independence of authority with the claim, "I can handle it" being a sort of emblem of making it in the modern college. Youth at college who do not use drugs or alcohol at all are seen as either "wimps" or as "having a problem," neither of which is a desirable status in the college culture. The highest status is often accorded to the student who uses alcohol and other drugs "under control."

The contemporary college counselor dealing with student drug and alcohol use is confronted with a difficult dilemma: to be nondirective and value-neutral about drug and alcohol use or to be an aggressive proponent of values opposing drug and alcohol use. The first approach commonly leads to enabling the chemical dependence syndrome to progress with often disastrous consequences for the student, the family, and the college. The second can lead to conflicts for both the counselor and the student as it violates the expectations and expressed values of the college community.

There is a third common and undesirable approach to this dilemma: for the counselor to accept or even to encourage the moderate use of drugs and alcohol. Sometimes this approach is taken with shy and socially isolated students by counselors who are themselves active users of drugs and alcohol. While this advice may lead to a break out of social isolation (and "moralistic rigidity") it all too often leads to serious problems of chemical dependence which are difficult for either the student or the counselor to face honestly.

Unfortunately, the most common way to escape this dilemma is *denial*; both the counselor and the student ignore the use of drugs and alcohol, focusing only on psychological aspects of the counseling experience instead on the consequences of alcohol/drug use such as poor grades, social failure, and conflicts with the parents and others in authority. Discouragingly, the common outcome of such counseling is termination of the student's education as the drug-using student leaves school to pursue what might be called the independent study of his or her own chemical dependence. A frequent variation on the theme of denial of chemical dependence is for the counselor to make a distinction between use and abuse of drugs and alcohol. In this view, students who apparently use drugs and alcohol responsibly and under control are seen as normal. Since counselors are often not sensitive to chemical dependence and since students often minimize both their drug use and its consequences, this approach leads to the reassuring, but often wrong, conclusion that chemical dependence is not the student's problem.

This dilemma—between denial of chemical dependence and aggressive assertion of non-drug values in conflict with commonly held values—is what I call the "counselor's dilemma." There is another, better, way for a counselor to handle chemical dependence at college. It is the subject of this chapter.

EPIDEMIOLOGY OF CHEMICAL DEPENDENCE AT COLLEGE

One of the important findings of the landmark study of drugs and youth conducted by Lloyd Johnston and his colleagues in the Institute for Social Research at the University of Michigan was that youth who leave school have higher rates of drug and alcohol use than those who stay in school and graduate. Thus, those who go to college have lower drug and alcohol use rates than those who do not (Bachman et al., 1980). This study also showed that while at college youth increase their use of drugs and alcohol, tending to catch up to the drug use rates of their peers who did not go to college (Engs & Hanson, 1983, 1985; Bloch & Untergleider, 1986).

The extent and trend of college drug and alcohol use from 1980 to 1985 in the United States is seen in Table 1 which shows the percent of college students using drugs at least once during the year before the annual survey. While there was a modest but reassuring drop in the rate of marijuana use over this six-year period (34% to 24% between 1980 and 1985), the use of other drugs, including cocaine, alcohol, and tobacco, changed little. The use of all four of these gateway drugs was distressingly common at college in 1985, the most recent year for which data is available: alcohol was used by 80% of American college students; marijuana, 24%; cigarettes, 22%; and cocaine 7%. These figures do not give adequate testimony to the seriousness, both in terms of extent and consequences, of college drug and alcohol problems partly because of the large number of students who leave college because of drug and alcohol use.

A CHEMICAL DEPENDENCE PRIMER

It is not possible to overcome the counselor's dilemma without a clear understanding of the chemical dependence syndrome (DuPont, 1984).

"Drugs" are chemicals which produce good feelings when used repeatedly in recreational settings. In this sense, alcohol is a drug. It is often useful to consider cigarettes to be drugs also although, un-

TABLE 1

Trends in Thirty-Day Prevalence of Twelve Types of Drugs
Among College Students 1–4 Years Beyond High School

	Percent who used in last 30 days						
	1980	1981	1982	1983	1984	1985	'84–'85 change
Approx. Wtd. N =	(1040)	(1130)	(1150)	(1170)	(1110)	(1080)	
Marijuana	34.0	33.2	26.8	26.2	23.0	23.6	+0.6
LSD	1.3	1.4	1.7	0.9	0.8	0.7	−0.1
Cocaine	6.9	7.3	7.9	6.4	7.6	6.9	−0.7
Heroin	0.3	0.0	0.0	0.0	0.0	0.0	0.0
Other Opiates[a]	1.8	1.1	1.0	1.1	1.4	0.7	−0.7
Stimulants[a]	13.4	12.3	NA	NA	NA	NA	NA
Stimulants, Adjusted[a,b]	NA	NA	9.9	7.0	5.5	4.2	−1.3
Sedatives[a]	3.7	3.4	2.5	1.1	1.0	0.7	−0.3
Barbiturates[a]	0.9	0.8	0.9	0.5	0.7	0.4	−0.3
Methaqualone[a]	3.1	3.0	1.9	0.7	0.5	0.2	−0.3
Tranquilizers[a]	2.0	1.4	1.4	1.1	1.2	1.4	+0.2
Alcohol	81.8	81.9	82.8	80.3	79.1	80.3	+1.2
Cigarettes	25.8	25.9	24.4	24.7	21.5	22.4	+0.9

NOTES: Level of significance of difference between the two most recent years: s = .05, ss = .01, sss = .001.
NA indicates data not available.

[a]Only drug use which was not under a doctor's orders is included here.

[b]Adjusted for the inappropriate reporting of non-prescription stimulants.

Source: National Institute on Drug Abuse

like the other drugs dealt with in this chapter, they are not intoxicating. Therefore cigarettes do not produce the behavioral toxicity (accidents, overdose deaths, crime, failed school performance, inappropriate sexual activity, and suicide) commonly seen from the use of alcohol, marijuana, cocaine, and other drugs.

There are two principal patterns to the chemical dependence syndrome which must be clearly understood. The first is the progression of substances. Use of chemicals to get high typically begins with alcohol (almost always beer) and/or with cigarettes. It progresses through marijuana to cocaine and ultimately to a wide range of other drugs, with heroin being, in the United States today, the end stage of this process. Not all people who take one step go on to the next. While much remains to be learned about the progression from one substance to the next, it is clear that the younger a person is at each step the more likely he or she is to progress to the next step, and the more heavily a person uses a drug the more likely he or she is to progress to the next drug in the sequence (Yamaguchi et al., 1984). For example, a 14-year-old who drinks alcohol heavily is far more likely to progress to marijuana use than is a 20-year-old who begins use of alcohol occasionally in small amounts.

The second pattern to the chemical dependence syndrome involves the stages within the syndrome itself, as opposed to the sequence of drugs. There are three stages to chemical dependence. The first is *experimentation*, which is generally limited to the ages of 12 to 21. These are the most vulnerable ages for initiation of drug use. Simply stated, if an individual does not begin use of a particular drug by the age of 21, the likelihood of his ever initiating use of that drug sharply decreases, and will continue to decrease for the rest of the person's life. (The only exception to this is the use of medically prescribed drugs which peaks later in life.) The second stage of the chemical dependence syndrome is *fooling around*. This stage lasts a variable time from weeks to years. The more frequent the use and the higher the dose used, the more rapid the progress out of this stage and into the next stage of the chemical dependence syndrome. Fooling around is characterized by the drug user's rather casual use of the drug and the belief that, "I can take it or leave it." This is the stage when the drug user is most likely to proselytize drug use because it is seen to be a problem-free way to have fun. It is not problem-free for many students. Accidents, especially automobile accidents, are common at this stage of the process.

The final stage, and in many ways the most mysterious in the chemical dependence syndrome, is *being hooked*. This last stage is not limited, as is commonly believed, to physical dependence. In fact, the belief that the drug problem is a problem of physical dependence is precisely the reason that we have the gateway drugs (alcohol, marijuana, and cocaine) that we do: they are commonly seen as being non-addictive. Recent research has shown that the problem the drug user has is not so much physical dependence as it is "falling in love" with the use of a chemical to get high. This new view focuses on loss of control of drug use and reinforcement, rather than on withdrawal symptoms, as the engine driving chronic, problem-producing drug and alcohol use. Most people who have lost control of their drug use are not physically dependent on the substance whereas, of course, all people who are physically dependent have, by definition, lost control.

Even this now more inclusive definition of dependence needs to be broadened. Some counselors consider loss of control to be the test of a problem with drugs. They often ask the student, "When you start to use the drug, can you stop use before you have a problem or do you keep taking it without the ability to stop?" If a student reports that he had a few beers (or a joint or a few lines of cocaine) at a party recently and "had no trouble stopping," all too often the student and the counselor are falsely reassured that a drug problem does not exist. Loss of control does not refer to "every time" the student uses, it means "any time." If a student *ever* drinks or uses drugs to intoxication, or ever has a problem because of drug or alcohol use, the student has a chemical dependence problem and is showing clear evidence of "loss of control." It is neither healthy nor normal for people of any age to become intoxicated on alcohol or any other drug.

This second type of progression within the chemical dependence syndrome is most likely to move to loss of control among youths who have a family history of drug or alcohol dependence but it can occur in anyone who regularly uses any of these reinforcing substances at intoxicating doses. The chemical dependence syndrome is a biological process largely outside the voluntary control of the drug user.

The most important concepts for the counselor to grasp to help a drug-using individual are *denial* and *enabling*. Denial refers to the process, shared by the substance user and by virtually everyone around that user, of simply ignoring or, if that fails, minimizing the importance of the use of the alcohol or drugs. The extent to which this process of denial dominates the user's experience is hard for most people to accept. It has pervasive and commonly devastating consequences that are all but unavoidable with continued drug use. The second concept that must be understood about the chemical dependence syndrome is enabling. It is closely related to denial. Enabling means that those who care about the substance user act, both wittingly and unwittingly, to promote the substance use. Again, the extent and consequences of this drug and alcohol use are often overlooked.

A typical example of denial and enabling is for a parent to help a college student fight a ticket for driving while intoxicated. Two parents recently told me, with pride, that they had hired an attorney to clear their college sophomore daughter when she was arrested for a DWI charge. At the time of the arrest her blood alcohol level (BAL) was 0.10. She told her parents that she had had "a couple of beers" while at a professor's house with a group of other students and that she was driving with no problems when arrested. After telling me that they first saw her drunk at the age of 14, her parents said, "She never had a drinking problem at all. In fact, she rarely drinks." They did not believe me when I told them that it was unlikely that she rarely drinks and that it requires many, many drinks over a short period of time to reach a BAL of 0.10. These parents did not consider it noteworthy that their daughter was under the legal drinking age at the time of the DWI charge or that she was drinking at a professor's house as part of a social gathering with other college students. They did not consider it possible that their daughter was lying to them. Instead, they simply mistrusted the police and the accuracy of the blood alcohol determination. This is an example of both denial of the drinking problem and enabling it to continue.

The drug chemical that produces the "high" acts on the user's brain to preempt the natural signals for pleasure. In fact, much of our modern understanding of neurotransmitters – the chemicals that pass signals between one nerve cell and another – has grown out of the research on drug abuse during the last decade. The mid-brain pleasure centers of the healthy human brain are designed to deal with such natural pleasures as eating and sexual activity. While it is now fashionable to see anything natural as safe and desirable and chemicals dangerous and frightening, this simplistic view is not warranted when it comes to the brain's pleasure or reward systems. Control of feeding and sexuality – the prototype for the brain's reward system – is powerfully managed by social control in all human cultures for thousands of years. This social control of personal pleasure is most powerfully expressed in the family, which I have come to think of as the preeminent pleasure-control social system. The family-based control is often reinforced by tradition, religion, and the law in cultures all over the world.

Not only have traditional social controls on drug and alcohol use been relaxed in America over the last two decades, but so have social controls over eating and sexual behavior. It is no accident that the drug and alcohol epidemic from which the U.S. suffers is part of a larger epidemic of pleasure-driven behaviors. Right along with the rise in drug and alcohol use has come disturbing increases in eating disorders (including anorexia nervosa, bulimia, and even obesity) and sexual problems (including sexually transmitted diseases and out-of-wedlock pregnancies). The list of pleasure-driven disorders which are now epidemic in America does not stop here. The same time period has seen unprecedented increases in crime, accidents, and even suicide, particularly among youth. In all these areas it is precisely the loss of social control and the substitution of personal and often impulsive control that underlies the rise of these problems. All of these pleasure-driven behaviors are particularly serious problems during adolescence because the brain's pleasure system is turned up during puberty and because social (usually family-based) control is lowest during this phase of the life cycle (DuPont, 1987).

Pleasure is the purpose of drug and alcohol use. People use drugs because they are happy and because they are sad, because they are rich and because they are poor, because they are gregarious and because they are shy. The common denominator is that drugs work – they make the drug user feel good on a powerful, biological basis. There is an interesting paradox here, however. The heavy drug user is an unhappy person who finds no significant pleasure in either drug use or in natural pleasures such as sex or eating. Why? Modern neuroscience offers some answers: chemical stimulation of the brain's reward system leads to its exhaustion so that neither drug use nor other pleasure-producing behaviors work any more. This biological view also helps explain why the early stages of drug and alcohol use are often associated with increased social activity as inhibitions are reduced, while at the later stages of the chemical dependence syndrome the user is more withdrawn from social activity (except as it relates to drug use) and achievement as pleasure of all kinds becomes elusive.

With this background in mind, it is not difficult to understand why the four factors described in the Introduction to this chapter make colleges such a fertile ground for drug and alcohol abuse. Colleges have concentrations of young people removed from adults in a setting where there is easy access to discretionary time and money, and in the obvious absence of social control exerted particularly by the family. Colleges in the last 20 years have literally abandoned any exertion of parental control, the so-called "in loco parentis" role, that was taken for granted by colleges in earlier years. More profound, however, even than these first three factors is the emphasis in modern American college life on the individual, personal control over one's behavior, rejecting control expressed through family, law, and tradition, and the equally powerful support for the more adventurous experimentation with lifestyles that are in conflict with parents and traditional values. This is all held together with the glue of the self-confident, if naive, assertion that, "I can take care of myself."

THE COLLEGE CONTEXT FOR PREVENTION AND TREATMENT

Colleges recently have begun, mostly reluctantly, a painful process of reevaluation of their relationship to students' behavior, including drug and alcohol use (University of Maryland, 1986; University of Virginia, 1987). The remarkable fact is that for many colleges it was the return of the legal drinking age to the traditional 21 that tipped the balance in the direction of reevaluation of alcohol use and secondarily of other drugs. So far these efforts, outside the few schools with strong traditional, often religious, orientations have been tentative and limited.

For the drug problem to be solved it is essential that the college make clear that drug and alcohol *use* are incompatible with the purposes of college and that they will not be tolerated. Related to that radical-sounding position is the importance of the college expressing support for the law, including both the law about the drinking age and the law about the use of purely illegal drugs. Such support for the law needs to be backed up by action to insure that the law is comprehensively enforced among the students, particularly, but by no means only, among those who live on campus or in university housing. Unfortunately, in the absence of such clear messages, many students find the climate at college either permissive of drug and alcohol use or encouraging of it.

THE COUNSELOR'S ROLE

An essential part of the psychotherapy evaluation of a college student is an assessment of the use of alcohol and drugs. Because of denial that drug and alcohol use are occurring, or are only moderate or under control, the student's initial statements should be viewed with skepticism. Nevertheless, direct inquiry about drug and alcohol use and associated problems is worthwhile in an initial evaluation since many students will admit their problems readily; even with a sense of relief. Any admission of alcohol or drug use should be dealt with directly with an expression of the counselor's views about this behavior. Such a direct expression of the counselor's own views about the student's behavior does not mean "imposing" the counselor's values on the student. It does mean that the views of both the student and the counselor are expressed and explored. All drug and alcohol use is, of course, illegal for all drugs other than alcohol and also for alcohol by students under the age of 21 virtually throughout the United States at this time. As a psychotherapist, I state clearly that I consider any use of intoxicants dangerous and contrary to my purposes of helping the student make the most of the college opportunity.

In considering drug and alcohol use by college students I use guidelines that are easy to understand, if hard for many students to accept.

Any use of illegal drugs and any underage use of alcohol is abuse and is simply unacceptable. For those who seek to be responsible social drinkers, I use my Four-by-Four Solution:

These four groups of people should not drink alcohol at all:

1. Anyone under the legal drinking age;
2. Pregnant or nursing women;
3. Anyone using any sedative drug such as a tranquilizer, sleeping pill, antihistamine, or painkiller; and
4. Anyone with a personal history of a drug or alcohol problem. Youth with a family history of drug or alcohol abuse pose a large and important population at higher risk. My approach to them is to suggest that their families have given them an important gift: an extra-strong reason not to experiment with drugs or alcohol.

For people who are not in any of these four categories and who want to drink socially I suggest these protective boundaries:

1. Drinking no more than three or four days out of any week;
2. No more than two or three drinks in any 24-hour period (one drink is defined as 12 ounces of beer, 5 ounces of wine, or 1-1/2 ounces of distilled spirits – all of which contain about the same amount of alcohol, about one-half ounce);
3. No drinking at all within four hours of driving a car, working, or going to school; and
4. Find someone who does not drink at all and ask this person to be your "alcohol monitor." If your monitor thinks you have a problem with alcohol, pledge that you will stop all alcohol use.

These guidelines are described in greater detail in *Getting Tough on Gateway Drugs* (DuPont, 1984). It is often helpful, even early in the psychotherapy, to include a friend or family member in the evaluation process. When I bring such people into psychotherapy I usually have the student present at the time, making it a joint interview, although on occasion I see significant others in separate sessions. I always ask directly about drug and alcohol use as well as problems which may be associated with such use. These questions will often elicit evidence of problems even when the student has denied use. This occurs because peers and family are often more sensitive and observant about problems than the student. It is also common to find friends of the student who are concerned about the student's drug use and feel helpless about being able to do anything about the problem. It is true that some of the student's peers may encourage drug and alcohol use. But it is also true that many peers are genuinely concerned about the drug-abusing student. I have many times been impressed by the compassion and concern of college peers. It is often possible for the counselor to identify, use, and promote the latent anti-drug attitudes in the college peer culture to aid the recovery of a student with a drug problem. It is especially useful to recruit to this task youth who have overcome serious drug or alcohol problems themselves. The youth culture has an easier time accepting and valuing abstinence when it is based on personal problems than when it seems abstract and moralistic. In this regard I often tell students that my best friend from high school was killed in an alcohol-related car crash and that I have seen many tragic results of drug and alcohol use, all of which has led to my views on this important subject.

As part of my evaluation of a student I include a urine test for drugs of abuse unless the student admits current drug use, in which case the initial drug test is unnecessary. I supervise these tests myself and send them to a clinical laboratory for analysis, for a "narcotic screen" (which usually includes opiates, cocaine, benzodiazepines, barbiturates, and amphetamines) plus a screening test for marijuana, such as radio immunoassay or enzyme immunoassay. These tests are positive for drug use for one or two days after the last use of a drug, except marijuana which may be positive for three to five days after use. An exception for marijuana occurs when the young person has been using marijuana heavily every day for long periods of time, in which case the urine test may be positive for several weeks after the last use of the drug because the THC, the psychoactive component of marijuana smoke, has saturated the user's fat. Usually a positive urine test means that the student is a heavy as well as a frequent drug user. I treat a positive urine test as a signal of a serious problem and explain that drug use must stop for psychotherapy to succeed. The best way to assess the achievement of this goal in psychotherapy is by repeated urine tests. Alcohol can also be detected in routine urine tests but since it is totally eliminated from the body (including the urine) within a few hours of use, this test is seldom positive except when the student has been drinking just before the urine test is taken.

Since no adverse action is taken as a result of a positive urine test for drugs in the context of ongoing psychotherapy, I do not use confirmatory tests. Students who test positive for drugs seldom deny use after I have explained the test and my use of it. When students with positive tests do deny drug use, I simply say, "We will continue the tests and see what sort of pattern develops in the future." If I have any question about the particular student, I observe the urine test myself for males or ask a female staff member to observe tests for females. Usually this is not necessary, however, as I check for the temperature of the specimen, making sure that it is warm after voiding.

It is certainly true that not all counselors working with college students agree with my Zero Tolerance stand. Whatever stand is taken about student drug and alcohol use, however, I suggest that it be made explicit to the student and to others the counselor deals with about the student, including college officials and parents. If some illegal drug use is acceptable to the counselor and/or if tests are not done to confirm non-use of drugs, these positions need to be made clear so that false assumptions by those who have a responsibility for the student are not encouraged.

Some college counselors ask me how a young person can "learn to drink alcohol responsibly." My answer is simple. The decision to be an adult social drinker needs to be made after the age of 21 and such drinking needs to be under clear personal guidelines such as those I have proposed in my Four-by-Four Solution. There is no good reason to begin to learn how to drink alcohol before the age of 21, any more than there is any reason one has to learn about drugs by trying them. Advice to the contrary, although common, is dangerous as well as scientifically unsound.

Assuming the student admits to drug or alcohol use, or if a urine test is positive, the first task of psychotherapy is to achieve a stable drug-free state. If this is not done, the common opinion of chemical dependence therapists is that the counselor is "talking to a chemical, not to a person."

The problem of the involvement of the student's parents must be faced immediately. I take the strong position that parents have a right and a responsibility to know what is going on with their children, so long as the children are being supported financially, including while they are at college. This means the parents need to know about drug and alcohol use and/or problems. This often controversial issue is dealt with in some detail in Chapter Six of my book, *Getting Tough on Gateway Drugs* (DuPont, 1984).

In working with a student, I explore this issue by asking if the parents know what is going on with respect to drug and alcohol use and if the student believes the parents are entitled to know the facts. If a student says "no" to either or both questions, I point out that this position involves lying to the parents. My simple rule in such cases is, "If you can't tell the people who love you what you are doing, you shouldn't be doing it." This rule certainly applies to parents of college students using drugs and alcohol. If a student claims that the parents are "old fashioned" or "unreasonable" I offer to help the student educate the parents in person or on the telephone. An alternative I suggest is that the student find a friend of the family member or a professional person (therapist, minister, rabbi, etc.) who can be a family advisor to help sort out any conflicts of values that occur. On the other hand, I will not accept lying to or deceiving the parents, especially if they are paying for the psychotherapy, which is usually the case whether the therapy is paid for by the parents directly or as part of the student's health services paid for through the college.

Some counselors will see my recommendations as violating the student's right to confidentiality or even the federal statute about the confidentiality of drug abuse treatment. These problems are overcome by insuring that all communications with the family are approved in advance by the student. This approval may take some time to achieve and it may have some restrictions placed on it. This is acceptable to me so long as both student and parent have a clear idea of what is and what is not being communicated, and so long as I am permitted by the student to tell the parents what I consider to be important to the student's welfare. If this permission is not granted after a few counseling sessions, I recommend that the student be referred to another therapist. This has rarely been a problem in my practice.

All of this, no doubt, may seem simplistic and even antitherapeutic to many counselors. I can only state that I have found this straightforward, value-based approach to be easily understood and appreciated by students and parents, both of whom are often relieved by such an understandable approach that emphasizes the family functioning together as a team to help the student make the most out of the college experience, including the substantial financial investment the family has usually made in the student's education.

It is quite common for therapists to misdiagnose chemical dependence problems, using labels such as "anxiety" or "depression" to define the problem. Typical problems associated with chemical dependence include poor school performance, limited or non-existent extracurricular activities, depressed mood, unrewarding peer relationships, and conflicts with teachers and/or parents. If a clear chemical dependence diagnosis is not made these problems are likely to continue unabated and are unlikely to respond to psychotherapy. Twenty-five years ago it was common for psychotherapists to believe that alcohol and drug problems were symptoms of underlying psychological disorders and that once these disorders were resolved through psychotherapy, the drug or alcohol use would stop. The dominant view today is exactly the opposite: before psychotherapy can be successful it is important that the client's mind be drug-free. Failure to achieve this goal almost always dooms psychotherapy.

In developing a therapeutic alliance it is important for the therapist and the student to come to some basic agreement about the purposes of the psychotherapy. There is no question that achieving a state of feeling good and high self-esteem are laudable goals. On the other hand, to simply focus on the feeling states and not to deal with the issues of relationships and achievement that are so important in the college student's life is to feed into the attitudes of many drug users – the entitlement to feel good without regard to what the person is actually doing. I find it helpful to focus the therapeutic alliance around goals the student would like to achieve during college, including goals related to academic achievement, the development of a personal identity, and the development of good relationships with both peers and adults. There is a tendency among many college students to act as if college is going to go on forever and that the major goal in college is to "have fun before I have to go to work." I find it helpful to emphasize that the college experience is brief, as well as important, and that it is essential to make good use of this opportunity in the student's life.

If a drug-free state is not achieved within three or four weeks of initiating psychotherapy, I find it useful to move to more specific chemical dependence treatment. My first effort is to encourage participation in Alcoholics Anonymous or Narcotics Anonymous, which have chapters on many college campuses. The traditional prescription for these self-help programs is "90 meetings in 90 days" if a person is to achieve a drug-free state. If this approach does not work or is not acceptable, I generally recommend an inpatient chemical dependence treatment program. I am intolerant of continued drug use. Continued psychotherapy on the assumption that somehow, if the goal of being drug-free is not achieved in the first few weeks it will be at some vague later time, is not in the student's best interest.

One of the more difficult problems faced by college counselors involves the use of alcohol by students whether or not the students have a drug problem. Although it is possible to convince many students that their drug use is a problem, they often cling to the belief that they can use alcohol with impunity. The college culture, often ambivalent about drug use, is all but universal in support of drinking alcohol. I make it clear that the student's problem is not a particular drug, such as marijuana or cocaine. The problem is using a chemical to get intoxicated or to get high. In this regard any alcohol use is equally undesirable. An attempt to solve the drug problem by attempting to control alcohol use, instead of being totally drug-free, is a bargain that is likely to lead only to frustration and disappointment for both the student and the counselor.

I do believe that psychotherapy is useful for students with chemical dependence problems. I have found, however, that psychotherapy is only likely to be successful after the drug-free state has been achieved or as part of a three- to four-week effort to get the student into a specific chemical dependence treatment program to achieve the drug-free goal. One abuse of psychotherapy is unfortunately common on campuses: some students who are under coercion either from the family, the courts, or the school administration will enter into psychotherapy on the assumption that they are solving their chemical dependence problems simply by being there. Such students may continue in psychotherapy, often lying about their drug and alcohol use, making the psychotherapy a cover for continued chemical dependence. It is important that this potential problem be identified and that the counselor not be an accomplice to such an abuse of the psychotherapy process.

I find it helpful to ask clients who are themselves recovering drug abusers to get involved with other students who are just coming into psychotherapy and to guide them to AA and NA meetings. This helps reinforce facing and overcoming chemical dependence problems. In the phrase of the Alcoholics Anonymous program, this is called "Twelfth Step Work" – helping others achieve recovery. As many of us who are therapists and teachers have learned, the best way to learn anything is to teach it. This is also true when it comes to the personal study of chemical dependence where helping someone overcome a chemical dependence problem helps the counselor learn about the problem of chemical dependence.

THE INTELLECTUAL AND HUMANITARIAN CONTEXT FOR CHEMICAL DEPENDENCE PREVENTION AND TREATMENT ON THE CAMPUS

When I was a college student a philosophy professor asked our class this question: "If someone offered you a way to feel good without cost and without harming your body for as long as you live, assuming that you would only feel good feelings and never bad feelings from that point on for life, would you accept that offer or would you not?" It was two decades before I was able to understand what that question meant. To answer the question one must understand not only the purposes of pleasure, or "good feelings," in one's life but also the important uses of negative feelings. Beyond this it is essential to understand the purpose of one's life beyond either good or bad feelings. Such questions are seldom asked explicitly in psychotherapy and yet it is difficult to work with a drug-using student without considering such important questions since this "deal" is the promise of drug and alcohol use. Of course, chemical intoxicants do not deliver on the promise but it is the promise itself that needs to be examined. The most sophisticated review of these questions that I know of was written by a poet and teacher, Richard Hawley, in a book entitled *The Purposes of Pleasure* (Hawley, 1983). This book can be a useful aid in psychotherapy with college students who have chemical dependence problems.

It can sound moralistic or even "anti-pleasure" for a counselor to oppose the use of chemical intoxicants. It is important that these issues be thought through by the counselor, including an honest review of the counselor's own use, past and present, of intoxicants. Such an exploration is highly valued, especially at college, and will improve the counseling process. It is also important for the counselor not to impose his or her values—one way or another—on the student. The criterion for good counseling of a student who has a chemical dependence problem is to have a clear concept of the student's own best interests. In my experience it is not reasonable to view the counseling process as simply passively promoting whatever the student may at any given moment believe is his goal. It is important to take a longer view and to consider the long-term interests of the student as best they can be seen by both the student and the counselor. This is a delicate matter involving the balancing of many factors. I have found that it is not difficult to articulate the issues and to engage in a lively and often productive discussion with the student as part of the counseling process. It is important also that this discussion be rooted in both an intellectual and humanitarian context, particularly in the college environment, since these values are preeminent.

Students who are confronting the Twelve Step programs of Alcoholics Anonymous and Narcotics Anonymous often need help in thinking through the concept of the "Higher Power" in these programs. Many secularly-oriented students find these ideas reminiscent of fundamentalist religion and, for many students, this is not a positive association. I find it useful to explain that the Higher Power can be anything that is outside the student's own skin. Thus, the Higher Power for some people is a parent, a teacher, a girlfriend or boyfriend, a parole officer, a counselor, or even a religious or secular group or tradition. It can be an AA group. The point is that the grounding of one's values needs to be in something bigger and more important—"higher"—than whether one feels good or not. It is often useful for the counselor to have attended several AA and NA open meetings as an observer and to have visited one or two nearby treatment programs for chemical dependence. Not only will such visits educate the counselor about chemical dependence, but they will facilitate referral when that is necessary.

CONCLUSIONS

The college environment offers a unique opportunity for the counselor to confront and resolve problems of alcohol and drug abuse. For this to occur, however, it is essential for the counselor to overcome the troubling dilemma – the counselor's dilemma – of either acting in a way that ignores values and unwittingly promotes drug and alcohol abuse or foisting the counselor's personal values willy-nilly on the student.

The solution to this dilemma involves a clear understanding of the nature of chemical dependence and the uses of college in the student's own long-term best interests. Once these two contexts are clearly understood, it is usually possible to form a vigorous and constructive therapeutic alliance around achieving a drug- and alcohol-free lifestyle while promoting values and achievements which are likely to lead to good feelings in the student's life, including a substantial increase in self-esteem and positive relationships with peers and adults.

REFERENCES

Bachman J. G., O'Malley P. M., & Johnston L. D. (1980). Correlates of drug use, part I: Selected measures of background, recent experiences, and lifestyle orientations in *Monitoring the Future Occasional Paper 8*. Ann Arbor, MI: The Institute for Social Research, University of Michigan.

Bloch S. A. & Untergleider S. (1986). The Brown University Chemical Dependency Project in *Integrated Research Services*, Eugene, OR, 32-34.

DuPont R. L. (1984). *Getting Touch on Gateway Drugs: A Guide for the Family*. Washington, DC: American Psychiatric Press.

DuPont R. L. (1987). Prevention of adolescent chemical dependency. *Pediatric Clinics of North America 34*, 495-505.

Engs R. C. & Hanson, D. J. (1983). The drinking patterns and problems of college students. *Journal of Alcohol and Drug Education 31*, 65-83.

Engs R. C. & Hanson D. J. (1985). Drinking related problems of college students:

Comparison over 2 years and between over and under 21 year old legal drinking age. *Health & Safety*, Bloomington, IN: Indiana University.

Hawley R. A. (1983). *The Purposes of Pleasure: A Reflection on Youth and Drugs.* Wellesley Hills, MA: The Independent School Press.

University of Maryland (1986). *Task Force on Drug Policies, Enforcement, & Education: Model University Program for Education & Prevention of Drug Abuse*. College Park, MD.

University of Virginia (1987). *Report of the Task Force on Alcohol and Drug Abuse and Education of the University of Virginia*. Charlottesville, VA.

Yamaguchi K. & Kandel D.B. (1984). Patterns of drug use from adolescence to young adulthood: II. Sequences of progression. *American Journal of Public Health 74*, 668-672.

Chapter 3

Inherent Problems in Substance Abuse Education on University Campuses: Student Perspectives

Harry Duran
John Brooklyn

SUMMARY. Substance abuse is a problem among college student populations. In spite of continued efforts to educate students about the dangers of substance abuse, preventive measures have been met with resistance. Reluctance to respond to these messages may arise from psychological defense mechanisms. However, the unique properties of university life and the student role are seen to contribute more significantly to this resistance. The processes of individuation, emotional development, socialization, and group membership appear to be significantly stabilized by the use of drugs and alcohol. These dimensions of student life are basic maturation processes. Successful campaigns for substance abuse prevention must consider the depth of these issues. Medical education in this area is complicated when these unresolved issues are confronted by the medical student in the classroom and clinical settings. More holistic approaches towards the personal and social dynamics of substance abuse must be developed to promote prevention among college youth. Alternative methods which incorporate these needs are mentioned.

Harry Duran, PhD, and John Brooklyn, BS, are affiliated with the Program in Medicine at Brown University.

Address reprint requests to: Harry Duran, Box G, Brown University, Providence, RI 02912.

INTRODUCTION

Substance abuse, the use of drugs and alcohol for the purpose of intoxication for whatever reason, is a common social phenomenon. On university campuses substance abuse has unique characteristics. These characteristics are derived from the influences which the role of the student, the university social structure, and environment have on substance abuse behavior. Although substance abuse may not be regarded as acceptable behavior by university officials, substance abuse is a common part of university life. Many claims have been made for recent declines in apparent drug and alcohol consumption on college campuses. However, the problem of drug and alcohol abuse on campus remains troublesome.

Resistance to Drug and Alcohol Education

The problem of resistance to substance abuse education programs in universities is large enough to leave many students unaffected by such efforts. Educational programs which have been designed to promote awareness of the problem of substance abuse, with the aim of bringing about a decrease in this behavior, have been met with resistance by students. Many of these resistant students consistently abuse drugs and alcohol. These students may be in trouble with these substances, or are on their way to having problems. The failure of substance abuse education designed for college audiences only complicates future campaigns. This is because repeated exposure to ineffective messages creates increasing levels of insensitivity and skepticism in actively abusing student populations. This increasing jadedness must be confronted in subsequent approaches. It is often the case that many of these students do not respond to messages about substance abuse hazards until professional help is sought for substance abuse related problems.

Some students may be apathetic towards information about the dangers of substance abuse because they do not use drugs or alcohol themselves. Other students may believe their use is minimal and not an issue. These particular groups may easily become trapped in the same cycle of skepticism and apathy that more regular drug abusers experience. This cycle may produce a sense of complacency which can result in drug and alcohol related problems. These problems may range from the dependency of initially occasional users, to the codependency of non-users involved with addicts.

Medical students, a subset of the university community, are uniquely faced with the personal issues of substance abuse. In addition to the need to make personal decisions, the medical student is confronted by diagnostic and therapeutic dimensions of substance abuse. These are aspects of medical education which may conflict with the personal values which the medical student has about substance abuse. Ineffective substance abuse awareness education in the medical curriculum may affect clinical judgement. In addition, the resolution of personal values, and the recognition of medical student impairment have been hindered by a lack of definitive treatment of substance abuse in medical education.

The University Environment Fosters Resistance

Resistance to drug and alcohol educational efforts may arise from defense mechanisms such as denial. However, resistance may also be the result of the unique characteristics which substance abuse has on university campuses. Substance abuse is a part of university life, and an element of the student role. These factors may attenuate the effectiveness of university substance abuse education campaigns if they do not include the social and personal issues of drug and alcohol use. These aspects need to be described, and their importance recognised in order to enhance the effectiveness of substance abuse education in universities and medical schools. In this paper, we will call attention to these mechanisms which we feel act to cause resistance to substance abuse education.

SUBSTANCE ABUSE AFFECTS THE DEVELOPMENT OF PERSONAL SKILLS

The university years are ones of maturation as well as education. The tensions of university life contribute to the unique nature of substance abuse phenomena on campus. In this novel environment, the student frequently encounters the belief that the use of drugs and alcohol are legitimate methods of coping with the demands of academic life. These demands surround the problem of identity, affiliation, emotional coping, academic performance, and pressure.

Identity Formation

A student entering university arrives with a set of personal values about substance abuse. These personal values are the product of the family, social, and educational environments in which the student has been raised (Vaillant, 1986). The entrance into university life is often the first experience the student has in leaving the home and supervision of parents or guardians. Consequently, the student is faced with the challenge of evaluating the beliefs and values which formed the nucleus of his or her prior family and community life. This process of evaluation is crucial to the adaptation which the student makes to university life. The choices which the college student makes about drug or alcohol use are a part of the process of evaluation.

The student is faced with the necessity to formulate personal judgements about substance abuse. This process helps the student to organize personal, moral, ethical, and social criteria which often conflict with familial, cultural, or religious values. This conflict demands scrutiny of one's position as an individual. This scrutiny lends credence to the assertion of independence by the student. The individuation process does not require the use of drugs or alcohol. However, making independent decisions about substance abuse is as important as making choices about sexuality, career, and marriage are to this process.

In addition to the personal challenge of asserting independence from the family, the student encounters a much wider range of behavioral norms. The backgrounds of individuals comprising a student peer group will yield a wider range of diversity in belief and behavior than the more homogeneous belief systems of a family environment. Each individual who asserts personal normalcy will be faced with accepting the normalcy of peers having different standards of acceptable behavior and beliefs. These standards may be widely divergent among students, and may at times seem to conflict. The varying attitudes which the student encounters about substance abuse among peers further necessitates the development of personal criteria for drug and alcohol use. These personal criteria affect the way the student defines his or her identity and the extent of peer affiliations.

Stress Management and Substance Abuse

The use and abuse of drugs or alcohol provides a convenient and readily available means of reducing the perception of pressure and relieving stress. Expectations of academic performance creates stress and anxiety in the university student. Substance abuse provides a quick remedy to feelings of anxiety about academic performance. The development of more adaptive skills in coping with stress are circumvented by the use of drugs and alcohol and a lack of availability of alternative methods in the university environment and the student's background.

Coping with Boredom

In addition to pressure to perform, student life consists of long periods of study. Boredom is a common complaint which arises from a need for stimulation to relieve the rigor of academic discipline. The unrelieved experience of boredom is a challenge which a young adult may meet for the first time in college. Prior to entering university, the diversions of family and high school life usually ward off the experience of long periods of boredom and isolation. The situation is quite different in university environments where boredom and isolation commonly accompany the meeting of academic obligations. Boredom is uncomfortable and stimulates pleasure seeking and affiliation. The fulfillment of these drives is one which the student must learn to deny until more appropriate times when study is not a priority. Thus, boredom plays an essential role in student development. The unfortunate fact remains that boredom is very easily and quickly relieved by the use of drugs or alcohol and the social activities which surround their use. If the student has not learned the value of seeking more fulfilling diversions, the alternative of substance abuse may seem preferable.

Meeting Needs for Affiliation

Uncomfortable emotions such as loneliness or sexual frustration which arise from the feelings of isolation in students are commonly associated with the phenomenon of boredom. Student depression frequently complicates the issues which arise with isolation, boredom and loneliness, and exacerbate substance abuse. In addressing the need for affiliation and intimacy, the college youth is expected to take social and personal risks. When the effort to maintain social and sexual relationships is avoided, a sense of tension arises in the student which is easily dulled or relieved by the experience of using and abusing drugs and alcohol. In this sense, substance abuse fills unmet emotional needs by substituting for more substantial social and psychological rewards. As a result, the student may learn that getting high or drunk provides an easy alternative to the challenge of pursuing more fulfilling experiences. Social substance abuse is a source of easily formed relationships. Relationships which are formed and stabilized around the use of drugs or alcohol lack the depth which affiliation based on meaningful social interaction provides. For the individual student, an important lesson in the formation of adult social skills is lost. The development of personal emotional resources which the adult professional needs to cope with stress, depression, loneliness, and isolation are similarly underdeveloped when substance abuse has provided a way to avoid dealing with these issues. This stunting of psychological and emotional development need not be confined to the problem substance abuser. Undoubtedly, this must be an effect which influences the development of all college students to some degree.

Developing Recreational Skills

For many students, the ready availability and lack of effort which goes into getting intoxicated outweighs alternative pastimes. These alternative pastimes may not provide the intensity of stimulus which drugs and alcohol provide. Students who do not yet understand that pleasure is something which requires a capacity in the individual to feel, appreciate, and interact over time will find these more subtle rewards to be inconsequential. This leads to the belief that one must be constantly entertained or amused and that boredom, loneliness, and isolation are always avoidable, and easily remedied by drugs and alcohol. Substance abuse requires little effort on the part of the student because of the grossness of the level of stimulation which it provides. In effect, substance abuse provides an easy escape which robs a developing mind of the ability to appreciate the subtlety of educational and environmental stimuli. The use of drugs and alcohol as escapes from boredom deprives the student of the opportunity to develop a valuable skill, the ability to enjoy life as it is.

Most substance abuse prevention programs do not address the issue of developing recreation and pleasure skills. When they do, it is usually limited to the development of tired axioms like "get high on life." Clearly, this approach engenders cynicism in substance abusing students because of the self-righteous and simplistic tone of such statements. No program has fully tried to instill a sense of responsibility in the student for his or her own feelings. This approach is one which would require more effort, but would in the end be more effective than the sloganizing approaches which have been so common in the past.

Devaluation of the Educational Experience

Because university life is an educational experience, the development of a refined capacity for appreciating aesthetic value, pleasure, or reward is bound to be enhanced as a result of the academic process. Appreciations develop from the interaction of the student with the material being studied. The use of drugs and alcohol often replace this appreciation of the rewards and satisfactions of academic accomplishment. The substance abusing student then is only able to see study as an unpleasant grind to be escaped by chemical means. The use of this chemical escape initiates a cycle which causes many students to flunk out, fail courses, or at best, to miss out on the full range of their educational experience. Substance abuse awareness programs frequently play on fear of failure in the student. Students are made to feel a threat of expulsion or academic failure as an incentive to not use drugs and alcohol. Rarely is an attempt made to instill a sense of reward in the nature of academic work. This is a change which cannot be mandated by the distribution of pamphlets and posters. The unpleasant reality is that academic life is one of few tangible rewards for accomplishment and all too many reprimands for failure. Students faced with a fear of failure as a motivation for study will be all too ready to seek escape in substance abuse.

Devaluation of Self-Worth

The process of substituting substance abuse for the value of self-fulfillment may diminish an individual's regard for achievement and self-actualization. Alcohol and drug awareness education programs often moralize and appear puritanical to students who have used substances as an emotional or psychological fulfillment. Because these individuals have found the personal skills that they were raised with to be inadequate, and consider substance abuse a valid personal goal, psychological resistance will occur when the dangers of drug and alcohol use are discussed. For these students the program represents the failed values and lack of fulfillment which have been replaced in their lives with drugs or alcohol. When challenged by information which does not consider these deep issues of inadequacy, the defense mechanisms of the affected student diminish the impact of the information. Eventually, these students may be confronted with the realization that drugs and alcohol have become the focus of his or her life. Often this realization is not reached until one is addicted.

Enhancement of Productivity and Achievement

The use of drugs and alcohol may also be considered instrumental in enhancing the ability of students to perform academically. The accepted use of coffee to enhance alertness, wakefulness, and energy in studies and the workplace is well known. The use of other, more powerful stimulants, like amphetamines may be preferred by the student as a superior alternative. The pressures of courseloads, deadlines, and examinations often cause the student to feel time pressure. The sense of time pressure may be aggravated if the student has not learned to effectively manage daily activities. The inability of some students to develop successful time management strategies leads to situations in which the student may feel compelled to study for periods of time beyond normal endurance.

The phenomena of cramming and the "all nighter" are good examples of time management gone awry. The use of caffeine as a stimulant may be legitimate in these circumstances. However, the panic stricken student may consider more potent stimulants preferable.

The use of amphetamines as aids in last minute, all night study sessions is common. The development of chronic use is a problem for some students. Because amphetamines do not cause the diminution of consciousness which alcohol does, and may seem to enhance performance, these students feel justified in using amphetamines.

The recent cultural phenomenon of cocaine use by business executives and other professionals provides acceptable role models and precedents for the use of cocaine and amphetamines by the student to enhance academic achievement. Transitorily improved academic performance becomes an incentive to continue using the drug as a reward. Consequently, abuse or dependence problems with cocaine or amphetamines may arise from their use as aids to achievement.

The common approach in substance abuse education and prevention measures has been to categorize all drugs as detrimental to social and personal success. When an individual experiences the temporary enhancement of performance from using cocaine or amphetamines, this experience appears to contradict the more generalized message of the antidrug campaign. This contradiction makes it easy for the abusing student to discount the validity of the message.

It may not be until the student has a problem with the use of cocaine or amphetamines that he or she realizes how these drugs are detrimental to success. In this sense, the message of the drug education effort is lost because of a presentation of facts which are seen as half-truths only. This establishes in the student mind-set a sense of mistrust which blocks receptiveness to well meaning messages of drug abuse prevention.

Psychological Barriers to Drug Abuse Education

In this psychological context, the diminution of the educational impact of substance abuse awareness programs is inevitable. This diminution of impact will occur regardless of the clarity or validity of the factual material being presented. The student is forming a world view and becoming an individual. The dogmatic approach of many substance abuse education and prevention programs is seen by students as a threat to the development of individuality. It is simplistic to assume that a student who has focused a large amount of personal definition around substance abuse will be receptive to, or even be able to perceive the messages of substance abuse education programs. Thus, substance abuse education and prevention must consider the level of voluntary and involuntary screening of information in the student.

Most often, however, these educational efforts do not cause the student to investigate the inadequacies of substance abuse as a personal choice of coping and socializing skills. The absence of being challenged to define one's own limits and values is glaringly apparent in the sloganizing and propagandizing processes which determine so many cultural, political, and religious beliefs. The unfortunate reality is that for many students, the choice to use or abuse alcohol and drugs is viewed in cultural, political, or religious contexts. Students who are disenchanted with these spheres of life will be more inclined to discount information about drugs and alcohol which reflect political and religious content. Other students who willingly accept the moral packages from these sources will be unable to adapt points of view derived from rigid dogmas to the realities of drug and alcohol consumption in their lives and the lives of their colleagues.

The Romance of Getting High

The experience of getting high or drunk for the first time may also have a special quality and significance for the student. The student may become nostalgic for the feeling of that experience. This nostalgic quality may resemble the recollection of one's first love or sexual encounter. This infatuation with the drug experience is different from the substitution of substance abuse for intimacy and affiliation mentioned earlier. In this framework the focus of the student's motivation to use the drug is the acquisition of the drug experience for itself. In attempts to relive the special quality of that high, the student will repeatedly abuse that substance or other drugs. By chasing this feeling, a student embarks on a quest to repeat an experience he or she believes to be of particular importance.

The magical quality of the initial high may be compelling enough to encourage the devotion of great amounts of time, money, and energy to the repeated attainment of that state. For some, the immense value of getting high takes precedence over the usual priorities of life and the person becomes addicted or dependent. The rapid development of a compulsion around the first high is characteristic of the use of crack cocaine (The Staff of the Medical Letter, 1986). However, the first love experience is commonly seen around alcohol, and other drugs.

The preventive aspects of drug and alcohol awareness education must consider that for some students, the effect of the drug is a competing message. The student who must choose between the message of the drug effect and the message of the dangers of the drug needs to be reached early, preferably before the first experience. Otherwise the cycle of repeated exposure to ineffective messages may be enough to prevent effective intervention.

THE EFFECTS OF ALCOHOL AND DRUG USE ON SOCIAL DEVELOPMENT

Substance abuse is important in the way it affects groups of students in the university community. Individual students will associate with other students for social and academic purposes. Social support is necessary and it provides students with a sense of belonging. These networks have protective effects on stress (Cobb, 1976). Absence of adequate resources allows for substance abuse to assume a major role in the development of social interactions.

Student associations and peer groups may form around formal or informal activities. Students will move among many different groups, depending on individual and group needs. The use of drugs and alcohol often influence the development and function of student groups, and the role of the individual student as a member of these groups.

The university community is undoubtedly affected by the choice of students to abuse substances individually or collectively. It may be said that substance abuse is as much a part of university life as course work, clubs, sports, and other extracurricular activities. The undeniable fact is that although one may individually choose not to drink or use drugs, the use of these substances in one's peer group is an inevitable encounter.

Dysfunctional Peer Groups and Codependency

The phenomenon of codependency in families is a clearly demonstrated pathologic process. The alcohol or drug addicted family member provides solutions to family crises with their substance abuse. Many unresolved family issues and conflicts are avoided by the use of the chemically dependent person as a focus of stability. In these situations, family members take on compensatory roles which enable the impaired family member to remain chemically dependent (Leipman, 1984). These roles have been carefully documented and may be found in other dysfunctional households where family members have been disabled by other disease processes (Smilkstein, 1980). The issues of codependency, and dysfunctional relationships may also be observed in the dynamics of student peer groups and organizations. How these relationships arise in the student body originates in the role substance abuse plays in the process of socialization and affiliation of individual students. The discussion of how the use of drugs and alcohol impairs individual development may now be viewed in the broader context of how it affects the formation of student relationships. From this perspective, codependent behavior and dysfunctional socialization contribute to the dynamics and structure of university communities composed of dysfunctional student peer groups.

Initiations and Rituals

An important contributor to the development of substance abuse networks in university communities is the sense of initiatory and ritualistic value for drugs and alcohol. Peer groups arise from a sense of common experience or purpose. The use of drugs and alcohol as one of these experiences contributes purposefulness and identification to student peer groups.

The importance which social substance abuse assumes among students cannot be underestimated. In a sense, the use of drugs or alcohol is an initiation into a peer group. Substance abuse then becomes a ritual around which the activities of this peer group stabilize. The chemical facilitates discussion, camaraderie, and provides a rationale for gatherings.

The initiatory significance of drug abuse binds the formation of peer group associations. In this way, the bonding of an individual student to a group is facilitated by the qualities of the drug and the group experience of the drug intoxication. The type of drug used and the nature of the group experience have a profound effect on how the individual student comes to view the role of mood altering substances as elements of social activity.

Rituals surrounding substance abuse in college student communities may take different forms. These differing manifestations of ritual substance abuse are determined by the effect of the drug, the expectations and psychological content of the students, and the environmental and social context in which the drug is used. These effects will influence the role which drug and alcohol use plays for the group.

Group Stabilization and Identity

The unique properties of certain drugs or combinations may fill the needs of group dynamics and provide stabilization better than other drugs. This filling of needs will depend on the composition of the group. For some student peer groups, one or more substances may be preferred to others. This functional aspect of the way drugs or alcohol are used may differ among groups. The use of a substance by a peer group will have different significance on various occasions. Certain substances may be disapproved of or forbidden in one context and used regularly in others. In this way minicultures surrounding the use of drugs and alcohol evolve and provide an easy way for a student to integrate into the social environment.

Students are often mobile among peer group associations. The individual student must accept the sets of rules and behavior surrounding substance use of each clique. These limitations are often not concisely verbalized or defined, but are established by informal group consensus. In each case, the student will need to learn and assume the standards of substance abuse behavior of the particular group for each occasion. For example, a student may drink moderate amounts of wine with some friends, but smoke marijuana, drink beer, and snort cocaine among others. The use of LSD may be important to some groups of students, while other students may prefer to drink, and regard the use of LSD as taboo. A sense of definition and purpose is given to the group by the mutual acceptance of these standards of behavior.

The choice one makes to participate or not in social drug or alcohol consumption depends on the structure of the group. Likewise, the extent to which one becomes intoxicated is mandated by the collective will. These rules regulate the intoxication of all participants, even to the extent that the absence of limitations implies a rule of liberality. Commonly accepted limitations on individual behavior in a substance abusing group maintains a sense of belonging, and the continuity of the relationships is assured.

The Hidden Dimensions of Peer Pressure

In understanding the ritual importance of substance abuse among college youth, the influence of peer pressure on the initiation and continuation of this behavior takes on added dimensions. Peer pressure may no longer be viewed as the simple coercion to use drugs and alcohol out of fear of rejection or desire for acceptance. Substance abuse in these small student societies is used in the same way that ceremonies, doctrines, and personalities are used to stabilize the identity of cultural, religious, and political groups in American society. With substance abuse as a focus of identification, the force of peer pressure has the equivalence of the criteria which gives one the sense of belonging in society. University peer groups are microcosms of larger social interactions, and the dynamics which govern larger cultural forces are in force in the substance abusing microculture. Substance abuse prevention campaigns must address the force which these sociologic interactions play in the university community. To merely attribute recalcitrance to peer pressure misses larger aspects of the importance substance abuse plays in the development of college student socializing skills.

Rites of Passage

As a rite of passage, the use of drugs and alcohol is not limited to initiating the student as a member of a peer group. Alcohol and drugs are viewed as an initiation into maturity. Many youth regard the approach of their 21st birthday with a high amount of anticipation because it marks the attainment of legal drinking age. The observation of this zeal surrounding the 21st birthday and legal drinking age reflects the importance which is placed upon the use of alcoholic beverages as a part of adult life. The common perception is that alcohol consumption is considered a right by most adults. This importance of alcohol is advertised as a central issue in the fulfillment of adult dreams.

The assault on the national consciousness by liquor, beer, and wine commercials gives the impression to college youth that intoxication is an essential element in the enjoyment of life. Legal drinking age is a milestone of maturity in many student minds and thus the starting point of adult life. The importance of the ability of students to pursue the adult activity of drinking is often underestimated by alcoholism awareness programs.

The University Enabling Environment

Although not all college students become alcoholic, the alcoholic-like drinking patterns of large numbers of students on many occasions provides an enabling environment. In this setting, potentially alcoholic members of the student body may quickly develop alcoholism. This setting is characteristic of almost any student organization or gathering. The unsupervised serving of beverage alcohol at university sponsored events confuses their efforts to educate alcohol and drug awareness. For many students, this discredits the messages about the dangers of substance abuse. It is only recently that many university officials have become aware of the magnitude of collegiate enablement.

The toll that uncontrolled student drinking takes on property, health, and academic achievement cannot be underestimated. The turning of a blind eye towards the excesses of campus alcohol consumption is no longer acceptable. Uncontrolled dispensing of alcohol at functions sponsored by universities and student organizations must be seen as problematic and enabling. Attempts to make consistent and enforceable guidelines for responsible student drinking are long overdue.

The leap from alcohol to other drugs is not a hard one to make for the university student. Many drug abusers will view their use of drugs as being no different than the use of alcohol. Other than the obvious differences in legality and the quality of intoxication, alcohol is viewed as one of many alternative drugs. The rationale behind substance use appears the same to these students.

Course Material as a Stimulus for Experimentation

University study is a period of personal and social development in which the student is challenged daily by academic material which forces the evaluation of one's personal values. In addition to social exposure, the student is exposed to the topics of substance abuse in course work. The use of substances by authors is commonly encountered in course material. The use of drugs or alcohol by authors such as Ernest Hemingway, Sigmund Freud, Aldous Huxley, Allen Ginsberg, and William S. Burroughs, to name a few, and their attitudes towards these substances is undoubtedly influential in the formulation of student attitudes towards issues of substance abuse, chemical dependency and addiction.

Some students may view the use of drugs or alcohol by prominent literary figures and scholars as an essential part of their creativity and greatness. Such students may seek to emulate these figures in hope of attaining similar greatness. Others may have their curiosity piqued by literary accounts. In the formulation of opinions about drug and alcohol use, the student may feel secure in his knowledge of the documented experience of literary greats and discount the widely publicized information about the dangers of substance abuse.

THE IMPACTS OF STUDENT SUBSTANCE ABUSE ON SOCIETAL STANDARDS

The maturing student as a member of society must personally evaluate the necessity to make judgements about substance abuse.

As the student matures and experiences the impact of university education, the incentive to question social and cultural values becomes more powerful. The acceptance of, or disenchantment with, accepted social values is a powerful influence on the student. The student returning to society from the university environment will bring values about substance abuse based on experiences at the university.

In early phases of academic development, the student frequently assumed many social roles. At this stage the student must successfully reconcile various roles as a member of the university community, as a member of a family, and of a culture. Thus, the student will be forced to accommodate personal values and experiences to university and non-university communities. Having observed the variability in social and substance abuse behavior in the contexts of university life, the student will need to acknowledge even greater vagueness in societal attitudes.

Alcohol as a Reward

One of the values which the student must evaluate is the societal use of alcohol as a reward. The consumption of alcoholic beverages is promoted as a right. This sense of entitlement is one method of promoting social approval towards substance abuse. The use of alcohol is viewed as central to the ability to enjoy life. The media fosters and exploits this attitude by claiming that alcoholic beverages are a legitimate reward and an essential element of any social interaction. The university student is often placed in conflict with this cultural belief when approached by substance abuse and education programs.

The prohibition of other drugs in view of the use of alcohol has been seen by many students as being arbitrary and another example of the failure of authority to be unbiased. The claims about the potential hazards associated with marijuana use, for example, clearly contrast with the proven and documented effects of alcohol on the lives and health of millions of Americans. To base a justification for the illegality of marijuana on the hazards of its intoxicating effects is patently absurd to the student familiar with the effects of alcohol and the devastating effects of alcoholism on society.

To justify the illegality of marijuana on the basis of pulmonary hazards appear ridiculous to the student juxtaposed against government subsidies for tobacco products. The inconsistency and hypocrisy of American legislation and societal standards about substance abuse clearly undermines the effectiveness of prevention and awareness education. The inability to rationally justify legal and illegal use is further complicated by the lack of consensus about what is considered legitimate use, abuse, dependency, and addiction.

The Importance of Developing Personal Criteria

The definitions of use, abuse, dependency and addiction are not clear in contemporary society. Previously, limitations were imposed by unquestioned religious and ethical authorities. The diminution of the effectiveness of religious and political leaders to define values for the social problem of substance abuse throws this responsibility to the student. The assumption that summary lists of cognitive information about substance abuse will effectively communicate their dangers is inappropriate. To assume that the dissemination of cold facts will accomplish the goal of diminished drug and alcohol abuse is erroneous. The information must appear relevant to the student and clearly state the importance of making personal choices.

However, the authoritarian presentation of many university drug and alcohol information programs does not provide the college student with the tools to personally evaluate this information. The old didactic model of communicating objective information cannot work in the field of substance abuse prevention. Students must be encouraged to develop critical faculties, and the nature of substance abuse information must be tailored to this mind set. Any campaign must be credible and take into account the developmental and educational needs of the university student. Many efforts are ineffective because of their simplistic approach. Often the information about the dangers of substance abuse is inaccurate, biased, or seen to be politically motivated. Students in a period of developing critical skills will be quick to seize upon these inconsistencies and discount this information.

When the student is assimilated back into society, the ability to make personal decisions about substance abuse will reflect the ability of the university to encourage independent thought and action in this area of life. Because of the erosion of traditional sources of authority, the university must increasingly take on the role of educating students to make and assume responsibility for their choices to use drugs or alcohol. These choices must be viewed as a decision which affect not only themselves but society. Current programs do not begin to appreciate the scope of the problem at hand and the dispensation of popular anti-drug propaganda material and moralizing panaceas are ineffective because they lack sufficient depth. Any attempt to educate students about the dangers of substance abuse and its prevention must consider the personal and social dynamics of substance abuse. The simple admonition to "Just Say No" is inadequate in a society which uses drugs and alcohol as a vehicle to help launch college youth into adulthood. Preventive education cannot view substance abuse as an isolated behavior which is preventable by issuing official proscriptions.

The problem is a dynamic element of society. Preventive education must consider the importance of drugs and alcohol in American culture. Attempts to regulate substance abuse will be ineffective unless relevant social values have been defined. Until this definition of values has been done, substance abuse will continue to be a problem for universities and for society as these students move into the workplace and positions of leadership.

SUBSTANCE ABUSE AND THE MEDICAL STUDENT

As a subset of the college student population, medical students occupy a more important position in the development of an education strategy. On the one hand, they must be educated about substance abuse in order to understand the pathophysiology and dynamics of abuse in order to aid their parents. On the other hand, they must be exposed to the delicate question of their own drug or alcohol use and grapple with the issue of personal impairment.

Shortcomings of Traditional Disease Models

The recent acknowledgement that alcoholism and drug addiction are disease processes is a welcome development (Lewis, Niven, Czechowicz, and Trumble, 1987). However this has led to their inclusion in medical curricula with other diseases with which they have little in common. Medical students, however, seem unusually resistant to learning about substance abuse, dependency, and addiction as disease entities. This resistance has perplexed medical educators. We believe that this resistance arises from the inability to consistently fit the disease process of addiction into the traditional medical model. The traditional model views illness as pathophysiologic and pathologic processes rather than due to a patient's lifestyle (Kinney, Price, and Bergen, 1984). The difficulty with drug dependency is that no pharmacologic cures exist and the treatment consists of an ongoing, chronic approach that is persuasive, supportive, and without guarantees. It is no wonder both patients and physicians are uncomfortable with a disease process which defies the traditional medical model.

A Holistic Approach to Substance Abuse and Dependency

A holistic approach is needed in dealing with substance abuse issues. This is extremely difficult to achieve in modern medicine where "pigeon-holing" of interests seems the norm. Rather than trying to understand the behavioral and social dimensions of substance abuse and dependency, there is a continuous attempt to retool these topics to fit the traditional medical model and preexisting "specialties." By including them in pharmacology, pathophysiology, neurobiology, and psychiatry, the information remains fragmentary. It is commonly assumed that the student will piece the knowledge together during clinical experience. Thus, the topics of alcoholism, drug abuse, and addiction remain curriculum orphans (Coggan and Davis, 1986).

Resistance to substance abuse education also involves the topic of personal use. Elsewhere, mention has been made of the college student's difficulty in accepting the issue of abuse. Medical students have the same impediments of age, level of maturity, and ego differentiation to contend with, but on a different scale. It can be said that depending on the subset of students in regard to legal, socioeconomic, and ethnic issues, that medical students feel that they have earned the right to smoke, drink or snort, especially following exams, because they have delayed themselves ego gratification. Their clinical understanding of the effects of drugs further justifies these attitudes. Having been involved in a continual succession of academic advancement, they have been unable to distance themselves from the university environment. Any substance abuse training meets a screen of unresolved issues and post-adolescent, untested theories that prevent important skills from being learned.

CONCLUSIONS

The use of drugs and alcohol play a crucial developmental role for the college student. These substances provide these youth with substitutes for emotional needs. They facilitate affiliation by helping the student overcome shyness and awkwardness. Drugs and alcohol use serve as rituals around which student communities develop. The full impact of the experience of these students on society has yet to be felt. However, the magnitude of the problem extends beyond the grasp of current university drug education and prevention campaigns. The inability of these programs to address the full scope of substance abuse results in the inability of these efforts to communicate their messages effectively.

Overcoming Stereotypes

The need to overcome stereotypes is essential. Many students have preformed ideas about substance abuse. Alcohol abusers are "skid-row" types, not high level business executives. Marijuana users are "pot-heads," "spaced out" and long haired, but not nuclear physicists. Cocaine users are flashy rich folks not blue collar or middle management workers. Opiate addicts are seen as "druggies" without purpose and losers, not nurses, doctors, princes or merchants. Tobacco and caffeine users are successful and productive, not addicted or dependent.

These preformed ideas and impressions allow the student some freedom. Freedom to experiment and use legal and illegal substances is accepted because their use does not conform to that of their image of other users/abusers. It allows them the freedom to reject those persons not fitting their stereotyped versions as not possibly being an abuser and accept those people fitting their stereotyped version as automatically being abusers. Humanity needs to make sense out of chaos and preformed values are an easy and primary defense.

Curriculum Alternatives

A new type of curriculum is needed at all levels of university education to inform students about substance abuse. This training is needed especially in medical school but is also important in undergraduate education. This training of college youth is necessary to mandate the needed change in perspectives about substance abuse. Change is needed for society to move forward in the way in which substance abuse is recognized and accepted.

Students learning about substance abuse on personal and professional levels need to be exposed to people in recovery. Stereotypes must be broken down and the student's attitudes modified so that the student can recognize the human side of dependency and recovery. If the student is an abuser this exposure may provide an opportunity to see the future consequences of substance abuse if their behavior continues. If the student is a user, the chance to examine one's value system may be invaluable in determining or establishing the limits of use. Students must challenge stereotypes and see first hand the processes of successful intervention and recovery (Kennedy, 1985).

Twelve-Step Resources

In this regard, Alcoholics Anonymous, Narcotics Anonymous, Al Anon, and Adult Children of Alcoholics meetings are seen as absolute necessities in education to reinforce the belief that the consequences of chemical dependency can be treated and successfully overcome. Twelve-step programs provide a holistic approach to the issues of personal and professional guidance. The interactive nature of the meetings allow people the chance to reevaluate their role in society. New parameters and guidelines for living are investigated in the twelve-step process. In this way the central role of substance abuse in the life of the dependent or co-dependent can be seen and accepted. This process removes the barrier to the development of more meaningful and successful ways of living. Any student having difficulty with their personal values about drug and alcohol use can benefit from attending open meetings.

Interaction Oriented Towards Prevention

The interaction between substance abuse education and prevention and the student must move beyond ivory tower proclamations and research oriented data. So much resistance develops to such because it stems from authority which may be the conflict which is causing substance abuse. Students turn it off as so much static.

A patient centered, direct contact approach brings these issues closer to home. Small group sessions, audience participation talks, and personal interaction allow for a sorely needed dialogue. College students exposed to an open dialogue may be more willing to confront such taboo issues as substance abuse.

PLME as a Model

The Brown University Program in Liberal Medical Education (PLME) allows eight years for completion of the medical degree. This is because PLME combines undergraduate and medical school programs. During this time, it is expected that the student will be less focused on premedical requirements and directed to more thoroughly pursue studies in liberal arts and social sciences. Early exposure to substance abuse training can be introduced to these students at all levels of their medical training. This has the dual capacity to benefit their professional as well as personal decision making. In this model, some inherent problems of substance abuse education can be overcome by introducing it during anthropology or literature courses in which open dialogue about values and beliefs could occur.

Suggestions for Novel Educational Approaches

University training is designed so that a student may enter society with professional skills and well developed personal values. Since the use of alcohol and drugs on campus is commonly accepted behavior among students, it is imperative for the university to have an open dialogue with students on their personal use and choices. Programs should be developed to incorporate the individual and social aspects of university life with the academic curriculum. A central focus should be the development of programs which promote more substantial understanding of the need for a sound mind and body. Courses in issues of drug and alcohol use must be designed. These courses could investigate and encourage personal choices through the use of literary works, personal essays, and group discussions. Role playing and discussion skills can be as important in developing a set of values as a philosophy course. Other possibilities include offering instruction in behavioral modification techniques, stress management, relaxation therapy, body imaging, biofeedback, meditation, and yoga. These are important because they give students other avenues for enjoying themselves.

Similar courses could be developed for medical curricula with the emphasis on developing a skills knowledge base which a physician can utilize when dealing with a patient having lifestyle associated difficulties (Hawkins, Catalano, and Wells, 1986).

The investigation of Asian, Native American, Indian, and other cultural traditions which have recognized the importance of mind/body interactions for centuries could be fruitful. Many disciplines and practices have been developed by these cultures to strengthen these interactions. When young adults set off into the world after college, or begin to practice medicine, an understanding of how mind states affect the body and vice versa can help in healthy living. The university must take a more developed approach to teach students how to take greater responsibility for their personal, physical, and mental well-being. University substance abuse prevention and education programs will succeed only when they provide a sound basis by which the student can make decisions.

REFERENCES

Cobb, S. J. (1976). Social Support as a Moderator of Life Stress. *Psychosomatic Medicine*, *38*, 300-314.

Coggan, P., and Davis, A. K. (1986). Alcoholism – a curriculum orphan forever? *Substance Abuse*, *7*(3): 28-33.

Hawkins, J. D., Catalano, R. F., and Wells, E. A. (1986). Skills training for drug users. *Journal of Consulting and Clinical Psychology*, *54*: 661-664.

Kennedy, W. (1985). Chemical Dependency: A Treatable Disease. *Ohio State Medical Journal*, *71*: 77-79.

Kinney, J., Price, T. R. P., and Bergen, B. J. (1984). Impediments to alcohol education. *Journal of Studies on Alcohol*, *45*(5): 453-459.

Leipman, M. (1984). Alcohol and Drug Abuse in the Family. In J. Christie-Seeley, M.D. (ed.) *Working With The Family in Primary Care. A Systems Approach to Health and Illness* (pp. 422-448). New York: Praeger.

Lewis, D. C., Niven, R. G., Czechowicz, D., and Trumble, T. G. (1987). A Review of Medical Education in Alcohol and Other Drug Abuse. *JAMA*, *257*(21): 2945-2948.

Smilkstein, G. (1986). The cycle of family function: a conceptual model for family medicine. *Journal of Family Practice*, *1*(2): 223-232.

The Staff of The Medical Letter (1986). Crack. *The Medical Letter on Drugs and Therapeutics*, *28*: 69-70.

Vaillant, G. (1986). Cultural Factors in Alcoholism. *Annals of the New York Academy of Sciences*, *472*: 142-148.

Chapter 4

Theory and Applications of Alcohol and Drug Education as a Means of Primary Prevention on the College Campus

Gerardo M. Gonzalez

SUMMARY. In the past, programs developed to prevent the consequences of alcohol and other drug use on the college campus have been hindered by a lack of theoretical orientation or consensus on goals. As a result, some of the educational judgements made in the development of campus prevention programs have been shown to be flawed. Although the current alcohol and drug education initiatives being sponsored by the U.S. Department of Education explicitly call for a focus on education as a means of primary prevention, this paper argues that such educational programs must be broad in scope and should be based on appropriate theoretical models. The Health Belief Model is presented as a useful theoretical construct for the development of college alcohol and drug abuse prevention programs. According to this model individuals engage in behaviors to avoid a health problem if they first believe that they are personally susceptible to the problem, that the problem can be severe, and that there are acceptable behavioral options available which will help reduce their susceptibility or the potential severity of the problem. These principles also affect institutional or social health policy changes. The author suggests that the growth in the level of attention given to alcohol and drug issues in higher education in recent years can be explained in terms of the Health Belief Model. While in the

Gerardo M. Gonzalez, PhD, is Associate Professor, Department of Counselor Education, University of Florida, Gainesville, FL.

past much of the attention given to alcohol and drug issues on campus was characterized by the perception that alcohol and drug education was needed but unaffordable. It is now apparent that this perception has changed, largely due to legal reasons, to one where alcohol and drug education is increasingly seen as something the colleges can't afford to be without.

INTRODUCTION

The attitude of benign neglect toward alcohol problems which prevailed on college campuses since the demise of in loco parentis has begun to change. This change has been the result of a growing alcohol education grassroots movement which has developed in higher education during the last ten years. The beginning of the modern college alcohol education movement can be traced back to the 50 Plus 12 Project sponsored by the National Institute on Alcohol Abuse and Alcoholism (Kraft, 1976). This project began with a national conference held on the campus of Notre Dame in 1975 in which college representatives from public institutions in all 50 states and 12 private and minority institutions participated. The 50 Plus 12 Project was extremely successful in encouraging colleges nationwide to discuss the impact that alcohol abuse was having on their campuses. As a result, alcohol abuse has been recognized as one of the leading social and health threats to college students today. Both the susceptibility of even the smallest and most conservative colleges to alcohol problems and the severity of these problems have been well established within higher education today. Moreover, the perception of beneficial program and policy options available to deal with alcohol abuse has also taken hold among the colleges. In the keynote address to the First National Conference on Campus Policy Initiatives held in Washington, D.C., Dr. John W. Ryan (1986), President of Indiana University, said: "Effective alcohol education programs and policy initiatives on campus have changed – from something we all wanted but could not afford . . . to something we cannot afford to be without" (pg. 78). The rapid growth of alcohol education programs and policies (Gadaleto & Anderson, 1986) since the 50 Plus 12 Project can be directly attributed to this changed perception on the part of the campus leadership. Furthermore, this level of motivation has been translated into action by the increasingly frequent incidents of both internal and external stimuli (e.g., liability lawsuits, survey results, media attention, Board of Trustees concern) experienced by the institutions as a result of a changing social environment. Precipitated most ostensibly by the raising of the drinking age to 21 and the increasing frequency of third-party host liability lawsuits, the colleges have responded to the alcohol problem with a heretofore nonexisting willingness to articulate standards of appropriate alcohol-related behaviors in their policies, and communicate these standards through alcohol education programs. It remains to be seen whether the same degree of response can be achieved on campus with regard to drug use other than alcohol.

On October 27, 1986 President Reagan signed into law the Omnibus Anti-Drug Bill of 1986 which provided a total of $1.66 billion to fund new anti-drug abuse initiatives in the United States (The Drug Abuse Report, 1986). This legislation established for the first time, an active federal role in drug education. The drug education initiatives spring from a section of the legislation titled the "Drug-Free Schools and Communities Act of 1986." This section, among other things, made available $16 million for grants to universities for drug abuse training programs, model demonstration programs with local schools, and drug abuse education and prevention programs for students at the college and university level. Such a focus on college students is important not only because of the high prevalence of alcohol and other drug use within this population (Kandel and Logan, 1984; Johnson et al., 1985), but also because college students represent the next generation of community leaders and parents. More than any other single group, college students will set the standards of social behavior for the future. In short, the development of attitudes against alcohol and drug abuse during college years is an extremely important topic for this student and for society at large.

Although the emphasis of the Drug-Free Schools and Communities Act is on illicit drugs other than alcohol, the recognition of prevention as an essential component of a comprehensive strategy, and the influx of funds for programs in higher education, will make an important contribution to the colleges' ability to confront both the alcohol as well as the other drug problems on American campuses. However, these program development efforts should be grounded on sound theoretical models of alcohol and drug abuse prevention for higher education. Historically alcohol and drug abuse prevention programs have tended to be atheoretical and based upon educational judgements which are not relevant to the correlates of alcohol and drug abuse found in the research literature (Bukoski, 1986; Saltz & Elandt, 1986). Therefore, the purpose of this paper is to discuss some of the research relevant to alcohol and drug abuse prevention on the college campus, and propose a conceptual model that may be adopted for program development efforts.

GOALS OF PREVENTION

Before meaningful prevention efforts can be developed on a college campus, the question of what is to be prevented must be addressed. It is not sufficient to say that the goal of prevention is to reduce alcohol and drug abuse. Prevention means different things to different people and is difficult to measure. Because of the ambivalence that exists about the use of alcohol and other drugs in American society, alcohol and drug education programs have often operated without clear-cut philosophy or goals (Freeman & Scott, 1966; Braucht et al., 1973; Botvin, 1983). Some researchers have recently proposed a focus on the problems or consequences of alcohol use (Mills et al., 1983; Gerstein, 1981). Moore and Gerstein (1981) point out that the idea of an alcohol problem brings various situations to mind which might include the drunk driver who causes a serious accident by ignoring a road sign or losing control of the car; the fraternity fight that, fueled by alcohol and the ready availability of a weapon, flares into bloody assault; the previously responsible student whose ability to meet the course requirements and expectations of teachers deteriorates as a result of increasingly frequent drunkenness and hangovers; the heavy drinker whose damaged liver becomes a chronic health problem; or the rowdy students whose behavior and loud parties offend others' sense of propriety and order.

Therefore, it is apparent that in order for alcohol to be a problem for a drinker or others, characteristics beyond just drinking and drunkenness come into play. Some of the consequences depend on unfortunate combinations of drunkenness with demanding environments which put the individual or others at risk or inconvenience. Others depend on being drunk frequently enough in situations in which sobriety is expected and demanded that the drinker repeatedly comes to be regarded as irresponsible and unreliable. In all cases, however, the environments in which the drinking is done as well as the frequency and degree of intoxication interact in determining whether bad effects occur (Moore & Gerstein, 1981).

While some people regard even the most temporary departure from sobriety as a significant moral and social problems in our society most people regard drinking and even short-lived infrequent periods of alcohol intoxication as acceptable behavior (Cahalan et al., 1969). In the case of illicit drugs, however, a different attitude prevails. The U.S. Department of Education (1986) has adopted the position and actively promotes the idea that any illegal drug use is harmful and wrong. This effort extends even to the use of alcohol by persons who are under the minimum legal drinking age. The expressed intent of the federal drug education and prevention initiatives for higher education is to develop programs on campus whose goals are to encourage non-users of drugs to continue to be non-users, to encourage occasional users to stop, and to encourage regular users to reduce or eliminate their use. These goals seem simple enough until one considers the research which indicates that, for the most part, by the time a student is in college the decision to use or not use drugs has already been made.

Johnson et al. (1986) reported that 92% of high school seniors have tried alcohol; 69% have smoked cigarettes; 54% have used marijuana; and 17% have tried cocaine. Moreover, Kandel and Logan (1984) reported significant age effects concerning the risk for initiation, continued use and discontinuation of drug use. Kandel and Logan found that the period of major risk for initiation of cigarettes peaks at around age 16, for alcohol at age 17, and for marijuana at age 18; in contrast, the risk for initiation into cocaine use continued to increase through the end of the surveillance period at age 25. The period of major risk for initiation to cigarettes, alcohol, and marijuana is completed for the most part by age 20, and to other illicit drugs except cocaine by age 21. Those who have not experimented with any of these substances by that age are unlikely to do so thereafter. Furthermore, a potential maturation trend in marijuana use was apparent with a decline beginning approximately at age 22.5 for most usage patterns. The period of highest marijuana and alcohol usage declines beginning at age 20-21 and contrasts sharply with cigarettes which exhibited climbing rates of highest use through the end of the surveillance period.

The implications of this research for college prevention programs are substantial. First, it would not be effective to spend a great deal of program resources in efforts to prevent the onset of alcohol and marijuana use, when most of those who are going to be users already initiated their use prior to college. Efforts to teach the consequences of regular use or abuse might be more appropriate for this group. On the other hand, preventing the onset of cocaine use may well be an appropriate goal for a population of young adults such as that found on most college campuses. Similarly, efforts to encourage discontinuation of use should take into consideration the data on maturation effects. Juniors and seniors are likely to begin maturing out of high rates of alcohol and marijuana usage. For upperclassmen natural interaction with their college environment is often characterized by changing priorities as well as increased concern for academic, social and career success. Therefore, prevention efforts targeted on this population might stress the effects of alcohol, cocaine and other drug use on employability, health and interpersonal relationships. Special attention might be given to the dangers of initiation into cocaine use. Information on the increasing use of preemployment drug screen urine tests by industry might also be appropriate.

It must be remembered that the use of alcohol and other drugs as well as the consequences of that use is not simply a function of individual characteristics, but more so of the interaction among the drug in question, the individual user, and the environment in which his or her use take place (Kumpfer et al., 1986). Therefore, while different types of prevention efforts should be carefully targeted on specific campus groups, the overall goal of a comprehensive prevention program may well be to create a campus environment that is conducive to responsible decision making concerning alcohol use or nonuse, and intolerance for illicit drug use. This focus on the environment would make it possible to identify and change those social conditions that interact with the individual student to put him or her at high risk for alcohol and other drug problems.

A FOCUS ON THE ENVIRONMENT

History tells us that what sounds good in alcohol and drug education does not always work. During the 1960s and 1970s many well intentioned alcohol and drug education programs were developed which resulted in either mixed, or in some cases, negative outcomes (Stuart, 1974; DeHaes & Shuurman, 1975). At best some of these programs increased the participants knowledge about drugs but did not change drug taking behavior and at worst some actually increased experimental drug usage (Halleck, 1970). Most of these "educational programs" were based on the knowledge-attitude-behavior model which assumes that an increase in knowledge about alcohol or drugs leads to an attitude change which in turn leads to positive behavior change. Goodstadt (1978) reviewed the literature dealing with alcohol and drug education efforts based on the knowledge-attitude-behavior model and concluded that many of the assumptions made under this model are seriously flawed. Other reviews of the empirical evaluation research literature on the effects of alcohol and drug education programs conducted during the early and mid-1970s reached a remarkable degree of consensus regarding the lack of effect on behavior. However, pervasive methodological flaws in these evaluation studies make any conclusions regarding the effectiveness of alcohol/drug educational strategies more a matter of reliance on faith than on credible empirical evidence (Braucht & Braucht, 1984).

Since these early studies, however, there has been growing evidence that carefully targeted educational programs can have a positive effect in reducing alcohol and drug-related problems. A review of the literature conducted by Goodstadt and Caleekal-John (1984) identified 14 studies that have experimentally assessed the impact of a definable campus-based alcohol or drug education program on college students. Although most of these programs focused exclusively on alcohol and the evidence concerning college-based alcohol and drug education programs is not extensive, the reviewers felt that there are sufficient experimental studies to begin to assess the potential for such programs. Nine of the 14 studies reviewed attempted to bring about change in individual knowledge levels regarding the effects of alcohol or drugs on the body, eight of the 14 studies focused on attitudinal change, and 13 studies were specifically concerned with behavioral change. All of the nine studies that attempted knowledge change were successful in achieving this objective. Seven of the eight studies that aimed at producing attitude change achieved this objective, and nine of the 13 studies that included a focus on behavior change were at least partially successful in this regard.

Goodstadt and Caleekal-John concluded that

> In contrast to alcohol and other drug education programs (see, Goodstadt, 1978, 1980; Schaps et al., 1981), campus-based alcohol education programs appears: (1) to be better designed, in employing at least one control group and some degree of random assignment; (2) to be more likely to be concerned with reported behavioral as well as attitudinal and knowledge change; (3) to be as (or more) intensive in their operation; and (4) to be more likely to be successful in achieving the desired behavioral, attitudinal and knowledge changes. (pg. 738)

In addition, they point out that the existing evidence suggest that programs which contain some amount of field or laboratory experience, along with factual information and effective experiential strategies provide a powerful stimulus for change among university students. Furthermore, they suggest that this effect appears to be more likely when the programs are intense, involving a considerable amount of input over a large number of hours, spaced over an extended period of time.

In another review of effective campus alcohol education strategies Oblander (1984) reached similar conclusions. She reported that the most successful strategies in terms of behavioral change were those that took place over time and involved more than one meeting with a facilitator or group leader. Oblander suggested that this translates into an overwhelming potential for alcohol and drug education academic courses as a form of prevention of alcohol and drug-related problems. Kraft (1984) found that concentrated alcohol education efforts could be successful in changing knowledge, attitudes and behaviors of college students. However, he commented that successful alcohol education efforts require multiple exposures to small groups of the target population over extended periods of time.

These findings regarding college-based programs are encouraging. Unfortunately, most of the existing evaluations of campus alcohol and drug education programs have followed a secondary school model. These are evaluations of classroom-based alcohol and drug education courses, workshops, or other forms of short-term interventions or units of instruction presented as part of academic courses. Most of these evaluations have emphasized cognitive, affective, or experiential modes of instruction focusing on knowledge, attitudes or behaviors of individual students. Evaluation efforts have generally ignored the effects of environmental pressures or environmental changes that may impact on individual behavior (Gonzalez, 1986). In a series of studies conducted at the University of Florida, Gonzalez (1982) found that a short-term alcohol education module and an academic course presented over the period of one semester were effective in producing positive attitude and behavior changes respectively. However, at a three month follow-up, the effects of the short-term module on attitudes began to reverse themselves (Gonzalez, 1980). Gonzalez concluded that the students need the opportunity to practice the alcohol-related behaviors discussed in the alcohol education program and be rewarded for such behavior in natural environments before the behaviors are actually learned. If, after exposure to an alcohol or other drug education program, students return to an environment that generally encourages excessive use of alcohol and tolerance for illicit drug use, the change in attitudes produced by the programs may well not be enough to offset the environmental pressures.

Thus, short-term programs and courses, even when effective, are not enough. Comprehensive campus-wide programs should be designed to impact not only on individual student attitudes but also to create environments that support moderation in the use of alcohol and intolerance for illicit drug use. Such comprehensive community-wide approaches have been tried for the prevention of smoking, heart disease, and other health problems (Johnson & Solis,

1983). Based on the premise that unhealthy behaviors are maintained through periodic social reinforcement, environmental cues, and in some cases physiological reinforcement, the most effective efforts have combined generalized community approaches with individualized instruction on life skills and healthful behavior. Therefore, a comprehensive campus-wide alcohol and drug education program should, at minimum, include an active public education media component; policy guidelines and instruction on proper party planning; individualized programs for alcohol and other drug-related disciplinary problems; small group training opportunities, including seminars and workshops; academic courses for credit; individual and group counseling for students with alcohol and other drug dependency; employee assistance programs for faculty and staff; and an active data collection and evaluation component. In addition, programs to influence faculty and staff attitudes toward intervention should be included. Faculty, counselors, deans, health personnel and student resident assistants are likely to encounter abusing students early on.

A FOCUS ON THE PERSON

Although the incidence and prevalence of alcohol and other drug related problems in a population is associated with the per-capita consumption of alcohol or other drugs in that population (DeLint & Schmidt, 1971; Musto, 1983), there are certain subgroups that are at greater risk for alcohol and other drug problems. Thus while the overall focus of primary prevention should be on the environment and its effect on the general population, there is growing recognition of the importance of identifying specific groups that are at high risk for alcohol or other drug problems in order to target these groups more efficiently (Bry, 1978; Office of Substance Abuse Prevention, 1987). For example, adult children of alcoholics often comprise a significant "at risk" population on a college campus. It is estimated that the chances of this population becoming alcoholic themselves is three to four times greater than the general population. In keeping with Miller and Nirenberg's (1984) contention that alcohol abuse prevention efforts have developed to the point where specific interventions should be matched up with specific populations, interventions can be designed to impact specifically on students who are children of alcoholics. Unfortunately, children of alcoholics or even students who may already bring substance use disorders to the campus cannot be readily identified unless they volunteer this information. And although self-disclosure by affected individuals in classes or special announcements for self-help group participation can sometimes motivate some affected individuals to seek help, the search continues for outwardly identifiable characteristics that might serve to recognize a person as a member of an at risk group.

Much of the research examining alcohol abuse in college students has been predicated on the assumption that there are characteristics of college students that will define them as either more or less "at risk" for alcohol problems. However, Brennan et al. (1986, pg. 451) point out that

> The findings of consistent but relatively weak relationships between certain demographic and personality variables and the measures of alcohol use/abuse support the notion that any one trait or personality characteristic is unlikely to account for a large proportion of the variance in college drinking behavior.

The one characteristic of the heavy college user of alcohol which is consistently found in the literature is that they are more impulsive, sensation seeking, and rebellious than the lighter user. Of 20 studies reviewed by Brennan et al. examining alcohol use in relation to impulse expression/sensation seeking, most came to the conclusion that college students who drink in greater quantity, drink frequently, and who experience more negative consequences as a result of drinking are more likely to be classified as impulse expressive, sensation seeking, or subscribed to the "hang loose ethic" as defined by the authors. Brennan et al. concluded that sensation seeking, more than the other variables considered, is a characteristic that predisposes a person to be extremely attuned to social norms or peer pressure. Therefore, these individuals are more susceptible to peer influences which may encourage excessive use of alcohol.

PEER INFLUENCES

There are a number of antecedent and environmental factors which are associated with alcohol and drug use among college students. As noted above, personality as well as environmental contexts exert some influence on problem drinking behavior. Jessor and Jessor (1977) have proposed a theory of "problem proneness" which combines certain personality characteristics such as lowered impulse control, lowered expectations of academic success, and greater value placed on independence with environmental and behavioral factors to predict when particular individuals will develop alcohol and other drug-related problems. For example, there is evidence that frequent-heavy drinking and intoxication is closely associated with the use of other drugs among college students. In a survey of 10,500 students enrolled in 34 New England colleges Wechsler and Rohman (1981) found that 91% of the frequent-heavy drinkers compared with 61% of other drinkers were current drug users. About 60% of the frequent-heavy drinkers and fewer than 30% of other drinkers were multiple drug users. The drugs most often used by frequent-heavy drinkers were marijuana (91%), amphetamines (48%) and cocaine (32%).

Berkowitz and Perkins (1985) cited reviews of the literature on alcohol and other drug use which found that while personality characteristics are an important component of alcohol and other drug usage patterns, in general, the influence of social context (peers, family and environment) among youth has been more powerful than personality correlates in predicting the initiation of and involvement in problem drinking and other drug usage patterns. Among social context variables, peer influences have outweighed the effects of family and environment and become stronger in adolescence and young adulthood. According to Perkins (1985) the influence of peers upon heavy drinking and other drug use is far greater than that of environmental or family characteristics. In a longitudinal study of adolescent drinking, Jessor, Collins and Jessor (1972) found perceived support for drinking from peers was the most important variable accounting for the change in drinking status of adolescents from abstainers to drinkers. Jessor and Jessor (1977) also found that adolescent drinking becomes more frequent and heavier as the extent of perceived drinking among peers increases. In a review of drinking and other drug taking behavior among youth, Kandel (1980) also found that perceptions of peer use rather than actual peer behavior may account for much of the influence that peers exert on alcohol and other drug usage patterns.

USE OF STUDENT PEERS IN PREVENTION PROGRAMS

Because of the findings that perceived alcohol and other drug use by peers have a powerful influence on the usage patterns of young people, a number of researchers have suggested that the effectiveness of alcohol and drug education programs can be enhanced by the use of peers in the implementation of the programs. This assumption has its basis in persuasive communication theory which identifies the source of the message as an important factor in developing communication strategies designed to affect behavior change (Smart & Fejer, 1972; Sheppard, 1980). Students are often perceived as highly credible sources of alcohol and drug information by other students. Early reports of positive results from alcohol and other drug education programs based primarily on informational methods suggested the promise of strategies involving a greater degree of active student participation, leadership and affective involvement (Kline, 1972; Swisher, Warmer & Herr, 1972; Williams, DiCicco & Unterberger, 1968). Since then, several approaches of this type have evolved. One such type of peer group strategy called the ombudsman approach is described in a report by Kim (1981). This strategy involves instructors or group leaders who are not regular teachers or otherwise part of the established school structure. In a comprehensive analysis of nine different models of drug education, Wong (1976) concluded that the peer approach is one of the few approaches that has consistently met with success. In a more recent study, Botvin et al. (1984) examined the effects of a peer-led and teacher-led "Life Skill Training" on seventh grade students' cigarette smoking as well as use of alcohol and marijuana. Results of this study showed that the peer-led program produced significantly less alcohol use per occasion, and significantly less monthly and weekly use of marijuana on the first year. Cigarette smoking was also significantly reduced for students in the peer-led program. Several successful college alcohol education programs have also utilized trained students as peer leaders (Kraft, 1984; Gonzalez, 1980; Rozelle & Gonzalez, 1979; Rozelle, 1980). In all of these studies students were trained in facilitative and group leadership skills and, under supervision, were encouraged to lead discussions with other students in workshops or classes.

Another form of peer involvement which has grown in popularity on the college campus recently is the formation of peer advocate groups. This type of peer approach frequently consists of student groups or social clubs whose main purpose is to raise awareness of alcohol or other drug problems. Student members of these groups most often serve as advocates for community standards of moderation and responsibility in decisions about alcohol use or non-use. One such national peer-based program in operation on college campuses throughout the United States and Canada is called BACCHUS (Boost Alcohol Consciousness Concerning the Health of University Students). BACCHUS consists of an international network of student organized chapters that are sponsored by the local college or university. This program, which was founded by the present author at the University of Florida, provides a mechanism for student involvement and support in efforts to combat commonly held attitudes toward alcohol that often make the entire college community tolerant of excessive drinking and drunkenness. BACCHUS recognizes that drinking is firmly rooted in college socializing. Moreover, BACCHUS recognizes that young people who drink excessively are not always alcoholics requiring medical and psychological treatment. These young men and women often drink too much because they feel that it is expected of them and are encouraged by their peers. Through BACCHUS, concerned students can communicate to other students that not everyone on campus views drunkenness as good fun and good form. BACCHUS chapter activities are often the focus of extensive media campaigns that feature students as having a good time without over-reliance on alcohol, and actually speaking out against excess.

The goal of BACCHUS is to impact on the campus environment so as to create a climate of positive peer pressure to discourage illegal or excessive drinking. BACCHUS is not a self-help group for student alcoholics or problem drinkers. Through a variety of small group activities, public debate, media campaigns, social events planning, alternative nonalcoholic programs, and role modeling BACCHUS student members convey their message. The components of this message are that excessive drinking and the resulting consequences are a severe problem, that everyone on campus is vulnerable to these consequences, and that students as well as the institution as a whole have reasonable options available to them which can effectively reduce the incidence and severity of these consequences. BACCHUS, and BACCHUS-like groups, are not intended to be a total campus program. Instead, these groups are designed to function as a mechanism for student involvement and support within what should be a comprehensive campus program. They provide for a visible student presence and cooperation with the administration in the promotion of a consistent message regarding alcohol use on campus.

A THEORY FOR PREVENTION

The BACCHUS message has its roots in the Health Belief Model. The Health Belief Model is a theoretical construct that has been used to explain health-related behavior in general (Rosenstock, 1974a) and prevention in particular (Rosenstock, 1974b). The Health Belief Model relates socio-psychological theories of decision making to an individual's perceived ability to choose from alternative health behaviors. The origins of the behavior motivation theory underlying the Health Belief Model have been attributed to Lewinian theory of goal setting in the level-of-aspiration situation. Lewin (cited in Maiman & Becker, 1974) hypothesized that behavior depends mainly upon two variables: (1) the value placed by an individual on a particular outcome and (2) the individual's estimate of the likelihood that a given action will result in that outcome. In the Health Belief Model an individual's motivation to act is analyzed as a function of the expectancy of goal attainment in the area of health behavior. Thus, the Health Belief Model provides a theoretical construct upon which health-related behavior might be predicted and altered. Rosenstock (1974a) described the Health Belief Model as based upon the phenomenological orientation which supposes that it is the world as it is perceived that will determine an individual's actions and not the actual physical environment. According to this model, in order for an individual to act to avoid a health problem, he/she would need first to believe that he/she was personally susceptible to the problem. Second, the perceived severity of the condition would influence the individual's disposition to take a particular action. And third, the probability of the health-related behavior is also determined by the perception of how beneficial an alternative behavior might be. An alternative is likely to be seen as beneficial if it is seen as likely to reduce one's susceptibility to or severity of a health problem. Finally, a "cue to action" such as an internal stimulus (e.g., perception of bodily states) or an external stimulus (e.g., interpersonal interaction, mass media communications, personal knowledge of someone affected by the condition) must occur to trigger the appropriate health behavior. The Health Belief Model assumes that motivation is a necessary condition for action and that motives selectively determine an individual's perception of the environment (Maiman & Becker, 1974). This approach to predicting behavior is often termed "value expectancy" and is closely related to social learning theory (Bandura, 1977) which conceptualizes alcohol and other drug use as socially learned, purposive, and functional behavior that is the result of the interplay between socio-environmental factors and personal perceptions.

In addition to its predictive value for individual health-related behavior, the Health Belief Model can be used to explain an institutional or social response to a health problem. For example, the development of alcohol education programs in institutions of higher education over the last ten years can be explained in terms of the Health Belief Model: As a result of the success of the 50 Plus 12 Project in encouraging colleges nationwide to discuss the impact that alcohol abuse was having on their campuses, alcohol abuse was recognized as one of the leading social and health threats to college students today. Thus, the first two principles of the Health Belief Model—susceptibility to and severity of the problems—have been well established within higher education today. The third principle of the Health Belief Model—the perception of beneficial alternative behavior—is also rapidly taking hold among the colleges. Encouraged by pronouncements such as those made by President John W. Ryan of Indiana University at the First National Conference on Campus Policy Initiatives held in Washington, D.C., the attitude of the campus leadership has changed from one of benign neglect toward alcohol to one of increasing concern. Moreover, this level of motivation has been translated into action by the increasingly frequent incidents of both internal and external stimuli (i.e., "cue to action" in the Health Belief Model) experienced by the institutions as a result of a changing social environment. One particularly strong stimulus has been the growing willingness of the courts to impose third party liability on colleges and college groups which sponsor or permit alcohol-related policy or law violations which result in injury or death. According to a white paper sponsored by the American Council on Education (1986) which was disseminated to college presidents nationwide, "The important point is that every school should appraise its policy in light of the changing temper of public policy toward alcohol abuse" (pg. 69). In addition to serving as a strong cue to action, such liability cases and warnings serve to underscore the susceptibility to and severity of the alcohol problems confronting higher education. Just as the Health Belief Model predicts, the colleges are taking considerable steps to protect themselves.

The Health Belief model has also been effectively applied to the design of small group and classroom interventions in alcohol education. Portnoy (1980) developed an alcohol education program for college students incorporating factors of the Health Belief Model and persuasive communication strategies. The results of a multivariate analysis of variance demonstrated the overall effectiveness of the program. Portnoy concluded that the program was effective for a population of college students who were not problem drinkers in that it increased alcohol knowledge levels, reinforced desirable attitudes and beliefs, and positively affected beer consumption patterns. He further suggested that the program could have had greater personal impact if more emphasis had been placed on the subjects' susceptibility to alcohol-related problems such as peer and parental relations, driving while intoxicated offenses, automobile accidents versus fatalities, and hangovers. These problems were seen as potentially more relevant than the presentation of the medical and psychological problems which often seem irrelevant to the college student.

Kleinot and Rogers (1982) also successfully applied the principles of the Health Belief Model to an alcohol education program for college students. They incorporated the crucial informational and motivational components of the model into a program that focused on (1) the noxiousness and severity of the consequences of excessive drinking, (2) the probability that these consequences would occur, and (3) the effectiveness of abstinence or moderation as a coping response in preventing these consequences from happening. In their experiment, Kleinot and Rogers examined in a systematic way the effects of this type of information on the students. They found that college students drinkers' intentions to moderate their drinking habits were positively affected by the information provided in the alcohol education program.

Although the Health Belief Model has not yet been extensively examined as a theoretical construct for alcohol and drug abuse prevention on the college campus, preliminary results do show that this is a promising area of study. In an ad hoc manner the principles underlying the Health Belief Model have been responsible for much of the progress made to date in alcohol education on campus. An empirical, purposeful examination of this model might provide an important first step in the development and application of theory to the growing number of alcohol and drug education programs now being created on college campuses throughout America. Without a sound theoretical model to guide these programs we are bound to repeat the mistakes of the past. We simply cannot afford to make programmatic judgements without basis on empirical fact. For too long alcohol and drug education programs have assumed that raising awareness of the problem is sufficient in and of itself to change behavior. On closer examination, however, it becomes evident that awareness is only a first step, perhaps a necessary but not a sufficient condition for behavior change. All three conditions of the Health Belief Model – awareness of the problems, belief in personal or institutional susceptibility, and availability of viable options – must be considered in program planning. Furthermore, it is not yet known just how these three conditions interact to produce behavior change, or what the most appropriate mix of emphasis for a college population might be. A large scale, collaborative college prevention program development study is needed to begin addressing some of these issues.

Given the influx of new federal funds and the potential costs in terms of both human and economic loss of failed efforts, there is simply no greater challenge for the academy today than the development of an effective response to the very serious problem of alcohol and drug abuse on campus. Unfortunately, the federal funding priorities for higher education encourage the continued development of atheoretical program efforts. The principles underlying the college federal initiatives are based on policy and programmatic assumptions designed for elementary and secondary schools (U.S. Department of Education, 1986). Higher education needs its own theoretical and programmatic approach to alcohol and drug abuse prevention. Furthermore, effective college approaches will require a meaningful long-term commitment on the part of the campus leadership to making alcohol and drug abuse prevention an integral part of the institution's mission and services. This commitment should extend to the creation of full-time alcohol and drug education specialists who can serve as coordinators for program efforts. Too often alcohol and drug education programs on campus are operated by committee without clear staff responsibility for overall coordination. Such efforts are usually short-lived at best.

Future alcohol and drug abuse prevention programs in higher education should not only be comprehensive and properly staffed, but they should also be based on appropriate theoretical models and the best available research. The information generated through this kind of academic study should then be applied in both preservice and inservice training of college student personnel professionals. Graduates of these training programs should have a thorough understanding of current prevention theory and research. They should possess the skills to apply this knowledge in the design of campus programs which encompass the whole spectrum of educational, policy, intervention and treatment efforts. Activities within each of these areas are complimentary and, when properly applied, enhance each other's effectiveness. For example, a viable alcohol and drug awareness campaign within the residence halls should be complemented with an increased willingness by the counseling center staff to respond to the needs of those who might feel susceptible to the problem. Likewise, a viable policy on alcohol and other drugs requires an active educational effort to explain the principles behind the policy and encourage student, faculty and staff acceptance of those principles. When all appropriate institutional resources are mobilized behind a prevention program, the campus environment, the individual members of the college community, and the conditions under which alcohol or other drugs are available in that community are impacted. Indeed, such a multifaceted impact should be the goal of a comprehensive prevention program. But this will only be possible within the framework of sound prevention theory, a meaningful institutional commitment, and a consistent educational message—a message that the entire college community can understand and is committed to support.

SUMMARY AND CONCLUSIONS

The initiation of alcohol and other drug use typically begins prior to college and appears to be the result of a complex interplay of social and personality factors. In the past, programs developed to prevent the consequences of this use in college have been hindered by a lack of theoretical orientation of consensus on goals. The result has been an undue program emphasis on increasing knowledge about alcohol and drug effects in the hope that such knowledge would lead to attitude change, which in turn would lead to behavior change. However, many of the assumptions underlying this knowledge-attitude-behavior model have been found to be flawed.

Although alcohol and drug education programs based on the knowledge-attitude-behavior model have not had an extensive record of success in the prevention of alcohol and other drug problems, education continues to be seen as an essential component of a comprehensive alcohol and drug abuse prevention strategy. The current alcohol and drug education college initiatives being sponsored by the U.S. Department of Education explicitly call for a focus on education as a means of primary prevention. However, the focus of alcohol and drug abuse prevention efforts must be broad in scope. Alcohol and other drug problems are seen as resulting from an interaction among the drug in question, the individual user characteristics, and the environment in which is or her use takes place. Therefore, individual perceptions and use patterns can best be modified by interventions directed at all three components. This can only be accomplished through the development of comprehensive campus-wide prevention efforts. Moreover, because of the powerful influence that students exert on their peers, students should be involved as an integral part of the service delivery systems in college prevention programs.

In addition, in order for the programs to be successful, a theoretical model must be developed and adopted. The Health Belief Model was presented as a useful theoretical construct for the development of alcohol and drug abuse prevention programs. According to this model individuals engage in behaviors to avoid a health problem if they first believe that they are personally susceptible to the problem, that the problem can be severe, and that there are acceptable behavioral options available which will help reduce their susceptibility or the potential severity of the problem. In addition, a "cue to action" such as an internal or external stimulus must occur in order to trigger the appropriate health behavior. These principles also affect institutional or social health policy changes.

An examination of the college alcohol and drug education programs developed to date makes it clear that while there has been substantial growth in the level of attention given to these issues over the last ten years, especially in the alcohol area, much of this attention has been characterized by the perception that alcohol education was needed but unaffordable. It is now apparent that this perception has changed, largely due to legal reasons, to one where alcohol (and other drug) education is increasingly seen as something colleges can't afford to be without. This is perhaps the first step in the evolution of a meaningful commitment to the prevention of alcohol and other drug problems on campus. The growing body of research on this subject can now provide the basis for a program development effort guided by theory, consensus on goals, utilization of effective campus-wide interventions, and involvement of all concerned including students. Moreover, these programs should be directed by trained personnel who possess the skills and theoretical knowledge necessary to make the programs work. These are the essential components for an effective, long-term strategy for the prevention of alcohol and other drug related problems on our nation's campuses. It is an idea whose time has come.

REFERENCES

American Council on Education (1986). Universities, colleges and alcohol: An overview of tort liability issues. In *Proceedings of the first national conference on campus alcohol policy initiatives* (pp. 63-70). Denver, CO: BACCHUS of the U.S., Inc.

Bandura, A. (1977). *Social learning theory*. Englewood Cliffs, NJ: Prentice-Hall.

Berkowitzs, A. D., & Perkins, H.W. (1985, May/June). *Problem drinking among college students: A review of recent research*. Paper presented at the annual meeting of the American College Health Association, Washington, DC.

Bill provides first major federal effort in drug education (1986, November). *The Drug Abuse Report*, p. 3.

Botvin, G., Baker, E., Renick, N., Filazzala, A., & Botvin, E. (1984). A cognitive-behavioral approach to substance abuse prevention. *Journal of Addictive Behaviors, 9*, 137-147.

Botvin, G. J. (1983). Prevention of adolescent substance abuse through the development of personal and social competence. In T. J. Glynn, C. G. Leukefeld, & J. P. Ludford (Eds.), *Preventing adolescent drug abuse* (Research Monograph number 47, pp. 115-140). Rockville, MD: National Institute on Drug Abuse.

Braucht, G. N., & Braucht, B. (1984). Prevention of problem drinking among youth. In P. M. Miller & T. D. Nirenberg (Eds.), *Prevention of alcohol abuse* (pp. 253-279). New York: Plenum Press.

Braucht, G. N., Follingstod, D., Brakorsh, D., & Berry, K. L. (1973). Drug education: A review of goals, approaches and effectiveness, and a paradigm for evaluation. *Quarterly Journal of Studies on Alcohol, 34*, 1279-1292.

Brennan, A. F., Walfish, S., & AuBuchon, P. (1986). Alcohol use and abuse in college students: A review of individual and personality correlates. *The International Journal of the Addictions, 21*, 449-474.

Bukoski, W. J. (1986). School-based substance abuse prevention: A review of program research. *Journal of Children in Contemporary Society, 18*, 93-115.

Bry, B. (1978). Research design in drug abuse prevention: Review and recommendations. *The International Journal of the Addictions, 13*, 1157-1168.

Cahalan, D., Cisin, I. H., & Crossley, H. M. (1969). *American Drinking Practices*. New Haven, CT: College and University Press.

DeHaes, W., & Schuurman, J. (1975). Results of an evaluation study of three drug education methods. *The International Journal of the Addictions, 18*, 1-16.

De Lint, J., & Schmidt, W. (1971). Consumption averages and alcoholism prevalence: A brief review of epidemiological investigations. *British Journal of Addictions, 66*, 97-107.

Freeman, H. E., & Scott, J. R. (1966). A critical review of alcohol education for adolescents. *Community Mental Health Journal*, *2*, 22-230.

Gadaleto, A. F., & Anderson, D. S. (1986). Continued progress: The 1979, 1982, and 1985 college alcohol surveys. *Journal of College Student Personnel*, *27*, 499-509.

Gerstein, D. R. (1981). Alcohol use and consequences. In M. H. Moore & D. R. Gerstein (Eds.), *Alcohol and public policy: Beyond the shadow of prohibition* (pp. 182-224). Washington, DC: National Academy Press.

Gonzalez, G. M. (1982). Alcohol education can prevent alcohol problems: A review of some unique research findings. *Journal of Alcohol and Drug Education*, *27*, 2-12.

Gonzalez, G. M. (1986). Proactive efforts and selected alcohol education programs. In T. G. Goodale (Ed.), *Alcohol and the college student* (New Directions for Student Services Monograph Number 35, pp. 17-33). San Francisco: Jossey Bass.

Gonzalez, G. M. (1980). The effect of a model alcohol education module on college students' attitudes, knowledge and behavior related to alcohol use. *Journal of Alcohol and Drug Education*, *25*, 1-12.

Goodstadt, M. S., & Caleekal-John, A. (1984). Alcohol education programs for university students: A review of their effectiveness. *The International Journal of the Addictions*, *19*, 721-741.

Goodstadt, M. S. (1978). Alcohol and drug education models and outcomes. *Health Education Monographs*, *6*, 263-279.

Halleck, S. (1970). The great drug education hoax. *The Progressive*, *30*, 18-21.

Jessor, R., Collins, M. J., & Jessor, S. L. (1972). *On becoming a drinker: Social-psychological aspects of an adolescent transition.* Ann, NY: Academy of Science.

Jessor, R., & Jessor, S. L. (1977). *Problem behavior and psychosocial development: A longitudinal study of youth*. New York: Academic Press.

Johnson, C. A., & Solis, J. (1983). Comprehensive community programs for drug abuse prevention: Implications of the community heart disease prevention programs for future research. In T. J. Glynn, C. G. Leukefeld, & J. P. Ludford (Eds.), *Preventing adolescent drug abuse* (Research Monograph number 47, pp. 76-114). Rockville, MD: National Institute on Drug Abuse.

Johnson, L. D., O'Malley, P. M., & Bochman, J. G. (1986). *Drug use among American high school students, college students and other young adults*. Rockville, MD: National Institute on Drug Abuse.

Kandel, D. B. (1980). Drug and drinking behavior among youth. *Annual Review of Sociology*, *6*, 235-285.

Kandel, D. B., & Logan, J. A. (1984). Patterns of drug use from adolescence to young adulthood: Periods of risk for initiation, continued use and discontinuation. *American Journal of Public Health*, *74*, 660-666.

Kim, S. (1981). An evaluation of the ombudsman primary prevention program on student drug abuse. *Journal of Drug Education*, *11*, 27-36.

Kleinot, M. C., & Rogers, R. N. (1982). Identifying effective components of alcohol abuse prevention programs. *Journal of Studies on Alcohol*, *43*, 802-811.

Kline, J. N. (1972). Evaluation of a multimedia drug education program. *Journal of Drug Education*, *2*, 229-239.

Kraft, D. P. (1976, Summer). College students and alcohol: The 50 Plus 12 project. *Alcohol Health and Research World*, 10-14.

Kraft, D. P. (1984). A comprehensive prevention program for college students. In P. M. Miller & T. D. Nirenberg (Eds.), *Prevention of alcohol abuse* (pp. 327-369). New York: Plenum Press.

Kumpfer, K. L., Moskowitz, J., Whiteside, H. O., & Klitzner, M. (1986). Future issues and promising directions in the prevention of substance abuse among youth. *Journal of Children in Contemporary Society*, *18*, 249-278.

Mariman, L. A., & Becker, M. H. (1974). The Health Belief Model: Origins and correlates in psychological theory. *Health Education Monographs*, *2*, 336-353.

Miller, P. M., & Nirenberg, T. D. (1984). Alcohol abuse prevention: Conclusions and future directions. In P. M. Miller & T. D. Nirenberg (Eds.), *Prevention of alcohol abuse* (pp. 503-510). New York: Plenum Press.

Mills, K. C., Neal, E. M., & Peed-Neal, I. (1983). *Handbook for alcohol education: The community approach*. Cambridge, MA: Ballinger Publishing Company.

Moore, M. H., & Gerstein, D. D. (1981). *Alcohol and public policy: Beyond the shadow of prohibition*. Washington, DC: National Academy Press.

Musto, D. F. (1983). The American disease: Narcotics in nineteenth-century America. In M. E. Kelleher, B. K. MacMurray & B. K. Shapiro (Eds.), *Drugs in society: A critical reader* (pp. 2-29). Dubuque, IA: Kendall/Hunt Publishing Company.

Oblander, F. W. (1984). Effective alcohol education strategies. *ACU-I Bulletin*, *52*, 17-25.

Office of Substance Abuse Prevention (1987). *Alcohol and drug abuse demonstration grants* (Announcement No. AD-87-01). Rockville, MD: Alcohol, Drug Abuse and Mental Health Administration.

Perkins, H. W. (1985). Religious traditions, parents, and peers as determinants of alcohol and drug use among college students. *Review of Religious Research*, *27*, 15-31.

Portnoy, B. (1980). Effects of a controlled-usage alcohol education program based on the Health Belief Model. *Journal of Drug Education*, *10*, 181-195.

Rosenstock, I. M. (1974a). Historical origins of the Health Belief Model. *Health Education Monograph*, *2*, 328-335.

Rosenstock, I. M. (1974b). The Health Belief Model and preventative health behavior. *Health Education Monograph*, *2*, 336-353.

Rozelle, G. R. (1980). Experiential and cognitive small group approaches to alcohol education for college students. *Journal of Alcohol and Drug Education*, *26*, 40-54.

Rozelle, G. R., & Gonzalez, G. M. (1979). A peer facilitated course on alcohol abuse: An innovative approach to prevention on the college campus. *Journal of Alcohol and Drug Education*, *25*, 20-30.

Ryan, J. W. (1986). Conference keynote address. *Proceedings of the first national conference on campus alcohol policy initiatives* (pp. 77-80). Denver, CO: BACCHUS of the U.S., Inc.

Saltz, R., & Elandt, D. (1986). College student drinking studies 1976-1985. *Contemporary Drug Problems*, *13*, 117-159.

Sheppard, M. A. (1980). Sources of information about "drugs." *Journal of Drug Education*, *10*, 257-262.

Smart, R. G., & Fejer, D. (1972). Drugs and drinking behavior among youth. *Annual Review of Sociology*, *6*, 235-285.

Stuart, R. B. (1974). Teaching facts about drugs: Pushing or preventing? *Journal of Educational Psychology*, *66*, 189-201.

Swisher, J. D., Warner, R. W., & Herr, E. R. (1972). Experimental comparison of four approaches to drug abuse prevention among eleventh graders. *Journal of Counseling Psychology*, *19*, 328-332.

U.S. Department of Education (1987). *Drug prevention program for students enrolled in higher education: Information and application guidelines*. Washington, DC: Office of Post-secondary Education.

U.S. Department of Education (1986). *Schools without drugs*. Washington, DC: U.S. Department of Education.

Wechsler, H., & Rohman, M. (1981). Extensive users of alcohol among college students. *Journal of Studies on Alcohol*, *42*, 149-155.

William, A. F., DiCicco, L. M., & Unterberger, H. (1968). Philosophy and evaluation of an alcohol education program. *Quarterly Journal of Studies on Alcohol*, *29*, 685-702.

Wong, M. R. (1976). Different strokes: Models of drug abuse prevention education. *Contemporary Educational Psychology*, *1*, 285-303.

Chapter 5

Difficulties of Diagnosis, Differential Diagnosis and Dual Diagnosis in the Late Adolescent and Young Adult Substance Abuser

Timothy M. Rivinus

SUMMARY. The role of alcohol or drug use has been underestimated in the etiology and diagnosis of the physical, academic and psychological problems of the college student; so has the fact of being the child of a parent with substance use disorder (SUD). SUD can masquerade behind a multitude of problems seen by college counselors such as depression, anxiety, eating disorders, social and academic difficulties.

The price of unrecognized SUD for the student is continued dysfunction. The price for the counselor, floundering therapy. Even when SUD and other or other problem(s) co-exist (dual diagnosis), treatment may still fail (or remain incomplete) if SUD is not identified and treated. The current principles of SUD diagnosis are outlined here with the purpose of raising the consciousness of counselors, deans, doctors, or other health or administrative personnel to the concern of college student SUD so that casualty among students may be minimized. Brief reference is also made to the problems of being the child of an alcoholic or other substance abusing parent.

Timothy M. Rivinus, MD, is Assistant Professor of Psychiatry, Department of Psychiatry and Human Behavior, Brown University Program in Medicine, 1011 Veterans Memorial Parkway, East Providence, RI 02915.

INTRODUCTION

One of three Americans are directly affected by alcoholism and drug abuse. Colleges and universities are where the substance use disorder (SUD) begins for many Americans who have had "higher education" (Vaillant, 1983). If, for affected students, a diagnosis can be made and these students helped while in college or university, a major impact could be made on a population who put themselves, the lives of their peers, and their children at risk. Not only diagnosticians, counselors, deans and administrators have a stake in knowing about SUD. Any better understanding of the power of alcohol and other mood-altering substances to affect the human organism allows us to better "know" the human condition. To that end, current thinking about SUD diagnosis, how SUD can "masquerade" under other diagnoses and the possibilities of "dual" diagnosis will be presented in this chapter.

Throughout the chapter both alcohol and other abused drugs are referred to as substances; hereafter, substance use disorder (SUD) is synonymous with alcohol and/or other drug use disorder.

DIAGNOSTIC CRITERIA

By current criteria (DSM III-R, 1987) many college students both seen in counseling and as yet unidentified by college administrators or counselors, already carry the diagnosis of psychoactive substance *abuse*. The criteria to make such a diagnosis positively are the following.

1. Duration of one month;
2. Continued psychoactive substance use despite knowledge of having persistent or recurrent social, academic, psychological or physical problem that is exacerbated by use of the substance;
3. Recurrent use in situations in which use is physically hazardous (e.g., driving while intoxicated). (DSM-III-R, 1987, p. 169)

A smaller but substantial number would fit the diagnosis for *dependence* on psychoactive substances. At least three of the following would qualify a student for the dependence category.

1. Chemical taken in larger amounts or longer period than the student intended;
2. Persistent desire or one or more unsuccessful efforts to cut down or control substance use;
3. Large amounts of time spent in getting the substance, taking the substance or recovering from its effects;
4. Frequent intoxication or withdrawal symptoms, often when the student is expected to fulfill major obligations (e.g., complete papers, take exams, etc.), or when substance abuse is physically hazardous (e.g., driving when intoxicated):
5. Important social, occupational or recreational activities are given up or reduced because of substance use;
6. Continued substance use despite knowledge of having persistent social, psychological, physical or academic problems.
7. Tolerance: need for markedly increased amounts of the substance in order to achieve intoxication or desired affect;
8. Withdrawal symptoms: hangovers, "shakes," hallucinations, etc.;
9. Substance taken to relieve or avoid withdrawal symptoms. (DSM III-R, pp. 167-8)

Any three of these symptoms persisting for *longer than one month* would qualify the student for a diagnosis of psychoactive substance dependence. Substitution of one psychoactive substance for another or abuse or dependence on more than one substance constitutes polysubstance abuse or dependence.

DIAGNOSIS

The present director of NIDAA, a pediatrician with special interest in the problem of substance abuse in adolescence, states that substance use disorder (SUD) is the most commonly missed diagnosis by clinicians working with adolescents (McDonald, 1984). Our experience corroborates this conclusion in reference to the college student. Therefore, the first principle of the diagnosis of SUD is: "Always suspect it! Always ask about substance use. If it is denied, ask again." In fact, when empathetically and routinely asked, students are most often candid about alcohol and drug use (Single et al., 1975).

Family history research suggests that symptoms of various psychiatric disorders such as affective disorder, dysthymic mood disorder, personality disorder, eating disorder and psychoactive substance use disorder cluster in certain families (Winokur, 1980). Alcoholism is also a familial disorder (Cotton, 1979; Goodwin, 1985).

What, also, of the psychological impact of growing up in an alcoholic family? Depression, dysthymia, chronic anxiety and proneness to repeat a pattern of psychoactive chemical use and family life style in the next generation are extremely common symptoms of the child of an alcoholic parent (COA) (Whitfield, 1981; Black, 1982, 1983; Deutsch, 1982; Fawzy et al., 1983; Cermak, 1986). Therefore, the second principle of diagnosis is: obtain from any student seen in counseling a careful history of psychoactive substance use both by the student *and* his/her family.

The development of chemical use and abuse is a *process*. This process begins with exposure to available drugs and a peer group who uses them. The decision to use, and experiment with alcohol and drugs is generally followed by a positive experience (Johnson, 1980; Schuckit, 1984a; Brown, 1985). Regular use of drugs or alcohol may, in the vulnerable student, gradually and inexorably flow into compulsive substance use (Wieder and Kaplan, 1969). "Self-medication" to relieve subjective experience caused by the absence of the abused substance occurs at this point in the process (Johnson, 1980; Khantzian, 1985). Dependence has begun. The likelihood of this sequence and its speed depends on many factors: including the biological susceptibility of the individual, his/her psychological state and traits, the addictive potency of the drug itself and the amount as well as duration of time over which the drug is used. Other factors include health, nutrition and age. There is ample evidence that adolescence may be a time when the individual is developmentally more, rather than less, susceptible to developing abuse of psychoactive substances (Boyd, 1972).

A student, when intoxicated with a drug or when withdrawing from a drug for days and weeks is under powerful psychological forces imposed by the biologic effects of the substance itself. It is well known among substance abuse clinicians that the assessment and diagnosis of conditions such as depression, anxiety, and even borderline and psychotic thinking and mood disturbance is extremely variable and difficult in the hours, days, weeks and even months following the last ingestion of an abused substance. Time is often required to allow essential factors to emerge.

> M came for counseling for panic attacks. They occurred prior to exams and had been treated while she was in high school with anti-anxiety drugs by a psychiatrist. She attended two sessions of counseling and when exams were over she stopped. During these sessions, her counselor had wisely deferred her request for "more valium" until a diagnosis could be made.
>
> M returned to counseling a year later, following a suicide attempt. During the course of five further counseling sessions, a family history (paternal) of alcoholism and her own five year history of alcohol, benzodiazepine (of which valium is one) marijuana and cocaine use and abuse emerged.

Therefore, a diagnosis of SUD requires that other primary diagnoses be delayed until the intoxicated state and withdrawal phase are completed. A drug-free state of at least one month prior to further diagnosis is recommended prior to entertaining other primary or dual diagnoses. During early abstinence many symptoms may be those of drug craving, the "building up to drink or drug" ("Budding") phenomena, flashbacks or other neurological, psychological or other behavioral instability of delayed withdrawal (Valles, 1972). The potency of the abused substance, the duration of abuse, and the severity of the dependence process are directly related to the number, severity and duration of abstinence symptomatology (Valles, 1972; Johnson, 1980).

Schuckit (1984b) suggests a classification which includes the concept of *primary substance use disorder and secondary substance use disorder*. In *primary* SUD, symptoms such as depression, anxiety, eating disorders or other behavioral manifestations are secondary to the primary problem of chemical use. The onset of "other problems" follow the first use of a substance or substances. *Secondary* SUD suggests that another problem existed prior to the onset of substance use for which substances are used as "self-medication." This group appears to be considerably smaller in number than those with primary SUD. There may be considerable diagnostic confusion of conduct disorder which may antedate the onset of SUD but which appear, along with substance use disorder, to have a "life of their own."

This suggests a third category in which *dual diagnoses* are possible, implying that two diagnoses, SUD and other primary diagnosis may exist side-by-side with a separate but interlocking course of development.

Table I outlines the co-existence of these three various diagnostic possibilities.

TABLE I

I. Primary Substance Use Disorder (with secondary symptoms similar to other psychiatric disorders)
II. Secondary Substance Use Disorder (secondary to other psychiatric disorder)
III. Dual Diagnoses (Substance Use Disorder co-existing with another primary diagnosis)

ACUTE TREATMENT ISSUES

In treatment, the most life-threatening and damaging diagnosis must be treated first. Whether a suicide attempt is a direct result of cocaine withdrawal or primary affective disorder, a student presenting with such a problem requires primary life support (Bean, 1982). However, to miss the diagnosis and the potent etiologic fact of cocaine dependence in the origin of suicidal depression would be a serious oversight in longer-term treatment planning. The diagnosis of suicidal depression in a case of primary cocaine dependence is, though primary in terms of treatment, usually a depression secondary to cocaine dependence. It would not warrant a long-term diagnosis of primary affective disorder which would imply a very different treatment course. Such a patient could only be classified as having primary affective disorder if the diagnosis *clearly* antedated cocaine use or appeared following cocaine use *despite* definitive and long-term treatment for cocaine use disorder.

Issues pertaining to specific dual diagnoses will be discussed in the following section.

Children of Alcoholic (COA) Parents

This is a large group–estimated between 20-30 million in the United States, and between 5-15% of college and university students. They are at high risk for developing SUD (Cotton, 1979; Fawzy et al., 1983) and other psychological problems which may co-exist with SUD. Their problems are accessible to group and individual treatment if recognized and revealed in the therapeutic process (Whitfield, 1981; Black, 1982, 1983; Deutsch, 1982; Cermack, 1986). Approach to their treatment in the university setting (see also Donovan, B.E., 1981) are discussed in Landers and Hollingdale, this issue.

Physical Disorder

A common presentation of SUD in the college student is a physical problem. This may range from the more obvious intoxicated state seen in an infirmary or emergency room, police headquarters, or in a dorm (Stephenson et al., 1984), to less obvious symptoms of neglected self-care and accidents. A student presenting with any physical problems resulting from lack of self-care or as a result of an accident, warrants serious consideration of SUD. Academic failure, the violation of the rights of others, antisocial or criminal acts such as driving under the influence of alcohol, or theft, are to raise suspicion of SUD. Brenner (1967) noted at least 50% of accidental deaths in adolescents are secondary to alcohol use. This percentage has increased with the increased use of alcohol in this age group and the rising use of other drugs (Jessor, 1985).

Psychiatric Disorder

Semlitz and Gold (1986) recently reviewed 153 adolescents admitted to a treatment center for SUD treatment. They noted that 46% had mixed (more than one drug) substance use disorder. Seventy-two percent were diagnosed as having conduct disorders. Sixty-three percent had developmental disorders. Twenty-one percent had attention deficit disorder, 10% had explosive personality disorders, 7% had schizoid personality disorder and 2% had affective disorder. Thirty percent were diagnosed as having borderline personality disorder, 8% narcissistic personality disorder and 4% schizotypal personality disorder. This sampling is probably *not* representative of most college student populations with SUD but is indicative of the wide range of simultaneous diagnoses made when substance use disordered adolescents are first seen.

Anxiety and Sleep Disturbance

When assessing the symptoms of anxiety in chemically abusing patients, the following observations must be made: first, anxiety disorder in college students, considering the developmental context in which it occurs, is a psychological problem. Anxiety or sleep problems should rarely, if ever, be treated pharmacologically in college-age students. In particular, anti-anxiety agents (*all* of which are cross-addictive with alcohol and other abused substances) should *never* be used in instances where the diagnosis of SUD is possible. Prescribed psychoactive substances can in fact increase anxiety, and produce depression and be substances of abuse themselves (Griffiths et al., 1983; Winger, 1986).

Second, next to family and peer group influences, the expectation that alcohol and other drugs can "relieve tension" appears to be a central cognitive feature of those college students who go on to develop substance use disorder (Brown, 1985). This suggests that patients who are anxious and expect relief from psychoactive substances are at risk for the development of or already have SUD.

Third, a cycle of anxiety and self-medication appears to be one of the moving dynamics of the use/abuse/dependency continuum (Johnson, 1980). Anxiety and drug-craving behavior is difficult to interrupt and may go on for weeks, months or years following the last ingestion of a drug (Valles, 1972; Johnson, 1980), particularly if a student is merely abstinent ("dry") but has not participated in active SUD treatment; this emphasizes the well-established point that recovery from SUD is rarely achieved without a "program."

Suicide

The role of substance use and its association with suicide attempts is dangerously underestimated in the adolescent population. Recent reviews of suicide statistics in college students make no reference to the role of abused chemicals in suicide attempters or completers (Schwartz and Reifler, 1984). Yet, others have demonstrated the connection between both substance use at the time of a suicide attempt and the presence of SUD in over 50% of adolescent suicide attempters (Garfinkel et al., 1982; Hawton et al., 1982). It is no coincidence that the largest number of suicide attempts in adolescents in the United States are made with substances of abuse.

Affective Disorder (AD)

To date, the relationship in young people between chemical abuse and AD is uncertain. Authoritative reviews of AD in children and adolescents make no mention of AD as an etiological factor in the onset of substance abuse or as a co-related factor (Rutter, 1986: Strober, 1985). Others have maintained, albeit with weak evidence, that depression plays a role in the onset of substance abuse in adolescents (Deykin, 1986). This finding can alternately be explained by the fact that epidemiological studies find clusters of pathology (which include AD, SUD personality disorders and eating disorders) in the same families (Winokur et al., 1975; Rivinus et al., 1984). Additionally, dysphoric mood and depression are common, if not "phase specific," to adolescence (Rutter, 1980; Offer, 1981). SUD has been said to predispose adolescents to develop AD (Smart and Fejer, 1974). Proneness to depression (as well as SUD) has been noticed in studies of children of alcoholic and other substance dependent parents (Booz-Allen and Hamilton, 1974; Sowder and Burt, 1978; Deutsch, 1982; Black, 1983).

Some researchers have advanced a "self-medication" hypothesis which suggests that patients will choose a substance "of choice" to treat the underlying premorbid symptoms (Wieder and Kaplan, 1969; Khantzian, 1985). Such thinking may be supported by the finding that AD is found in as many as 50% of patients recovering from cocaine abuse (Gawin and Kleber, 1985; Mirin and Weiss, 1986). However, this research cannot conclude that a need for self-treatment *caused* the onset of cocaine abuse. It may be that AD was either caused or released by cocaine abuse. Nevertheless, it can be concluded that at least in cocaine abusers, AD may be a co-morbid factor which would warrant the consideration of pharmacological treatment. Both Lithium and Desipramine have been found to be useful in recovering cocaine users (Gawin and Kleber, 1984).

All observers would agree that once diagnosed, continued active SUD can only exacerbate the symptoms of AD and without treatment of SUD there can be little hope of treatment success of AD (Ablon and Goodwin, 1974).

Eating Disorders

Increased incidence of bulimia has been noted to be frequently associated with SUD in adolescents and college students (Pyle et al., 1983; Clarke and Palmer, 1983). The incidence of anorexia nervosa and substance use disorder is higher in families where either diagnosis is found (Rivinus et al., 1984). A higher incidence of alcohol abuse and dependence has been noted in patients with anorexia nervosa (Eckert et al., 1979). It is noteworthy that many now classify the eating disorders with "the addictions"; and many of the treatments for the eating disorders follow the principles of the self-help groups which have worked successfully with SUD (e.g., Alcoholics Anonymous, Narcotics Anonymous).

Attention Deficit Disorder (ADD)

ADD has been noted with increased incidence in the children of alcoholic parents (Goodwin et al., 1975; Tarter et al., 1984). ADD appears to be a risk factor in the onset of SUD (Weiss et al., 1986). Khantzian et al. (1984) have noted that a sub-group of cocaine abusers appear to have ADD. It was unclear whether this was a preexisting diagnosis, coexisting diagnosis, or a diagnosis as a result of cocaine use. Administration of methylphenidate (Ritalin) aided the remission in both cocaine abuse and ADD.

Personality Disorders (Conduct Disorders)

The increased incidence of conduct and personality disorders in substance users have been noted (Robbins, 1978; Hartocollis, 1982; Hoffman et al., 1987). The earlier the onset of the one, the more likely it is to be correlated with the other (Robbins, 1978). However, SUD without a pre-morbid history of conduct disorder *can lead to* conduct, behavior, and personality disorders. It is important for college counselors to examine the early history of substance using patients for conduct problems as well as to determine whether conduct and personality traits are "ego-syntonic" or "ego-dystonic" to a patient. Those patients with a co-existence of personality or conduct disorder that is ego-syntonic require longer and more intensive treatment (Rounseville et al., 1982).

Borderline Personality Disorder

Clinical (Masterson, 1972) and epidemiologic (Goodwin and Guze, 1979) studies have shown an association between borderline personality disorder and SUD. Not only do many patients share the same diagnosis but many of the behavioral symptoms of both disorders overlap (Hellman, 1981). Vaillant (1987) suggests that the better part of wisdom may be to withold the diagnosis of borderline personality disorder or traits until the etiology of those symptoms can be determined. Many relate etiologically to traumatic childhood experiences. The trauma of growing up in alcoholic or substance abusing families is common, but often an overlooked, traumatic childhood experience (Black, 1982, 1983). Symptoms of borderline personality disorder coexist with the unstable symptomatology of SUD. With rehabilitation and remission of the SUD many of those symptoms disappear.

Psychosis

It is well known that abused chemicals can cause psychosis states, hallucinosis, delusional disorder, amnestic disorder and other disorders of mood and perception (DSM III-R, 1987, pp. 127-

61; Davison, 1976; Tsuang et al., 1982; Siegal, 1978; Connell, 1958). These can occur both during acute intoxication, withdrawal and during post-withdrawal abstinence, remaining for periods of days, weeks, or months following the last ingestion of a drug. Some cases of chronic drug-induced psychosis have been known to follow the ingestion of certain drugs such as LSD and phencycledine (PCP) (Siegal, 1978). Multiple drug ingestions and intoxications have also been known to be releasing factors in the etiology of chronic psychosis in pre-morbidly schizotypal individuals (Teffert, 1978).

CONCLUSIONS

1. Always and repeatedly ask about and look for SUD when assessing college students who are having trouble;
2. Delay other diagnostic considerations until SUD considerations are clear;
3. Treat life-threatening symptoms first; but,
4. Recall that treatment of other disorders without simultaneously treating SUD where it exists is usually unsuccessful or only partially successful;
5. Accidents, anxiety, depression, eating disorders, "borderline" disorders, can often be SUD in disguise;
6. Psychoactive substances particularly those with abuse potential should *never* be prescribed unless SUD has been excluded as a diagnostic possibility;
7. The special vulnerability and treatment considerations of the large group of college and university students who are children of alcoholic (and other substance abusing) parents should be kept in mind when assessing students;
8. SUD is an eminently treatable diagnosis, requiring treatment persistence, but responding well when taken seriously by student and counselor alike.

SUMMARY

Psychoactive SUD may be caused by or cause other psychiatric and psychological disorders; or they may be concomitant with other psychiatric disorders. The need for research in the areas of cause and effect is in its infancy. The association of mood disorders and SUD particularly needs research.

There is increasing understanding that suicide attempts and accidents in college students have high relationship to chemical (alcohol and other drug) use. SUD in a student (or having a parent with SUD) may lower a student's threshold for other physical and psychological problems. Careful attention to diagnosis of SUD may begin a process of healing and spare considerable pain for those whose future can be so powerfully shaped by the college experience.

REFERENCES

Ablon, S. L. & Goodwin, F.K., High frequency of dysphoric reactions of tetrahydrocannabinol among depressed patients. *Am. J. Psychiat.* 131: 448-453, 1974.

Bean, M., Identifying and managing alcohol problems of adolescents. *Psychosomatics* 23: 389-396, 1982.

Black, C., *Repeat After Me*. MAC Publications, Denver, CO., 1983.

Black, C., *It Will Never Happen to Me!* MAC Publications, Denver, CO, 1982.

Booz-Allen & Hamilton, Inc., *An Assessment of the Needs of an Resources for Children of Alcoholic Parents*. NIAAA, Rockville, MD, 1974.

Boyd, P., Adolescents-drug abuse and addiction. *British Med. Journal*, 4: 540-543, 1972.

Brenner, B., Alcoholism and fatal accidents. *Quart. J. Stud. Alcohol*, 28: 517-528, 1967.

Brown, S., Expectancies versus background in the prediction of college drinking patterns. *J. Consult. Clin. Psychol.*, 53: 123-130, 1985.

Cermak, K., *Diagnosing and Treating Co-Dependence*. Johnson Institute, Minneapolis, MN, 1986.

Clarke, M. G., Palmer, R. M., Eating attitudes and neurotic symptoms in university students. *Br. J. Psychiat*. 142: 399-404, 1983.

Connell, P. H. *Amphetamine Psychosis*. Maudsley Monograph, No. 5, Chapman & Hall, London, 1958.

Cotton, N. S., The familial incidence of alcoholism. *J. Stud. Alcohol*, 40: 39-116, 1979.

Davison, K., Drug-induced psychoses and their relationship to schizophrenia. In *Schizophrenia Today*, Kali, D. (Ed.) Pergamon, New York, 1976.

Deutsch, C., *Broken Bottles, Broken Dreams: Understanding and Helping the Children of Alcoholics*. Teacher's College Press, Columbia Univ., New York, 1982.

Deykin, E. Y., Levy, J. C., Wells, V., Adolescent depression, alcohol and drug abuse. *Am. J. Pub. Health*, 77: 178-182, 1986.

DSM III-R, *Diagnostic and Statistical Manual of Mental Disorders*. Third Ed., Revised, American Psychiatric Association Press, Washington, DC, 1987.

Donovan, B. E., A collegiate group for the sons and daughters of alcoholics. *J. Am. Col. Health Assoc*., 30: 83-86, 1981.

Eckert, E. D., Goldberg, S. C., Halmi, K. A., et al., Alcoholism in anorexia nervosa. In Pickens, R. W. & Hoston, L., (Eds.) *Psychiatric Factors in Drug Abuse*. Grune & Stratton, NY, 1979.

Fawzy, F. I., Coombs, R. N., Gerber, B., Generational continuity in the use of substances: The impact of parental substance use on adolescent substance use. *Addict. Behav.*, 8: 109-114, 1983.

Garfinkel, B. D., Froese, A., Hood, J., Suicide attempts in children and adolescents. *Am. J. Psychiat*., 139: 1257-1261, 1982.

Gawin, F. H., Kleber, H. D., Cocaine abuse: Abstinence symptomatology and psychiatric diagnosis. *Amer. Gen. Psychiat.*, 43: 569-573, 1985.

Gawin, F. H., Kleber, H. D., Cocaine abuse treatment: An open pilot trial with lithium and desipramine. *Arch. Gen. Psychiat*., 41: 903-910, 1984.

Goodwin, D. W., Alcoholism and genetics. *Arch. Gen. Psychiat*., 42: 171-174, 1985.

Goodwin, D. W., & Guze, S. B. *Psychiatric Diagnosis*, 2nd Ed. Oxford U. Press, New York, 1979.

Goodwin, D., et al., Alcoholism and the hyperactive child syndrome. *Journal Nervous and Mental Disorders*, 160: 349-53, 1975.

Griffiths, R. R., Bigelow, G. E., Liebson, I., Differential effects of diazepam and pentobarbital on mood and behavior. *Arch. Gen. Psychiat*., 40: 865-873, 1983.

Hartocollis, P. C., Personality characteristics in adolescent problem drinkers. *J. Am. Acad. Child Psychiatry*, 21: 348-353, 1982.

Hawton, K., O'Grady, J., Osborn, M., et al., Adolescents who take overdoses: Their characteristics, their problems and contacts with helping agencies. *Br. J. Psychiat*., 140: 118-123, 1982.

Hellman, J. M., Alcohol abuse and the borderline patient. *Psychiatry*, 44: 307-317, 1981.

Hoffman, N. G., Sonis, W. A., Halikas, J. A. Issues in the evaluation of chemical dependency treatment programs for adolescents. *Ped. Clin. N. A*., 34: 445-459, 1987.

Jessor, R., Adolescent problem drinking: psychosocial aspects and developmental outcomes. *Alcohol, Drugs, Drinking*, 1: 69-96, 1985.

Johnson, V. E., *I'll Quit Tomorrow*. Harper Row, New York, 1980.

Khantzian, E. J., The self-medication hypothesis of addictive disorders. *Am. J. Psychiat*., 142: 1259-1264, 1985.

Khantzian, E. J., Gawin, F. H., Kleber, H., et al., Menylphenidate (Ritalin) treatment of cocaine dependence: A preliminary report. *J. Subst. Abuse Treatment*, 1: 107-112, 1984.

Mc Donald, D. I., *Drugs, Drinking and Adolescents*. Year Book, Chicago, 1984.

Masterson, J. F., *Treatment of the Borderline Adolescent: A Developmental Approach*. Wiley, New York, 1972.

Mirin, S. M., Weiss, R. D., Affective illness in substance abusers. *Psychiatric Clin. N. A.*, 9 (3): 503-514, 1986.

Offer, D., Ostrov, E., Howard, K. I., *The Adolescent: A Psychological Self Portrait*, Basic Books, New York, 1981.

Pyle, R. L., Mitchell, J. E., Eckert, E. D., et al., The incidence of bulimia in freshman college students. *International J. Eating Disorders*, 2: 75-85, 1983.

Rivinus, T. M., Biederman, J., Herzog, D. B., et al., Anorexia nervosa and affective disorders: a controlled family history study. *Am. J. Psychiat.*, 141: 1414-1418, 1984.

Robbins, L. N., Study of childhood predictors of adult antisocial behavior. *Psychol. Med.*, 8: 611-622, 1978.

Rounsaville, B. J., Weissman, M. M., Wilber, C. H., et al., Pathways to opiate addiction: an evaluation of different antecedents. *Br. J. Psychiat.*, 141: 437-446, 1982.

Rutter, M., Izard, C. E., Read, P. B. (Eds.) *Depression in Young People: Developmental and Clinical Perspectives*, Guilford, New York, 1986.

Rutter, M., *Changing Youth in a Changing Society: Patterns of Adolescent Development and Disorder*. Harvard U. Press, Cambridge, MA, 1980.

Schuckit, M. A., Subjective responses to alcohol in sons of alcoholics and control subjects. *Arch. Gen. Psychiatry*, 41: 879-884, 1984(a).

Schuckit, M. C., *Drug and Alcohol Abuse: A Clinical Guide to Diagnosis and Treatment*. Plenum, New York, 1984 (b).

Schwartz, A. J., Reifler, C. G., Quantitative aspects of college mental health: Usage rates, prevalence and incidence, suicide. *Psychiat. Ann.*, 14: 681-688, 1984.

Semlitz, L., Gold, M. S., Adolescent drug abuse. *Psychiat. Clin. N. A.*, 9 (3): 455-473, 1986.

Siegel, R. K., Phencyclidine and ketamine intoxication: a study of four populations of recreational users. In *Phencyclidine (PCP) Abuse: An Appraisal*, Petersen, R.C., and Stillman, R. C. (Eds.), U.S. Gov. Printing Office, Washington, DC, pp. 119-147.

Single, E., Kandel, D., Johnson, B. D., The reliability and validity of drug use responses in a large scale longitudinal survey. *J. Drug Issue*, 5: 436-443, 1975.

Smart, R. G., Fejer, D., *Drug Education: Current Issues Future Directions*. Addiction Research Foundation, Toronto, Ontario, 1974.

Sowder, B., Burt, M., *Addicts and Non-addicts: A Comparative Investigation in Five Urban Sites*. (Report to NIDA), Burt Associates, Bethesda, MD, 1978.

Stephenson, J. N., Moberg, D. P., Daniels, B. J., et al., Treating the intoxicated adolescent. *J.A.M.A.*, 252: 1884-1888, 1984.

Strober, M., Depressive illness in adolescence. *Psychiat. Ann.*, 15: 375-378, 1985.

Tarter, R. I., et al., Adolescent sons of alcoholics: Neuropsychological and personality characteristics. *Alcoholism: Clin. & Exper.*, 8: 216-222, 1984.

Treffert, D., Marijuana use in schizophrenia: A clear hazard. Presentation at 130th Am. Psychiatric Assoc. Annual Meeting, Toronto, Ontario, 1977.

Tsuang, M. T., Simpson, J. C., Kronfol, Z., Subtypes of drug abuse with psychosis: Demographic characteristics. *Arch. Gen. Psychiat.*, 39: 141-147, 1982.

Vaillant, G., The beginning of wisdom is never calling a patient borderline. Address given at Butler Hospital, Providence, RI, May 28, 1987.

Vaillant, G., *A Natural History of Alcoholism*. Harvard U. Press, Cambridge, MA, 1983.

Valles, J., *From Social Drinking to Alcoholism*. Tane Press, Dallas, TX, 1972.

Weiss, G., Hechtman, R. J., *Hyperactive Children Grown Up*. Guilford, New York, 1986, pp. 118-141.

Whitfield, C. L., Children of Alcoholics: Treatment Issues. In *Services for Children of Alcoholics*, NIAAA, Monograph 4, (DHHS Publ # Adm.81-1007), U. S. Gov. Printing Office, Washington, DC, 1981, pp. 66-80.

Wieder, H., and Kaplan, E. H., Drug Use in Adolescents: Psychodynamic meaning and pharmacologic effect. *Psychoanalytic Study of the Children*, 24: 399-431, 1969.

Winger, G., *Valium, The Tranquil Trap*. Chelsea, New York, 1985.

Winoker, G., Cadoret, R., Baker, M., et al., Depression spectrum disease vs. pure depressive disease: some further data. *Br. J. Psychiat.*, 127: 75-77, 1975.

Chapter 6

Treatment Alternatives for University Students with Substance Use/Abuse Problems

David Suchman
Elizabeth Broughton

SUMMARY. The authors present the University of Florida treatment program which is the result of cooperative efforts by the Psychological and Vocational Counseling Center and the Alcohol and Drug Resource Center.

This program includes outreach programs and a Student Assistance Program as well as individual and group treatment for ACOA and substance abusing students.

Illustrative case material is presented. Some general principles drawn from the development of a university based substance abuse counseling program are presented as well.

The importance of understanding the social context of a student substance abuse, psychological awareness, and the need for multidisciplinary cooperation in the treatment and prevention of student substance abuse are emphasized.

David Suchman, PhD, is Professor and Coordinator, Alcohol and Substance Abuse Counseling Program, Psychological and Vocational Counseling Center, 311 Little Hall, University of Florida, Gainesville, FL 32611.

Elizabeth Broughton, EdS, is Assistant Dean for Student Services, Director, Campus Alcohol and Drug Resource Center, 124 Tigert Hall, University of Florida, Gainesville, FL 32611.

INTRODUCTION

The development of treatment alternatives for university students requires the awareness that one is serving the largest segment of a university community rather than simply treating a group of individuals who have been identified as suffering from addictive disorders. Decisions about the use or avoidance of intoxicating substances are a part of the rites of passage that confront all students and, for a part of the student body, these decisions are complicated by the need to react to the substance use/abuse of a friend. An alcohol and substance abuse program in a university setting must consider developmental issues associated with substance users who are experiencing problems. It needs to offer services to students experimenting with substances as well as offer treatment to substance dependent students. Further, developing treatment alternatives requires an understanding of the university setting, an environment with its own peculiar characteristics.

The university environment can be characterized as permissive in terms of control of behavior and demanding in terms of performance. It is a high stress environment with a broad range of possible lifestyles. Most students, whether they are "traditional" or "non-traditional" (e.g., older, international or disabled) enter the university at a point in which they are open to questioning or altering their personal norms and value systems. The role of a student is, in and of itself, a transient role with the expectation that the student will emerge at some point as "an educated (if not mature) person."

In addition many students have left family or community networks with stable social controls to be transients in an environment in which lifestyle experimentation is the norm. University students are constantly confronted by decisions related to lifestyle issues, such as career choice, sexuality and dating styles, as well as the conscious or unconscious selection of stress management techniques.

Since being a student implies some degree of social experimentation, students often experience some degree of lack of awareness or denial that problems exist when their substance use begins to meander toward substance abuse. Substance abuse does not become an issue for a student unless defense mechanisms and/or coping styles begin to fail. A student must reach some sort of "bottom" in which some event occurs which confronts resistance to the concept that a problem exists. In the same way that primary prevention programs keep the issue of substance abuse in the foreground of public awareness, secondary prevention programs can assist the campus community by bringing problematic substance use on the part of individuals to the attention of professionals. These programs "raise the bottom" and provide opportunities for students to question their substance use behavior.

Surveys of student alcohol use show that 70-95% of students drink beverage alcohol (Blane, 1982; Blane and Chafetz, 1979). Brigman and Knox (1987) reported lifetime use for Arizona State University students to be 95% for alcohol, 56% for marijuana, 27% for cocaine, and 24% for amphetamines. Broughton (1987) found a similar pattern at the University of Florida. She reported that 95% of the student body ascribes to lifetime use of alcohol, 42% lifetime use of marijuana, 19% for cocaine and 12% for amphetamines. Further, Kandel and Logan (1984), relying on retrospective reports of their longitudinal study, found that for most illicit drugs, the period of highest risk for initiation of use peaks at 18 years with cocaine initiation occurring somewhat later. The fact that risk of initiation to illicit drugs is high in the college population underscores findings that approximately 25% of the 18-21 year old population experience some difficulties with their use of alcohol (Williams et al., 1987).

Until recently, most institutions of higher education assumed that college student drinking or substance abuse was a precursor to adult behavior and focused mainly on primary prevention activities. Fillmore's (1974, 1975) longitudinal study of individuals during and after college found that students classified as problem drinkers in college were problem drinkers in middle age. Therefore, primary prevention activities were concerned with changing college student's knowledge, attitudes, and behavior towards alcohol and other drugs. However, a growing trend in higher education is the examination of the consequences of substance abuse and identifying or intervening with treatment alternatives. Several studies have highlighted the negative consequences of alcohol and substance use behavior (Engs, 1977a; Wechsler, 1979; Kraft, 1981). Problem behavior has been noted as lower grades, physical problems or accidents, trouble with the law, drunk driving arrests, relationship problems, and damage to property. Due to these reports, there appears to be an increase in developing student assistance programs and treatment programs modeled after successful employee assistance models.

The University of Florida's model of treatment alternatives focuses on targeting its community through:

1. Outreach Prevention Programs
2. Student Assistance Programs
   (a) Driving under the influence (DUI) "at risk" students
   (b) Judicial "at risk" referred students
3. Alcohol and Substance Abuse Treatment Program
   (a) Adult Children of Alcohol or Substance Abusing Parents (ACOA) group
   (b) Alcohol and Substance Abuse group

The 5 main targeted populations are:

1. Education and information for experimental users and non-users.
2. Programs for students who abuse alcohol and other drugs whose use is causing problems.
3. Programs for students who are affected by the substance use or abuse of others.
4. Assistance for recovering students who need assistance in adapting to the college environment.
5. Assistance for students who are chemically dependent.

OUTREACH PREVENTION PROGRAMS

Some of the most highly valued outreach programs offered by the Campus Alcohol and Drug Prevention Project (a program funded by The Florida Department of Health and Rehabilitative Services) and the University of Florida's Counseling Center substance abuse program have been directed toward students who are concerned with the alcohol and drug use of another student. Outreach programs are closely associated with treatment alternatives because it brings treatment closer to students who may be concerned about their alcohol and drug use. In some cases, students present their own alcohol and drug use as though they are concerned about a friend. Some of the students are personally concerned by their perception of alcohol and drug abuse by other students.

Methods of outreach include media awareness campaigns, informational campaigns, and workshops. Campus and community media have assisted attempts by professionals to help students confront these behaviors successfully. Radio and television news and public service announcements with titles such as "Holiday Drinking" or "Party Safe" have been valuable examples of the role that the electronic media can play in influencing student substance abuse behavior. Campus and community newspapers have published columns by professionals which present techniques and ideas related to confronting substance abuse behaviors in friends.

Finally, workshops using concepts from assertiveness training, intervention (Johnson, 1986) and substance abuse prevention (e.g., Gonzalez, 1984, BACCHUS Guide) have been frequently requested by campus organizations and the Division of Housing. These workshops are part of a broad range of outreach programs designed to support decisions for responsible use of alcohol on the part of students who have chosen to drink. The workshops on confronting substance abusing peers often lead to referrals to the treatment programs.

STUDENT ASSISTANCE PROGRAM

The University of Florida's student assistance program is designed to bring two groups of "at risk" students into contact with professionals. These two groups are students who have been arrested for Driving Under the Influence (DUI) offenses and students who have had conduct offenses (e.g., fights, damaging property, etc.) in which alcohol or substance use is considered to be a component of the behavioral problem. Students with conduct offenses may be referred by a campus agency, such as the Division of Housing or the student conduct court. Most frequently, referrals come from the Office for Student Judicial Affairs. The DUI offenders may be referred by the regional safety council, the community addictions programs, or the campus police. There are separate programs for each of these groups but they follow the same general format (Broughton and Suchman, 1983).

The "at risk" students are required to attend an "alcohol and drug education workshop." Attendance is required. The Office for Student Judicial Affairs will take disciplinary action if a student fails to attend. The ambience of these workshops is informal and although it is made clear from the outset that substance abuse is an issue to be considered, it is also stressed that the leaders do not necessarily assume that the student is "alcoholic" or a habitual substance abuser. Rather, the workshop presents the philosophy that people may have substance use problems when they begin to have problems associated with their substance use and that addiction is only one of the problems that one might experience with alcohol or drugs. The philosophical basis of this workshop is similar to that of Marlatt (1977) who encourages clients to take an active role in treatment planning and decision-making. The workshop becomes an opportunity for the student to examine his or her substance use and decide if he or she might benefit from substance abuse treatment. Further, the workshop provides a relaxed atmosphere in which a student can examine the place that substance use has in his/her lifestyle. This creates an opportunity for the student to reflect on their values and attitudes toward alcohol and drug use as well as their substance use behavior. Students generally do not resist discussing their views of substance use because the workshop climate is not viewed as threatening. The program has been in effect since 1979. The workshops are designed to meet for three 2-hour sessions. Each session has specific objectives. The film *Chalktalk*[1] is used as an informative, entertaining introduction to alcohol and drug education and a discussion of the process involved in addiction.

The final component of the workshop is one in which the student writes a biography of his or her alcohol and drug use and discusses it with a professional. This gives the student an opportunity to examine the historical development of his or her substance use and to

---

[1]*Chalktalk*: A Father Martin film, Kelly Productions, 8 Howard Street, Aberdeen, MD.

experience a meeting with a professional. This final meeting is an individual session with a counselor. At the completion of the workshop, students are not obligated to seek treatment unless they have been referred by the courts and the professional believes substance abuse treatment is necessary.

The student assistance program is reviewed each year to reassess its goals and objectives. Since 1979, more than 400 students have utilized these workshops with five reported second offenses. Overall, about one or two students in each workshop refer themselves for further substance abuse treatment.

ADULT CHILDREN OF ALCOHOLICS OR SUBSTANCE ABUSING PARENTS (ACOA)

Counseling of students with a parent or parents who are or have abused alcohol or other substances is provided by the University Counseling Center. Outreach programs such as "ACOA" are offered on campus by the Counseling Center and the Campus Alcohol and Drug Resource Center. Many of the students who finally seek ACOA counseling have attended one or more of these workshops. Others respond to advertising in the campus newspapers, seek counseling for other problems or hear about the ACOA program through the campus grapevine. ACOA counseling has been offered since 1978 and so a relatively large group of students have experienced this aspect of the alcohol and substance abuse program.

Offering counseling to ACOA students requires a commitment to an ongoing therapeutic relationship which is not offered in the outreach or student assistance programs. Students who request ACOA counseling receive an initial intake interview. They are asked to set their experiences growing up in the family of an alcoholic or substance abusing parent in the context of their lives in the present. The majority of these students indicate that they experience some form of difficulty in their social relationships, especially in the area of dating relationships. If it is ascertained that a student is abusing alcohol or other substances, he or she will be referred for substance abuse counseling.

ACOAs often present the same relationship issues that one sees in general counseling groups with the added stress of problems in the family of origin. Anxiety about returning home for holidays is a typical student concern which is exacerbated when a student has a substance abusing parent. In some cases, this takes the focus of anxiety about "being pulled back into it again." In other cases, the student does not articulate this fear but experiences a "holiday depression." This depression can be the result of the student's unhappy resignation that he or she has not been able to "rescue" the parent.

Most students who request ACOA counseling prefer group counseling. Group members are usually helpful in supporting one another during anxious periods and the intimacy level in these groups is similar to that in a general therapy group which has met for several sessions. Although group leaders underscore the notion that not all ACOAs have had the same family experience and that ACOA is a generic term, the students indicate that they appreciate the fact that they are not alone. Further, many of the students who attend ACOA groups have had positive experiences with Alateen or other self-help groups. This, coupled with the fact that there are usually one or two students who have attended a previous UF ACOA group contributes to the sense of community which results in a high intimacy level. The intimacy and bonding of these groups provides a safe background for the confrontation of unrealistic expectations and self-defeating behaviors which are revealed in group meetings.

Group leaders approach the ACOA groups developmentally. That is the students are presented with the notion that childhood in a dysfunctional family requires that one learn certain survival skills. As one matures, the survivor begins to take on a particular role in the family. Concepts based on the work of Black (1982) are presented as well as the concept that going away to college represents an opportunity for students to become aware and change those aspects of their survival patterns that are no longer useful to them.

Assertiveness training techniques including role-playing of problematic family situations or problems occurring in present day university life, provide opportunities for students to release emotions associated with painful experiences. These "mini-psychodramas" also provide opportunities for students to experience empathy for their parents or other participants in re-enacted scenes by playing their roles and to experiment with new responses in situations that have been troublesome.

ACOA Case Example

N. came to study in Florida from her family home on the west coast in the hope that the distance would help her to, in her words, "heal up" from the pain of living with an alcoholic mother. Instead, N. found herself becoming more and more depressed and came for counseling with depression as her presenting problem. During an intake interview, she revealed her family background and decided that an ACOA group might be useful to her. During the early "bonding" phase of the group N. complained that she was from a high achieving family and that she was expected to do well in school. In addition, she stated that she would receive a visit from the family in November and that she was expected to fill her mother's role and serve Thanksgiving dinner. N. was anxious about this but wanted to fulfill this expectation.

In the next phase of treatment N. was able to look at her depression and became aware that depression represented a mixture of anger at her mother for not being available as a parent and for being self-destructive. For the first time N. was able to see the connection between her unfulfilled expectations of her parents and their demands on her, anger which was never expressed in her family, and her depression.

In the next phase of the group N. participated in a series of role-plays in which she would have to learn from her mother via telephone the secrets of the annual Thanksgiving dinner. She was able to use her role-play experiences in real life and was satisfied with the family visit. Afterwards, she still experienced some "sadness" at her mother's poor physical health but she discovered that her depression had become less severe as she was able to express her anger and gain some empathy for her mother.

ALCOHOL AND SUBSTANCE ABUSE GROUP

Students come for substance abuse counseling with a range of issues related to their use of alcohol or drugs. Some mention having attempted to control their substance use and having failed. They want counseling to help them in their attempts to "improve their will power." Other students may come for counseling after having been in residential treatment or otherwise attaining sobriety and want counseling for the purpose of maintaining abstinence. For some of these students the issue of abstinence has been resolved. They are not so much concerned with relapse as they are in other aspects of their lives such as relations with same or opposite sex friends, career choice, etc. These students are generally "group wise" and want to work on general counseling issues in a substance abuse group because it is more comfortable for them. Some students come for counseling with the awareness that they are misusing alcohol or drugs but not at an addictive or even habitual level. With this mixture of students, it is probable that a therapist might lead a group composed of students who are abstinent, those who want to be abstinent, and those who want to drink or use drugs in a controlled fashion.

In addition to the range of concerns that students have vis-à-vis alcohol or drugs, there is also a range of levels of involvement that students have with their drug(s) of choice. The most severe cases provide the simplest disposition. The student who is physiologically addicted is in need of immediate detoxification. There is no point in recommending outpatient psychological therapy for such a student.

A student who is consistently using alcohol and/or drugs at a level which will allow him or her to abstain from these substances without experiencing symptoms of withdrawal presents a more complex decision as to disposition. Is residential treatment required or could this student be seen as an outpatient? These decisions require some experience on the part of the therapist. One goal in the decision for a particular treatment modality is to attempt not to disrupt the most positive aspects of the student's life. If possible, treatment should be offered while the student remains in school and continues to attend classes. However, the therapist's estimation of the student's involvement with the drug(s) of choice, with a social milieu that supports continued drug use, and the student's degree of determination to break his or her self-destructive habits are also factors in the decision. A student who does not appear to be able to sustain abstinence at this point will need residential treatment.

If abstinence seems to be possible and the student appears to have enough psychological organization to continue in school, it may be appropriate to suggest outpatient psychotherapy and an intensive involvement in Alcoholics Anonymous (AA) or Narcotics Anonymous (NA). In the case of a student whose drug of choice is alcohol, antabuse[2] may fit into this plan of treatment.

A number of students request substance abuse counseling when they become aware that they are beginning to lose control of their substance use. These students can be treated in outpatient counseling and may choose to attend AA or NA meetings. In brief, the mid-range of these cases, the student who is habitually abusing his or her drug of choice but who, for one reason or another (support group, regular attendance at classes, psychological strength, etc.) may be able to withdraw successfully and maintain sobriety poses the most complex disposition decisions. Although the assessment of the degree of the student's involvement with alcohol and/or drugs precedes decisions as to treatment dispositions, the understanding of the psychological or lifestyle issues underlying the abuse of intoxicants is a major part of substance abuse treatment. Treatment is a form of education in which a patient becomes aware of psychological, emotional, behavioral, and social aspects of their use of intoxicants. There are also aspects of this process that include social skills training, such as assertiveness training, drug education, and, insight-oriented psychological therapy.

Case Examples

1. B. is a 29-year-old female junior who came for counseling at the beginning of the Autumn semester. She had been at her parent's home in a resort area during the summer. She de-

---

[2]Antabuse (disulfiram) is a drug which results in an extremely unpleasant reaction to alcohol.

scribed a lifestyle in which she worked the dinner shift as a waitress in a beachfront restaurant. After work she would go out with her friends until early morning and she felt that her use of alcohol was becoming somewhat excessive. In treatment B. revealed that she felt constricted by being in her parent's home when she had much more freedom at school. She described her relationship with her parents as positive but that they tended to treat her more as a child than as an adult. She described her drinking behavior as part of the typical social behavior of restaurant personnel in her home town and that she was avoiding going home until her parents were asleep. Treatment consisted of some reflection on the developmental phase in which she was involved. She was coming into adulthood and her parents were treating her as though she was somewhat younger. There was an element of assertiveness training in her treatment as well as some "dutch uncle" talk about coming into adulthood gracefully.

B. found that her use of alcohol began to moderate when she was back at school and was making her own lifestyle decisions. She continued in treatment until she had been home for two or three vacations in which she was able to suggest to her parents that they begin to "promote one another to the rank of equals." The therapists in this situation saw B. as a student who did not need extended treatment. An interesting aspect of B.'s treatment came from some experienced AA and NA members of the substance abuse group who thought that B. was in denial of a more serious alcohol problem and respectfully suggested that the therapists might be enabling B. to continue to abuse alcohol.

2. J. was an undergraduate who was close to graduation. He came for substance abuse counseling because he was losing control of his use of cocaine. During treatment J. became aware that his life had become consumed by his cocaine. An average student, with strong interests and abilities as an athlete, J. saw that between the support network in which he sought out coke and the friends that he "used" with, most of his life was oriented toward cocaine. After reducing his use to what he thought was an acceptable "controlled" level, J. had

a "slip" (relapse to uncontrolled cocaine use). The slip was valuable because it illustrated a few truths about his substance abuse behavior to J. The first was that he could not control his use of cocaine. When one of the therapists provocatively suggested that there might be an appropriate amount of coke that he could handle, J. stated that he knew he had to be abstinent. He did not wish to try, once again, to moderate his use of cocaine. Further, the slip was precipitated by J.'s use of alcohol. J. had never abused alcohol and did not think of himself as "alcoholic." However, this slip brought him to the awareness that after he had had a few drinks he would begin to experience a craving for cocaine and that he was less able to withstand the cravings he was experiencing. J. decided that he had better "get out while I'm still able." He decided to become abstinent. He made contact with N.A. through another group member and remained abstinent for the remainder of the academic year. The final months of his counseling were oriented toward relationships with family, dating behavior and attitudes toward relationships with the opposite gender. As J. began to reactivate his interest in sports he used some of his time in the substance abuse group for some sport psychology.

3. R. was referred for substance abuse counseling by the county court. He had been responsible for a serious automobile accident which had resulted in a death. R. made a great deal of progress at first. He was able to see that use of drugs was a long-standing pattern which was associated with his ambivalent relationships with his parents. His father had abandoned the family when R. was quite young and so R. had grown up with an absent father and an intensely oppositional relationship with his mother.

After a few group meetings R. was confronted with the facts of his long-standing polydrug abuse. He admitted that he had a problem with alcohol and abstained from alcohol use. R. did not believe that he had a problem with other drugs and continued to use marijuana regularly and psychedelic drugs episodically. After a few months it became clear that R. was not able to work on the family issues that were associated with his substance abuse. His probation officer did not object to R.'s use of other drugs since he was attending classes, was employed, and was not "getting into trouble." The therapists reluctantly terminated counseling with R., noting that he had made "moderate progress."

CONCLUSION

These brief case summaries illustrate some of the diverse concerns that students bring to substance abuse counseling. It might be useful to elucidate some of the general counseling principles which have been drawn from the development of a university based substance abuse counseling program.

1. The authors were trained as generalists and began substance abuse counseling after experience with mental health clients. It became apparent almost from the outset that substance abuse counseling is a metaphor for all psychological counseling. All clients or patients have a lifestyle which includes longstanding cognitive and behavioral habits. When these habits become self-defeating or self-destructive the counselor functions very much like a specialist in the field of addictions. The client is asked to endure the discomfort of giving up some long-standing, albeit painful, patterns with the expectation that this discomfort and possible disorganization will be followed by a period of well-being. Trust is invaluable in developing this expectation.
2. There is a natural tension between the expression and control of any set of behaviors. In the case of substance abuse/and other self-destructive behavior, the client has learned to bypass some natural warning signs that are intended for the protection of the organism. Gestalt work has proved to be highly valuable in bringing the self-protective side of this natural dichotomy to the client's awareness.
3. Awareness of the effects of specific drugs are important. For example a cocaine abuser who becomes abstinent will have to come to grips with the boredom and apathy that follows withdrawal from a stimulant. An alcohol abuser will have to come to grips with thoughts and feelings which have been anaesthe-

tized with alcohol. In the case of B. the anaesthetized feeling was anger.

4. Students in the process of abuse/dependency often feel that they are not able to depend on others. The path away from dependency is intertwined with the path toward healthy interdependence with other human beings. This may require social skills training like the assertiveness skills required by B. or it may require a longer term healing process in which the client learns to trust and to be trustworthy.
5. It follows from this that students will present differing types of substance abuse issues. Some students will be strongly dependent on their use of intoxicants. Some find their use of intoxicants to be a *component* of a problematic set of behaviors. The authors use the example of a student who drank to intoxication only twice a year and had a fight or an automobile accident each time to illustrate that one can have problems with alcohol without being "alcoholic."
6. In general the authors prefer group to individual treatment. However, there are times when issues are raised in group sessions which can be best worked on in individual counseling sessions. Individual counseling has the advantage that the client and therapist can concentrate directly on a special issue for an extended period of time. Group counseling has the advantage of multiple role models, and a wider basis for support and confrontation.

The development of a university based substance abuse counseling program requires a broad view of substance use and abuse as being part of the development of a student's lifestyle in a university environment. This view requires an understanding of student development, the university environment, the effects of specific drugs and the psychology of the individual student.

Further, this view of student substance abuse implies that treatment personnel will consider efforts in the areas of primary prevention and early case findings as well as in the development of creative treatment alternatives. The outreach and student assistance programs noted above represent the authors' attempts to broaden the base of substance abuse services at the University of Florida.

This has required integrating these services with those of other campus and community agencies. At times the treatment professional must leave the realm of psychological treatment and enter into the realm of creative program development, marketing, consciousness raising, and multidisciplinary efforts with college administrators, legal agencies, and the self-help movement. This requires that one maintain an open mind to the thinking of professionals and lay people from various backgrounds who are creating exciting new developments in the complex field of substance abuse.

REFERENCES

Black, C.A. (1981). *It Will Never Happen to Me*. Denver: M.A.C. Publications.

Blane, H.T. (1982). *Chronicle of Higher Education*. Vol. XXIV, No. 21, July 21, 1982.

Blane, H.T. and Chafetz, M.E. (1979). (Eds.) *Youth, Alcohol and Social Policy*. New York: Plenum.

Brigman, S.L. and Knox, R.W. (1987). Drug use study. *Arizona Studies in Student Affairs*, No 2.

Broughton, E.A. (1987). University of Florida. Unpublished Survey.

Engs, R.C. (1977). Drinking patterns and drinking problems of college students. *Journal of Studies on Alcohol*, *38*, 2144-2154.

Fillmore, K.M. (1974). Drinking and problem drinking in early adulthood and middle age. *Quarterly Journal on Alcohol*, *35*, 819-840.

Fillmore, K.M. (1975). Relationships between specific drinking problems in early adulthood and middle age. *Journal of Studies on Alcohol*, *36*, 882-907.

Gonzalez, G.M. (1984). *The BACCHUS Program Guide: A How to Manual for Alcohol Abuse Prevention on Campus*. Third edition. University of Florida.

Johnson, (1986). *Intervention: How to Help Someone Who Doesn't Want Help*. Minneapolis: The Johnson Institute.

Kandel, D.B. and Logan, J.A. (1984). Patterns of drug use from adolescence to young adulthood: Periods of risk for initiation, continued use and discontinuation. *American Journal of Public Health*, *74*, 660-666.

Kraft, D.P. (1981). *Demonstration alcohol education project: September, 1975 to August, 1980.* Summary report and evaluation report, University of Massachusetts, Amherst, Massachusetts.

Marlatt, G.A. (1977). Alcohol use and problem drinking: A cognitive-behavioral analysis. (Ed.S.) *Cognitive-Behavioral Interventions*. New York: New Academy Press, Inc.

Williams, G.D., Stinson, F.S., Parker, D.A., Harford, T.C. and Noble, J. (1987). Demographic trends, alcohol abuse and alcoholism 1985-1995. *Alcohol Health and Research World*, 11(3), 80-83.

Chapter 7

Integrated Treatment Approach with the Chemically Dependent Young Adult

Elena V. Gonzales

SUMMARY. An integrated treatment approach to the treatment of the chemical dependent college student is presented. Attention is given to the impact of chemical abuse on the developmental task of identity formation. Specific phases of the addictive recovery process are outlined in a stage framework. These are: (I) development of attachment to addictive object without conscious awareness of harm; (II) attachment to addictive object with growing awareness of harm; (III) beginning detachment from addictive object and engagement in a change program; and (IV) program of maintenance of change. The therapeutic task is derived from the effect on psychological, cognitive, behavioral and physiological factors in each stage of the addictive recovery process. Case examples are detailed to illustrate the application of the integrated approach in the treatment of the chemically dependent college student.

INTRODUCTION

In the United States drinking and drug use has become an integral part of the process of adolescent development (Jessor & Jessor, 1975). Data suggest that drinking to the point of drunkenness may peak at about age nineteen or twenty just as the adolescent is mak-

Elena V. Gonzales, PhD, is in private practice South Kingston Office Park, Suite C-6, 24 Salt Pond Road, Wakefield, RI 02879.

ing the transitions to young adulthood (Crowley, 1985). Many college age students (traditionally from seventeen to mid-twenties) follow the drinking and drug use pattern of their age mates (Milman & Su, 1973), initiating drinking in adolescence followed by heavy drinking in young adulthood and gradually settling into regular but moderate drinking. However a small percentage of students become dependent and require intervention and treatment. To adequately service this special population we need to combine our knowledge of developmental issues and treatment of chemical dependency.

The conceptualization of alcoholism/drug addiction has gone through many transitions and still remains controversial. Different models have been proposed to define the cause and appropriate treatment of chemical dependence. A number of the more prevalent models will be briefly described before outlining a framework used to develop an integrative treatment approach.

The prevalent conceptualization of chemical dependence for many centuries was the moral model. This came from the perception of the alcoholic as a morally weak person who lacked the will power to stop drinking. Detrimental effects of this model still remain. It is not uncommon for the addict and family members to believe that excessive alcohol and drug use is a result of poor will power and a weak moral character.

The disease model of alcoholism was first presented by Benjamin Rush in the early nineteenth century. Yet it is E.M. Jellinek (1960) and his associates at the Yale Center for alcohol studies who are credited with articulating and elaborating this model. The disease model of alcohol and drug abuse has been recognized and accepted by the American Medical Association since 1956, the year that association officially declared alcoholism and other drug dependence a disease. The important contribution of the disease model is to lift the moral stigma from addiction to alcohol or drugs. As a result the treatment of addiction has become a legitimate medical function. This model conceptualizes chemical dependence as caused by an underlying biochemical disorder. It also outlines chemical dependence as a progressive disorder that if left unchecked will lead to life threatening or health threatening physical disorders or even death.

Similar to the medical model is the Alcoholics Anonymous (AA) model. AA is not a formal model but it is one of the oldest and most widely used self-help programs for treatment of alcoholic/chemical dependence. AA defines alcohol and drug dependence as a disease not only of the body but also of the mind and spirit. The central concept is loss of control over one's drinking and drugging, concept of surrendering and practicing abstinence with the support of other recovering alcohol drug dependent members (Alcoholics Anonymous, 1955).

Chemical dependence as defined within the traditional psychoanalytic framework places compulsive drinking or drugging as a symptom of an underlying and unresolved conflict or as a symptom of underlying personality disorder (Cahn, 1970). Treatment involves the uncovering of the underlying conflict with the assumption that conflict resolution will lessen or alleviate the symptomatic behavior "compulsive drug use." Though the classical neurosis model is seldom used exclusively, many psychodynamic concepts are still employed (defenses, unconscious motivation) in treatment of alcohol and drug abuse.

There have been a number of sociological explanations for chemical dependence. The various social factors that have been implicated are: socioeconomic status, ethnicity, subcultural mores, and family (Ward, 1980, p. 10). Sociological models emphasize the interactive social processes as determinants of behavior. Chemical dependence is seen as caused by an imbalance in the social structure as it is relative to cultural norms. Treatment therefore involves change in the social structure.

The behavioral model emphasizes the factors that sustain compulsive drinking and drug use. Treatment is based on a set of principles stemming from behavioral psychology. Behaviorists are sometimes reluctant to use the term addiction because of its disease connotations. They often refer to "problem" drinking or drugging to emphasize the behavioral aspect of addiction and the possibility of the achievement of moderate alcohol or drug consumption as a treatment goal.

In this article chemical dependence is conceptualized as an interactive process whereby many factors are implicated. The controversy in regards to disease and behavioral models is put aside; as neither is seen as completely correct or inclusive. Psychological, cognitive, behavioral and physical factors are all important in the understanding of etiology and in developing a treatment approach. Since there is no definitive model the clinician must choose from each model what has been proven to be sound and clinically useful. The purpose of this article is to present an integrative treatment approach to working with the chemically dependent young adult. The rationale for this integrative approach comes from an understanding of the complexity of addictive disorders and a belief that no one theory explains all aspects of chemical dependency.

The article is organized in two main parts. First, a general discussion on how chemical dependence impacts on the major developmental task of identity formation for the adolescent/young adult. Second, an articulation of an integrative treatment approach to chemical dependence is presented. Four stages of the addiction recovery process are identified. The stage and subsequent effect on psychological, cognitive, behavioral and physiological factors defines the appropriate therapeutic task. Each stage is discussed in detail and illustrated with a case example of a college student. The article ends with a summary and discussion of the limitations and advantages of this approach.

SPECIAL ISSUES OF THE YOUNG ADULT

The college age student typically aged from seventeen to the mid-twenties presents many challenges in integrating what we know about addictive disorders and developmental issues of the adolescent and young adult. The central difficulty for the young adult abuser is the way that the chemical use both interferes with and confuses the normal developmental process. The young abuser and those around him/her lose sight of what is a result of usual developmental issues and what results from chemical use. For parents (and clinicians) it is difficult to distinguish between the chemical abuser's defenses of denial, rationalization, defiance and grandiosity and normal youthful rebellion. Defiance and grandiosity are an aspect of youth that seem natural and in many ways can be beneficial; but when combined with an addiction and accompanying defense system they can become deadly. This combination interferes with development of a strong ego identity and hides the poor self-esteem and insecurity that may lie underneath.

As part of the struggle for self-definition, adolescents seek to link their current sense of self with a perception of self dating from earlier periods, with their biological make up, and cultural heritage and current life situation. This task is especially difficult at the beginning of college because there is so much disruption of environment, peers and role (Waterman & Waterman, 1971). This disruption occurs at a time when adolescents are attempting to maintain a feeling of inner sameness and continuity across time and across the many situations in which they find themselves. Confidence emerges when the adolescent is able to integrate their self-perceptions with the feedback they receive from others and with a known past. Indeed, Erickson articulates the main purpose of identity (1968) as providing "a subjective sense of invigorating sameness and continuity" (p. 19).

If a subjective continuity is the organizing principle of identity formation, it can readily be seen how drug abuse and addiction can interfere with the adolescent's quest of an integrated and stable identity. The drug abusing adolescent usually experiences radically different perceptions of self in different contexts, with different people, or at different times. He may overidentify with cliques, heroes, crowds or causes putting himself at a severe disadvantage in the struggle to develop a secure identity. Two factors appear to be important in recent research on identity formation: (a) the extent of exploration of alternative roles and perspectives and (b) whether and which type of a commitment is made to certain roles and points of views (Marcia, 1966; Orlofsky, Marcia & Lesser, 1979; Bourne, 1978a, 1978b; Grotevant, Thorbecke & Meyer, 1982). The abusive use of drugs by the adolescent or young adult can impact on both factors in a detrimental manner.

Abusive use of chemicals severely limits the exploration of alternative roles and perspectives. Alcohol and drug abuse often are accompanied by a peer group that requires the adoption of a certain world view or attitudes. Likewise, learning to make choices and commitments to one's choices is often missed by the addicted youth when the defensive structure that develops to protect drug use requires an antagonistic stance toward different roles or perspectives.

> The complexity of these issues can be seen in the case of a young black man in his junior year of college. He had a great investment in athletics and came to college on a scholarship. He had been struggling with depression for most of his life. Depression was the outcome of a disruptive alcoholic family life. His father was actively alcoholic and abusive. The depression had intensified after the death of his mother in the middle of his sophomore year in college. The young man had used alcohol abusively in high school and had episodes of uncontrolled drinking for extended periods of time while in college. He had become addicted. On the one hand he loathed his father's drinking and consciously wished not to be like him. On the other hand alcohol provided him with an escape from feelings and companionship with other males. Unconsciously the drinking appeared to offer him an identification with his father and was part of his identity conflict. He had sought out other role models in high school and in college. Usually these were male figures whom he tended to idolize. At one point he had become very close to an older camp counselor he had worked with during the summer. The intensity of his feelings confused him and he feared that he was homosexual.

The difficulty in teasing out identity issues from alcohol abuse and subsequent addiction is demonstrated by this case. Exploration of alternative roles and perspectives for this young man searching for his identity was restricted by the role model of an alcoholic father. Prejudice against the young mans's minority status and low economic status were other factors. Role models in the sports world and his hard work to become an athlete were enhancing factors, impressive enough to earn him a scholarship in spite of the progressive alcohol abuse. The strong attachment to his mother and his wish to be successful to make up to her for the shame and hurt of his father's alcoholism were important driving forces in his ambition to be successful. These forces were lost with her death. The efforts that he had previously made to contain his drinking began to diminish. Likewise his motivation to perform at school lessened. Abetted by alcohol abuse he began to default in his commitment to growth enhancing roles and views. Instead he chose a "foreclosure pattern" with an avoidance of exploration of alternatives and a taking on of other's (his father's) roles and views without commitment to his own. The assessment and understanding of identity issues for this young man will help guide the subsequent treatment of his alcoholism and depression.

INTEGRATIVE TREATMENT APPROACH

The addictive process is conceptualized as progressive and pervasive. Various systems are implicated and effected. These include psychological, cognitive, behavioral, environmental and physiological systems. Just as the acquiring of an addiction is progressive, so too is the relinquishing of the addictive object (Brown, 1985).

A conceptual framework of four stages can be used to assess the progression of the addiction and to formulate the appropriate therapeutic task. These stages are outlined in Table I. These stages are: (I) development of attachment to addictive object without conscious awareness of harm; (II) attachment to addictive object with growing awareness of harm; (III) beginning detachment from addictive object and engagement in a change program and; (IV) program of maintenance of change. Each stage is reflected in the related psychological, cognitive, behavioral and physiological system. The stage defines the appropriate therapeutic task.

Stage I: Development of Attachment to Addictive Object Without Connection to Harm

If an addiction has developed the related systems will reflect this dysfunctional attachment. Psychologically the patient denies the strength of the attachment to the abused chemical and the harm to oneself or others. In support of the denial a student defines himself as being in control and nondependent. Behaviorally, there is a pattern of repetition – compulsion in regards to the addictive object. The chemically dependent person plans his day, week and month around alcohol or drug consumption. Protecting one's supply and source of chemicals and anticipating how not to drug or drink when necessary become consuming psychological and behavioral preoccupations. The preoccupation with the addictive object is reflected

TABLE 1: PROCESS OF ADDICTION AND RECOVERY

STAGE	RELATED SYSTEM	THERAPEUTIC TASK
STAGE I: DEVELOPMENT OF ATTACHMENT TO ADDICTIVE OBJECT WITHOUT CONNECTION TO HARM	1) Psychological: Denial.	1) Breaking through denial.
	2) Cognitive: I'm in control	2) Assessing addictive disorder without threatening ego. Paradox of control.
	3) Behavioral: Obsessive and repetitive acts.	3) Gaining understanding of pattern of drugging/drinking.
	4) Environmental: Constricting family, peers, work.	4) Acknowledging loneliness, isolation, unhappiness. Recognition of how these factors are negotiated to support addiction. Introducing group support.
	5) Physiological: State of health, drug hunger. Influence on mood, judgment, memory and learning.	5) Assessing health needs: referral to appropriate physician. Understanding the drug experience as defined by the addict.

TABLE 1 (continued)

STAGE	RELATED SYSTEM	THERAPEUTIC TASK
STAGE II: ATTACHMENT TO ADDICTIVE OBJECT WITH GROWING AWARENESS OF HARM	1) Psychological: Denial/shame/guilt.	1) Changing internal attributes of being "weak person." Issue of control vs. responsibility.
	2) Cognitive: Fear of not being in control.	2) Facilitating admission of loss of control. Paradox of Control.
	3) Behavioral: Rearranging of obsessive, repetitive acts without relinquishing addictive object.	3) Challenging rituals and experiencing outcome.
	4) Environmental: Increased isolation. Increased Conflict.	4) Breaking isolation. Group support - AA, NA.
	5) Physiological: Increased drug hunger. Poor health. Blackouts. Poor memory and concentration.	5) Identifying triggers. Educating on detrimental affects on health.

TABLE 1: PROCESS OF ADDICTION AND RECOVERY (Continued)

STAGE	RELATED SYSTEM	THERAPEUTIC TASK
STAGE III: BEGINNING DETACHMENT FROM ADDICTIVE OBJECT/ ENGAGEMENT OF CHANGE PROCESS	1) Psychological: Confrontetion with self.	1) Facilitate surrender. Acceptance of loss of control.
	2) Cognitive: I'm not in control. I'm addicted.	2) Integrating loss of control with new identity.
	3) Behavioral: Stopping repetitive acts. E.g., stops drinking.	3) Taking action.
	4) Environmental: Family, peers, work introduced to change.	4) Breaking isolation. Integrating AA/NA in life. Modifying systems.
	5) Physiological: Improve health. Monitors triggers.	5) Developing skills for stress management. Practicing good health habits.

TABLE 1 (continued)

STAGE	RELATED SYSTEM	THERAPEUTIC TASK
STAGE IV: PROGRAM OF MAINTENANCE	1) Psychological: Self-esteem. System of self-reward, self-punishment.	1) Teaching moderation and accurate self-evaluation.
	2) Cognitive: Postive self-statements and expectations. I'm responsible & capable.	2) Enhancing self-efficacy. Developing/practicing realistic expectations--trial & error learning and here and now focus.
	3) Behavioral: Constructive obsessions and repetitive self-monitoring.	3) Developing relapse plan. Sustaining attentional focus on change program.
	4) Environmental: Learning to cope with situational factors without addictive object.	4) Making necessary adaptation to family, friends, work, to support change. Working a recovery program in AA.
	5) Physiological: Improve health. Coping with drug hunger and memory or concentration problems.	5) Same as in Stage III plus compensating for memory and concentration problems.

in the progressive constriction of the environmental factors. Peers may be selected or avoided based on how they restrict or enhance the ongoing addiction. Likewise former non-abusing peers may begin to avoid contact with the abuser. Long-term relationships may become conflictual. There is the development of emotional dishonesty with family members in order to protect the ongoing addiction and denial. As a result the student will experience a growing physical and psychological isolation. Sometimes work and school relationships are affected. Physiologically, there may be a deterioration of health and a decline in ability to think clearly. Memory loss and blackouts may occur. There may be an experience of craving or drug hunger. With any chemical addiction the physiological effect of the drug is important in understanding the overall experience of the addict. For example, the depressive effects of alcohol may result in ongoing experience of depression. Its use may also numb a student's inhibitions resulting in an ongoing grandiosity or unemotionality. With cocaine there is the high and subsequent crash resulting in an experience of extreme mood variability from euphoria to suicidality. It is not within the scope of this paper to address the physiological effect of various drugs but to emphasize the necessity of being informed and knowledgeable about drug effects on mood and behavior to understand their effect on the drug dependent person. (See Radcliffe & Rush, this issue.)

In stage I the therapeutic task is primarily one of assessment. Once the diagnosis of chemical abuse or dependence is made each related system is examined to determine how it has been effected. The overall goal is to facilitate student's movement to stage II which will bring the abusing student to heightened awareness of the harm done to self or others as a result of the ongoing abuse.

> A young man in his early twenties presents to the University counseling service with anxieties and loneliness. He is worried because he hasn't been able to focus and concentrate on his studies. Academically he has done well, burying himself in his work. He now finds himself restless, fearful and lonely. As he begins to tell his story he places his anxieties in the context of a long-standing problem dating back to junior high school. Relationship with parents have been conflictual. His choice of

> friends and his early experimentation with drugs and alcohol had been an issue between him and his parents since his early adolescent years. The young man presents this information as historical data, qualifying it with the statement that he no longer drinks or uses any heavy drugs. When asked if he is completely drug free he admits to regular use of marijuana which he sees as "no big deal." His focus during the interview is on the many fears he has, social isolation, and poor social skills, especially with women, that have resulted in deep loneliness.

In the process of assessing and diagnosing this young man's problem there are many variables to be sorted through. The questions therapists ask in this process follow a usual process of elimination. Is his a life adjustment problem? Does he have an anxiety disorder? Is he depressed? Is there a personality disorder? The difference between the therapist who is knowledgeable about alcohol and drug addiction and one who is not is that in that assessment process the diagnosis of a drug addiction will also be considered.

Since this young man presents in distress it is necessary to first address the immediate feelings, to support the present reaching out and need to be heard. The therapist keeps in mind the necessity of addressing the drug abuse issue but understands that timing and readiness of the client is essential. For most adolescents and young adults the best approach is to provide a positive first encounter with a counselor so that they will return and begin to engage in the helping process.

After determining that this student wasn't in immediate danger, it was important to let him express his unhappiness and help him recount the various ways he had dealt with his anxiety and depression. In this first encounter simply to identify the role that marijuana has played in his recent life is sufficient. Usually a question can be framed in a positive nonthreatening manner such as "I heard you say that your smoking grass isn't a problem to you. How have you managed to not let it be a problem?" This is sufficient to give the counselor a clearer picture of the drug use while indicating that the student's relationship with his drug of choice may not be normal. This approach is advised in the case of someone who presents in distress and has not yet identified that they are addicted.

At a later session more complete assessment of drug addiction was made. In the case of this young student it was determined that he was dependent on marijuana and alcohol. He had symptoms of generalized anxiety disorder, although without a drug free sample of behavior and mood the diagnosis of an anxiety disorder could only be tentative. The student could admit that smoking grass was a bad habit but didn't connect it to contributing to his unhappiness or causing any harm.

This young man fell very clearly in Stage I. Psychologically, denial was present. The assessment established that marijuana use was a daily activity and alcohol was abused episodically. Cognitively despite everyday use of marijuana the young man felt that he was in control and could stop if he wanted. He simply felt that he didn't need to not smoke and had many rationalizations for how daily smoking was a help to him. Behaviorally, regular drug use was repetitive and obsessive. His world had become restricted and lonely. He responded to loneliness with more marijuana use. Physiologically, he craved marijuana. Cognitively and emotionally he was aware that the drug helped him to feel less anxious and allowed him to "mellow out."

Given that contact would be brief (as is usual in college counseling) the therapeutic task in this stage was to reframe the problem for the student. Alcohol and drug abuse were introduced by his therapist as personally harmful in a straightforward way.

The therapist uses her status and experience to identify and educate the student about the addictive process. This is an important first step in breaking through denial in particular the "belief in control" at this stage of drug use. This allows the student to relinquish blame and helps him regain self-esteem. The pattern of drug use is explored in detail so that the student can have an opportunity to articulate possibly for the first time the extent and obsessionality of drug or alcohol use. With time and help the student begins to make a connection between their use of drugs and the losses and pain they may be experiencing.

The use of other support services within the college is not only helpful to the student but also supports the counselor in the therapeutic task of breaking through denial. In this case the health service provided a physical evaluation of the student. He had many physical symptoms that were frightening to him. The evaluation indicated that he was physically healthy. The attending doctor supported the diagnosis of abusive use of drugs and anxiety as causal to the various physical complaints that the student presented with. As a result of the contact with the counseling service the young man was able to vent his feelings and connect his abusive use of drugs as a separate but contributing problem to his ongoing anxiety.

Stage II: Attachment to Addictive Object with Growing Awareness of Harm

In stage II the drug attachment or addiction is still denied but there is a growing awareness of harm and as a result all related systems have some disequilibrium. Denial is still the predominant mechanism underlying and sustaining the addiction, however it is weakening. The struggle with shame and guilt of injury to self and others is beginning. Cognitively, the conflict is between the belief of having control and fear of not being in control. The student attempts to demonstrate control by rearranging the obsessive and repetitive acts without relinquishing the addictive object. For example the alcohol abusing student stops drinking during the week but continues to binge on weekends. Periods of abstinence ("going on the wagon") are attempted to demonstrate control. Environmentally the family, peer or work area that have been constricting may become more openly conflictual. A relationship loss will occur or grades will drop considerably. Parental anxiety may increase with expressed demands for some change. The original pay-off of the chemical, namely, "to feel good" is no longer present. The worse the dependent person feels, the more he craves "going back for more" hoping for the original pay-off. Drug hunger may be experienced more intensely or not at all (especially if there now is a pattern of maintenance drinking or drugging whereby a certain amount of the chemical is always in the system). There may be a growing awareness of the drug obsession, memory difficulty, concentration problems, interference with studies and healthy interpersonal relationships.

A nineteen-year-old female was referred by the college counseling service to a private practitioner because of academic problems. She had presented academic problems to the counseling service but actually came because her parents had given her the choice of seeking help for abusive cocaine use or being withdrawn from college.

An attractive and mature looking young woman dressed stylishly and with care, she had difficulty with eye contact, looking embarrassed, with downcast eyes and a nervous inappropriate smirk. She was quick to point out that cocaine abuse was "in the past" as she had decided to stop. She wanted to come to treatment to reassure her parents of her sincerity in relinquishing cocaine use and wish to finish college year. She felt that cocaine abuse was not the central problem. She felt that lack of self-confidence was the core issue. The young woman's focus was on negative feelings about herself and her sorrow in disappointing her parents with whom she had always had a good relationship.

She believed that the acquired addiction was an indication of her weak character. There had been many humiliating episodes that had begun to undermine her sense of self. She wanted to demonstrate to herself, her parents and her therapist her ability to control and exercise her "strong will" over her drug use. This didn't mean she wanted to relinquish the drug altogether. It meant that she could regain the choice when, in what amounts, and at what times she could use cocaine.

The student was able to articulate her thinking in regards to the issue of control once she felt secure that the therapist understood the nature of her struggle. Admitting to having incurred losses or pain because of abusive use of a chemical is wholly different from accepting that you are addicted. This young woman had begun to experience hurt and losses, her academic standing was threatened, friends were avoiding her, family members were angry and disappointed, men were rejecting her. These losses made her feel sad, hurt, and undermined her self-esteem. Yet she saw relinquishing the chemical as another kind of loss which, in this stage, seemed unnecessary, only adding to her hurt.

The awareness of harm is the main distinguishing factor from stage I to stage II. In the case of this young woman it became clear that all related systems reflected the disequilibrium that is characteristic of stage II.

With the addicted young adult in stage II it is important from the onset to begin to address the issue of control. This is both to give the young adult the appreciation of the difficulty of relinquishing an addiction and to begin to educate in regards to the issue of control. It would be naive of the therapist to simply congratulate the young woman on her decision to give up cocaine use and go on to helping her pick up the pieces. It is important to recognize the fragility of her present position. The therapeutic task is to recognize the ambivalence and conflict of the drug dependent person in stage II. In this case it is important to help the young woman gain an understanding of what brought her to the point of identifying the abusive use of cocaine as problematic for her. Therapeutically, the question of what the patient thinks she can or wants to do about chemical use needs to be raised so as to address her ambivalence and the issue of control. By doing this the therapist allies with that part of the patient that is the emerging young adult and needing to make decisions for herself. This allows her to separate from her parents as superego figures and begins to elicit her own observing ego in regards to chemical use. Chemical abuse is reframed as an outside and harmful stressor as opposed to an internalized necessity and comfort.

It may seen contradictory but the therapist needs to establish that control is not simply an issue of free will and is not vested in either the abuser or the healer. The abuser can't simply "will" himself to stop and the healer can't likewise command cessation. The first alliance with a young adult abuser in stage II is with the acceptance of the contradiction in admitting that abusive use of a chemical is actually harmful but still can be a wished-for (physiologically and psychologically) relief (or comfort).

Another central issue is the growing shame and self-deprecation that usually is born of the moral model that frames abuse or dependency as a "weakness" of character or will. This concept is as prevalent among young people as for older generations. It may be "cool" or in to use drugs or alcohol but the repeated chemical abuse, especially by a female, is seen as a negative attribute. The experience of intense shame impedes the process of identity formation. Shame is intensified by behaviors while chemically intoxicated that compromise one's values in regards to what is acceptable. Young males often behave in a loud and obnoxious manner. Their drunken grandiosity may lead to major assaults and accidents harmful to their sense of identity. A young intoxicated woman is seen as sexually available and often is taken advantage of or becomes a victim of assault. Ongoing drug use places students in high risk situations with impaired judgment. For females the usual vigilance that a young woman must have regarding safety is temporarily suspended. The violence of rape can be particularly painful and detrimental to ego development. A chemically dependent female who has been raped while drunk or high usually feels so bad about their high or drunken state they blame themselves and remain silent about the episode. The prevailing social norms blame the drunken female. The issues are particularly complicated if the violence occurred in the circumstance defined as "date rape."

Once dynamic conflict is articulated and an alliance is formed with the student the therapeutic task of stage II is to deal with the issues of shame and guilt by educating the patient about how an addictive disorder is formed. Once there is a lessening of shame and guilt the process of dealing with the fear of "losing control" can begin.

A major environmental effort is needed to reduce social isolation. Isolation has supported the denial and ongoing sense of being in control, i.e., by confining oneself to drug-using peers or drugging and drinking alone. Use of a self-help program is important in each stage but particularly in this stage. The use of AA, NA or "drug free" peer support groups in college introduces the patient to recovery concepts and group support in ways that individual counseling cannot. It is important that the individual work support the affiliation with drug-free self-help groups by emphasizing the need for ongoing support and the difficulty in relinquishing a chemical addiction alone.

Stage III: Beginning Detachment from Addictive Object/ Engagement of Change Process

In Stage III there is beginning detachment from the addictive object and an engagement in change. Psychologically denial and the struggle with guilt and shame have precipitated a confrontation with self. There is a coming to terms with the futility of pursuing control and being confronted with repeated loss of control. Different authors describe this internal experience in different ways. Bateson (1971) describes this point as a collapse of the system of denial that had perpetuated the belief in control. Tiebout (1949, 1953) speaks of it in AA terms as a "surrender" or "conversion," a coming to terms with one's inability to control the obsessive-compulsive behavior (drinking or drugging) alone. Brown (1985, p. 13) refers to this phenomena as the "paradox of control" the alcoholic admits to defeat at their effort to control their drinking. They "surrender in order to win."

Cognitively, the student accepts the premise "I'm not in control and need help to change." Along with this is a redefinition of self as someone who is chemically dependent and is in need of help to change. Behaviorally, there is cessation of ongoing abusive behaviors, stopping of chemical use, a breaking of rituals connected with the addiction, and replacing these behaviors with constructive activities. Environmentally, it is important to engage the student support system (family, friends, work, academic situation) in the change process. There must be change in these systems also if there is to be success in the student's change program. Physiologically, the promotion of good health and the management of acute and chronic stress becomes the focus. There still may be need to address drug craving and a program of monitoring triggers to relapse. Learning to adapt to moderation, avoiding extremes and fatigue helps the student become less vulnerable to a "slip" (relapses in to drug using behavior).

The focus in stage III is to help the student to cope nonchemically. Students in stage III are in a transition. They recognize the need to relinquish chemical dependency but don't yet feel they have the skills to manage without chemical use.

A twenty-year-old Hispanic college junior was referred by her college peer counselor because of anxiety and depression. She was anxious about poor academic performance and procrastination. She had a pattern of dropping courses and lived in constant worry over unfinished work. She saw herself as a professional student: fearful of never being able to graduate and equally fearful of graduating and being on her own. Two years previous to contacting the counseling service she had been in treatment for issues related to her mother's pending death. During this therapy her mother had died, but the student's anxiety and depression did not lessen but escalated. The earlier therapy was terminated by the therapist who had identified the young woman as having had "borderline" characteristics who had used therapy as a means of avoiding making any commitment to change. The young woman felt rejected by the former therapist but could acknowledge that she had seen therapy as an opportunity to vent unhappiness with an underlying hope, that often became a demand, that the therapist would change the situation.

In early interviews at the counseling service she realized how much her focus had been on her mother's illness throughout her adolescent years and not on herself. During adolescence she had been truant and ran away from home. This had resulted in juvenile court involvement, a brief stay in detention and foster home. She had minimized this in her former therapy. Additionally she hadn't spoke of her long history of alcohol and drug abuse. She had seen her early involvement with drugs as a normal part of teenage rebellion. She had always attributed the great emotional turmoil she struggled with to the family disruption caused by her mother's illness. Now she could no longer use that as a rationale for her ongoing emotional distress. She began to see the deep involvement she had always had with drugs and alcohol, and was amazed at the way she had rationalized her abuse.

The young woman was entering stage III of the addiction model. Her first therapy had bypassed Stage I issues and had initiated stage II. Her former therapist was correct in having assessed the lack of commitment to a change process but failed to identify drug dependence as a problem. That therapist apparently only understood the amount of turmoil and conflict in terms of "borderline" characteristics, a premature conclusion which foreclosed the correct diagnosis. Yet the earlier therapy was critical in moving this young woman into stage III initiating a confrontation with herself. She had tired of the struggle and pain and could see that she wasn't "in control" of chemical use or her life. She readily accepted a suggestion to attend AA where she was amazed to hear her own story being told by others. She had learned by the termination experience in her previous therapy that she was responsible for changing herself but because of an insufficient grasp of her specific "disease" didn't know how.

This young woman's readiness to engage in change and her inability to relinquish drug and alcohol use completely as an outpatient met the criteria for inpatient alcohol/drug rehabilitation as a way to start anew. The rehabilitation program provided the structure and opportunity to focus on the addiction as the central problem. She understood that the referral was not a termination of the therapeutic relationship but the initial step in an intervention program for her. Once she completed that program she would need to return to college and continue in outpatient therapy.

Stage IV: Program of Maintenance of Change/ Ongoing Recovery

All authorities on chemical dependence agree that stopping addictive behavior is not as difficult as the maintenance of abstinence and the promotion of a "sober" drug-free life style. Fortunately more research and formulation from a number of perspectives is focused on the ongoing recovery process (Brown, 1985; Marlatt & Gordon, 1985; Kirschenbaum, 1987). In stage IV the student attempts to synthesize the various factors that have been found to be important in a program of maintenance of change. The overall goal is to help solidify self-regulation mechanisms and group identity so that change will be maintained over time and in different situations. As these mechanisms are solidified the role of therapy will diminish and can eventually be terminated.

Psychologically, the extent to which the person has experienced and internalized nurturant or punitive parental figures is important in governing one's behavior. Behaviorally it is the systems of self-reward or self-punishment by which behavior is regulated. For some theorists the ability to administer appropriate consequences to oneself according to favorable self-evaluation or unfavorable self-evaluation is considered a necessary ability in maintenance of change (Bandura, 1977; Kanger & Karoly, 1972). An addicted individual functions at extremes. Self-evaluation is either too critical or too lenient. The system of self-reward or self-punishment therefore is skewed to one extreme or the other. Learning to moderate and self-evaluate accurately is an important task in this stage. The adolescent in particular has great difficulty in this area. The sense of invincibility and incomplete identity formation make accurate self-evaluation difficult. Complicating factors are past issues that may have fostered a tendency toward negative self-evaluation. This is particularly true if parental figures have been rigid, strict, invalidating or abusive. Identifying these past issues gives both the therapist and patient understanding of the underlying dynamics that may undermine the process of accurate self-evaluation. The emphasis is on supporting the behavioral changes necessary to remain drug-free. It is not appropriate to engage in in-depth "insight" oriented therapy in early recovery. In her approach to the patient the therapist encourages the handling or managing rather than analyzing of symptoms of past conflict or trauma (Hellman, 1981).

Cognitively, the enhancement of self-efficacy is most helpful in this stage of therapy. The development of positive expectations and cognitions of self have been articulated as important factors in the maintenance of change (Carver & Scheir, 1981; Abramson, Seligman & Teasdale, 1978). In general success in any change program is more probable if self-encouraging and positive expectancies are acquired and enhanced (Blittner, Goldberg & Merbaum, 1978).

Clinical experience indicates that all or none thinking can be detrimental in a change program. It is more helpful to accept the basic learning principle of trial and error. "Slips" or returning to old behaviors is seen as an opportunity to reevaluate the change program rather than failure (Donovan & Chaney, 1985).

Another attitude to foster in a change program is a "here and now" focus. This philosophy enhances self-efficacy by encouraging the patient to take control of the present and relinquish the impossible task of changing the past or predicting the future. For the young adult the task of integrating and balancing a healthy past, present and future orientation is a particular developmental focus. Fostering a realistic present orientation can be helpful in developing competency and supporting the change program.

Behaviorally the literature indicates the necessity of sustaining an active program of change. Ongoing self-monitoring is a necessary condition to generalized and maintain changed behavior (Kirschenbaum & Karoly, 1977). Kirschenbaum (1987) advocates continual, systematic self-regulation which utilizes the client's obsessive-compulsive defenses to generate the intensity needed to maintain behavioral change. The AA program is helpful in advocating an ongoing recovery process with intense vigilance against returning to old attitudes and behaviors and in encouraging practicing new attitudes and behaviors (Brown, 1985).

Social pressure and stressors, interpersonal conflict are all important factors that influence whether a program of change will be successful. It is often necessary to develop coping skills to manage stressful life events (Chaney, O'Leary & Marlatt, 1978). Where necessary and possible, some environmental changes will need to be made to support the change program. Some of these are obvious (e.g., not associating with previous drinking/drugging peers, not having drugs on hand, etc.). Others are subtle and idiosyncratic (association of drugging or alcohol use with certain music, drinking in certain bars, etc.). It isn't possible to eliminate social pressure and stressors or interpersonal conflict. Learning how to cope nonchemically (maintaining the change program in face of the environmental stressors) will determine success. Chemically dependent students who become "sober and clean" have the same life and relationship stressors as others. Being sober and clean of drugs only affords them an opportunity to deal more effectively with their lives.

The young adult who has been drinking and drugging through

most of their adolescence may have missed experiencing the usual developmental anxieties. When drug-free they begun to have many unfamiliar feelings. Reassurance and support in accepting and developing nonchemical ways to cope with these feelings is necessary during this "catch up" phase.

Using the case introduced in stage III, the therapeutic task of stage IV will be explored.

> This young woman's sense of self was poor and negative. She experienced her father as punitive, rigid and strict and her mother as lenient and emotionally unavailable. She had internalized her father's high and unrealistic standards and sought his approval by trying to meet those standards. Her experience with her mother had fostered anger and mistrust toward women. She saw women as weak and ineffectual. As a result her tendency was to self-evaluate in extremes using very high unrealistic standards. When she couldn't meet these standards she felt as if she were a disappointment to her father and a failure to herself. Even if she met these standards she attributed this to luck or her ability to "fool" others (be a manipulative and covertly controlling woman), not to competency. Her drugging and drinking which originally provided escape from her sense of failure had become another indication that she was a "weak" and "bad" person.
>
> The behavior that resulted from these psychological issues was the focus of therapy. How she used high and unrealistic expectations to set herself up for failure was identified as "perfectionism." The perfectionistic behavior that undermined the process of accurate self-evaluation was identified, labeled and managed. She could understand and accept her "perfectionism" and the necessity to develop realistic expectations. This approach provided a safe nonthreatening way to deal with behaviors that were an outcome of painful and threatening issues without engaging in "insight" oriented therapy.
>
> As a result of her many experiences of failure the patient had learned to anticipate failure. She had many negating cognitions of self. In her perfectionistic stance she saw mistakes

as intolerable and validating her worst fears of being a failure. The development of realistic expectations, positive cognitions and an ability to tolerate mistakes was applied to the goal of reestablishing herself academically. A cognitive behavioral program was developed to monitor and systemize her approach to completing her academic work. As she worked on completing her course work she learned how to moderate her expectations and to be more realistic in her assessment of her performance. These skills were applied to her ongoing recovery program. Her tendency was to expect too much too soon. She needed the therapist's help to define and understand normal feelings in a relationship as well as realistic expectation. Behaviorally the patient's participation in AA sustained the ongoing recovery program. AA provided group support, models, means of coping and reinforced positive expectancies.

The student had accepted the recommendation to participate in an inpatient rehabilitation program for both psychological and practical reasons. In stage III she had come to the point of feeling that her life was out of control. Her anxiety was such that she was constantly battling fear and emotional turmoil. She couldn't cope with either academic or family demands. With the therapist assistance she recognized that she needed a safe and therapeutic environment to help her withdraw from all chemicals. Practically the means was there, her college insurances paid for such care and she could use an upcoming academic break period for the 30 day rehabilitation stay.

The inpatient program had been helpful in engaging her large family in the recovery process. They had been brought in for family sessions and had participated in a one week educational program for families. The patient continued to live at home while attending college and so family participation (which is always recommended) was necessary and possible.

The physiological concerns were mainly in the area of developing good health habits and stress management. The patient was healthy and didn't suffer from drug hunger or "cravings." Also she did not have ongoing memory or concentration problems. She did experience ongoing fatigue and chronic stress.

She had developed poor and erratic eating and sleep habits. She had never practiced a regular exercise program.

These physiological concerns were rectified by regularizing eating and sleeping habits, learning progressive relaxation and incorporating regular exercise in her routine by riding her bike to classes.

For this student alcohol/drug abuse had isolated her from family and friends. Her concealment of her addiction had meant that a habit of avoidance or outright dishonesty had developed. Reengaging with family members and peers meant breaking the secret of her drug dependency and reestablishing trust.

RELAPSE PREVENTION

A relapse program isn't simply a plan for dealing with what happens if drugging or drinking occurs. It articulates the necessity for ongoing monitoring and practicing of change in each area, psychological, cognitive, behavioral, environmental and physiological. Drug-dependent patients set themselves up for a slip by not attending to the program of change. There is a process of relapsing where attention to monitoring of attitudes, expectations, beliefs and behavior begins to wane and then stop before drugging and drinking is actually resumed.

SUMMARY AND DISCUSSION

This paper presents an integrative approach to the treatment of the chemical dependent college student. Special emphasis is placed on the effect of chemical abuse on the developmental task of identity formation.

Four stages of the addiction recovery process are proposed as a helpful framework from which to develop appropriate treatment interventions. It is the movement from one stage to the other that directs the treatment. The tenacity and recidivism of chemical dependence along with the evolving identity issues of the adolescent/young adult makes treatment of the chemical dependent college student challenging if not difficult. Negative expectancy by both the therapist and patient can be avoided by focusing on the process of recovery and flexibility and versatility in the treatment approach.

The multidimensional approach means that there is a role for dynamically trained therapist as well as the behaviorist, educator, physician and community based support system. The counselor in the college/university setting is at a particular advantage in having access to a number of expert team members. Responsibility for servicing the different needs of the chemically dependent student need not be solely the therapist/counselor's. Indeed it is important to utilize resources within the college/university community to address the different therapeutic needs of the chemically dependent student. These include the health service, deans in charge of resident living and academic affairs, student organizations and support services.

In sharing responsibility and in accepting recovery as a process the therapist is less likely to become discouraged or feel a failure and avoids the pitfall of setting up a win/lose struggle over control of drugging/drinking.

What we gain in organization we may lose in oversimplification when employing a stage framework. In this regard the framework presented here is considered a working and evolving outline that is open to modification with increased clinical experience and research data.

REFERENCES

Abramson, L.Y., Seligman, M.E.P., and Teasdale, J. Learned helplessness in humans: Critique and reformation. *Journal of Abnormal Psychology*, 1978, 87, 49-74.

Alcoholics Anonymous. AA World Services, Inc. New York, 1955.

Bandura, A. Self-efficacy: Toward a unifying theory of behavioral change. *Psychological Review*, 1977, 84, 191-215.

Bateson, G. The cybernetics of self: A theory of alcoholism. *Psychiatry*, 1971, 34 (1), 1-18.

Bissell, L.C. Recovered alcoholics counselors. In: E.M. Pattison and E. Kaufman (Eds.), *Encyclopedic handbook of alcoholism*. New York: Gardner Press, 1982, pp. 810-821.

Blittner, M., Goldberg, J., and Merbaum, M. Cognitive self-control factors in the reduction of smoking behavior. *Behavior Therapy*, 1978, 9, 553-561.

Bourne, E. The state of research on ego identity: A review and appraisal. Part I. *Journal of Youth and Adolescence*, 1978a, 7, 223-252.

Bourne, E. The state of research on ego identity: A review and appraisal. Part II. *Journal of Youth and Adolescence*, 1978b, 7, 371-392.

Brown, S. *Treating the alcoholic: A developmental model of recovery*. New York: Wiley and Sons, Inc., 1985.

Cahn, S. *Treating the alcoholic: A developmental study*. New York: Oxford University Press, 1970.

Chaney, E.F., O'Leary, M.R., and Marlatt, G.A. Skill training with alcoholics. *Journal of Consulting and Clinical Psychology*, 1978, 46, 1092-1104.

Crowley, Joan E. The Demographics of Alcoholic Use among Young Americans: Results from the 1983 national Longitudinal Survey of Labor Market Experience of Youth. Ohio State University, Columbus, Center for Human Resource Research, April 1985.

Donovan, D., and Chaney, E. Alcoholic relapse prevention and intervention: Models and methods. In: Marlatt A. and Gordon J. (Eds.), *Relapse prevention*. New York: The Guilford Press, 1985.

Erikson, E. *Identity: Youth and crisis*. New York: W.W. Norton, 1968.

Grotevant, H.D., Thorbecke, W., and Meyer, M.L. An extension of Marcia's identity status interview into the interpersonal domain. *Journal of Youth and Adolescence*, 1982, 11, 33-47.

Hellman, J. Alcohol abuse and the borderline patient. *Psychiatry*, 1981, 44, 307-317.

Kanfer, F.H., and Karoly, P. Self-control: A behaviorist excursion into the lion's den. *Behavior Therapy*, 1972, 3, 398-416.

Jellinek, E.M. *The disease concept of alcoholism*. New Haven: College and Universities Press, 1960.

Jessor, R., and Jessor, S. Adolescent development and the onset of drinking. *Journal of Studies on Alcohol*, 1975, 36, 1, 27-51.

Kirschenbaum, D.S. Self-regulatory failure a review with clinical implications. *Clinical Psychology Review*, 1987, 7, 1, 77-104.

Kirschenbaum, D.S. and Karoly, P. When self-regulation fails: Tests of some preliminary hypothesis. *Journal of Consulting and Clinical Psychology*, 1977, 45, 1116-1125.

Marcia, J.E. Development and validation of ego-identity status. *Journal of Personality and Social Psychology*, 1966, 3, 551-558.

Marcia, J.E. Identity six years after: A follow-up study. *Journal of Youth and Adolescence*, 1976, 5, 145-160.

Marcia, J.E. Identity in adolescence. In: J. Adelson (Ed.), *Handbook of adolescent psychology*. New York: Wiley Press, 1980.

Marlatt, A.G., and Gordon J.R. *Relapse prevention*. New York: The Guilford Press, 1985.

Milman, D.H., and Su, W. Patterns of drug usage among university students. *Journal of American College Health Association*, 1973, 21: 131-7.

Orlofsky, J.L., Marcia, J.E., and Lesser, I. Ego identity status and the intimacy versus isolation crisis of young adulthood. *Journal of Personality and Social Psychology*, 1973, 27, 211-219.

Tiebout, H.M. The act of surrender in the psychotherapeutic process with special reference to alcoholism. *Quarterly Journal of Studies on Alcohol*, 1949, 10, 48-58.

Tiebout, H.M. Surrender versus compliance in therapy with special reference to alcoholism. *Quarterly Journal of Studies on Alcohol*, 1953, 4, 58-68.

Ward, D.A. *Alcoholism: Introduction to theory and treatment*. Dubuque, Iowa: Kendall and Hunt Publishing Company, 1980.

Waterman, A.S., and Waterman, C.K. A longitudinal study of changes in ego identity status during the freshman year at college. *Developmental Psychology*, 1971, 5, 167-173.

Waterman, A.S. Identity development from adolescence to adulthood: An extension of theory and a review of research. *Developmental Psychology*, 1982, 18, 341-358.

Chapter 8

Substance Use Disorder and College Students: Inpatient Treatment Issues – A Model of Practice

William T. White
David Mee-Lee

SUMMARY. The college student population is at high risk to develop substance use disorder. A sizable minority of students will manifest addictions of major severity. Lacking sophistication in the process of substance use disorder assessment precludes objective identification of students requiring intensive inpatient treatment. A multivariate model of alcohol and other drug addiction is proposed. A multidimensional comprehensive assessment and treatment matching instrument is presented. A working inpatient addictions treatment unit is outlined to demonstrate intensity of tertiary intervention.

William T. White, RN, MSN, CS, is Director of Program Development and Marketing, New Day Center for Addictions at Fuller Memorial Hospital, South Attleboro, MA, and Adjunct Faculty, University of Rhode Island, College of Nursing Science.

David Mee-Lee, MD, is Vice President, Monarch Health Corporation, Marblehead, MA, and Instructor in Psychiatry, Harvard Medical School.

Address reprint requests to: William T. White, RN, MSN, CS, Rural Route 3 Box 1409, Foster, RI 02825.

INTRODUCTION

The abuse of alcohol and other drugs by college students is well documented (Friend & Koushki, 1984; Hughes & Dodder, 1984; Humphrey, Stephans & Allen, 1983). While recent research suggests undergraduate use of alcohol may have peaked (Temple, 1986), others report student intake of sedative drugs has doubled in the past ten years (Nicholi, 1984). Young adult cocaine abuse is epidemic; college graduates report the heaviest use, with median use onset between 18-20 years of age (Clayton, 1985). A significant number of students suffer adverse consequences from alcohol and other drug abuse (Humphrey et al., 1983; Nicholi, 1983); one college survey revealed 25 percent of the student body experienced problems from alcohol use alone (DEAP, 1980). Concern regarding alcohol and other drug (alcohol/drug) use and its associated problems prompted the American College Health Association to release in 1986 "Statement on College Alcohol and Drug Use" (Policy Statement, 1986). This statement strongly supports primary and secondary prevention measures aimed to provide education and early intervention for high risk students. Conspicuously absent is any direct reference regarding tertiary prevention with students in serious trouble with substance use disorder (SUD). While many colleges have developed organized programs to address alcohol and drug prevention, those with formal treatment and intervention services are in the vast minority (Claydon, 1984). This is despite SUD being the most common psychiatric disorder diagnosed among 18-45-year-olds, independent of education or social class (Robins, 1984).

The first year of college finds most students dramatically increasing alcohol/drug use (Friend & Koushki, 1984). One school of thought postulates freshmen escalate use to reduce tension precipitated by academic and social expectations in the face of lacking familiar social supports. Another hypothesis proposes students augment use to enhance sensations in the context of a peer environment supportive of alcohol/drug abuse. Both explanations may be equally valid, discriminating two types of student alcohol/drug abusers (Brennan, Walfish & AuBuchon 1986). Regardless of dynamic, increased alcohol/drug intake by college students predisposes SUD vulnerability; those students with moderate/heavy high school drug use histories are perhaps at greatest risk (Humphrey & Friedman, 1986).

According to the author's clinical experience, very few SUD college students receive inpatient treatment. The more typical young adult SUD history represents a 25-30-year-old who reports dropping out of college as a function of drug abuse. Summary anecdotal data from hospitalized students finds the majority exhibited out of control behavior long before inpatient referral was suggested. Why does it appear that college administrators and adjustment counselors, community based helping providers, and parents, demonstrate a lack of awareness that inpatient treatment may be necessary prior to total loss of control? There are three primary reasons for such a knowledge deficit among this diverse group. Firstly, there exists a lack of sophistication about SUD in general and how this problem is exhibited in college students in particular. Secondly, some professionals and other helpers believe alcohol/drug users must "hit bottom" (lose everything) before they can accept treatment. This philosophy encourages a binary model of SUD; either one is an active out of control alcoholic/addict or not. Instead, viewing alcohol/drug addiction as a multivariate syndrome with early, middle, and late stages encourages sooner and more aggressive interventions (Pattison, 1985). For the college student, "hitting bottom" operationalizes to losing critical supportive relationships, flunking out of school, and all too often, serious accidental injury or death. Finally, most college helping providers are unacquainted with SUD inpatient programming. This fact, in association with limited understanding of SUD, precludes comprehension of why inpatient clinical intensity is necessary for certain student SUD presentations.

This chapter provides a reference for how inpatient treatment can help the college student with SUD. Salient points regarding student inpatient assessment are discussed in detail. Generic inpatient care issues are framed according to student psychosocial development. A working inpatient Addictions Treatment Unit is outlined to serve as a context for more specific issue examination.

STUDENT INPATIENT CARE ASSESSMENT

A multivariate model of alcoholism/drug addiction provides a context for matching intensity of student SUD presentation with intensity of treatment. Effective treatment matching is dependent on comprehensive assessment of accurate substance use data. Reliable student substance use history is best obtained with self-report corroboration. Very few students self-refer for SUD evaluation, yet professionals often do not involve significant others for self-report validation (i.e., best friends, dorm counselors, girl/boyfriends). The use of breathalizers and urine drug toxicology screens can also be helpful.

Mee-Lee's (1985, 1986) Recovery Attitude and Treatment Evaluator (RAATE) is an efficient yet comprehensive assessment and treatment matching instrument (see Appendix 1) which can be used with college students. The RAATE is comprised of five specific dimensions (A, B, C, D, E) representing the key clinical areas relevant to assessment of addictions severity. Patients are scored in each dimension according to severity (1-5) of corresponding beliefs, attitudes, and behaviors relative to addictions recovery. Higher scores indicate serious SUD pathology whereas lower scores reflect mild symptomatology. Taken as a whole, the instrument represents a comprehensive addictions severity profile which can be correlated with appropriate treatment intensity. A review of RAATE severity dimensions will underscore the clinical features germane to student SUD inpatient evaluation.

RAATE A – Degree of Resistance to Treatment

RAATE A assesses level of awareness that an addiction problem exists and some form of treatment is necessary. Student denial of SUD is common and extremely difficult to treat. This is partly caused by student perception (albeit incorrect) that colleagues drink/drug at equivalent or greater levels (Perkins & Berkowitz, 1986). The belief that ones' drinking/drugging is not outside of the college norm often precludes meaningful processing that any form of treatment is necessary. Since most undergraduates have had little life experience or education about SUD, it is difficult to mediate such perceptions even with professional help. Students with severe SUD consequences (i.e., two driving while intoxicated arrests in the past ten days with near serious auto accident; accidental overdose with barbiturates; post seizure from excessive cocaine intoxication) scoring severity levels of 4 or 5 on RAATE A are inpatient treatment candidates.

RAATE B – Degree of Resistance to Continuing Care

RAATE B determines degree of acceptance that SUD recovery is a process and not an event. Realizing that recovery involves continued vigilance and ongoing responsibility for abstinence can be overwhelming for college students. Sensation seeking tendencies (Brennan et al., 1986) and peer influence vulnerability (Kandel, 1980) are college student psychosocial developmental realities. The SUD student's predisposition to increase arousal level in tandem with peer pressure to use drugs potentiates impulsive relapse. Most college students are novices at providing self-imposed structure and limits, essentials of SUD recovery. Students concentrating on external factors to facilitate abstinence rather than intrapersonal efforts are unlikely to maintain continuing motivation for recovery. Undergraduates scoring 4 or 5 on RAATE B will require high intensity treatment to increase emotional insight and improve personal motivation.

RAATE C – Degree of Acuity of Biomedical Problems

RAATE C severity generally discriminates college students from younger high school students. In general, college students drink and drug in much greater quantities and frequencies than younger adolescent counterparts. SUD college students are therefore more prone to demonstrate physiological addiction and other serious medical consequences from substance use (i.e., overdoses, pancreatitis, hepatitis). Although the potential for serious medical sequelae from withdrawal is limited (Liepman & Whitfield, 1984) student detoxification can be uncomfortable. Students dependent on alcohol, opiates, or cocaine are at greatest risk for withdrawal induced relapse. Regardless of etiology, biomedical problems distract from student focus on recovery. Student RAATE C scores of 4 or 5 are not uncommon and are indicators for inpatient treatment.

RAATE D–Degree of Acuity of Psychiatric/Psychological Problems

RAATE D evaluates psychological status within the context of SUD. A small minority of addicted students demonstrate concomitant psychiatric disorders (i.e., major affective disorders, anxiety disorders) requiring careful assessment and treatment during early recovery. Protracted stress is a part of college life; roommates, academic pressure, lack of familiar supports, and conflicted love relationships are all potential stressors. Many students use substances to medicate anxiety and overwhelming feelings surfacing under such stress. The propensity for psychiatric disorders and unresolved issues (i.e., arrested grief, children of alcoholic, abuse/neglect) to exacerbate is great.

The severity of psychological problems must be measured in terms of how they might impact, or be impacted by, student recovery attempts. In extreme eases, (i.e., suicidality, psychosis) intensive treatment settings are required to support the limits and alternative coping strategies necessary to prevent serious self/other harm.

RAATE E–Extent of Social/Systems/Family Problems

Dimension E evaluates level of interpersonal support for recovery. Most undergraduates are distanced from familiar social supports while experiencing high stress in a drinking/drugging environment. Students modeling abstinence are viewed as social deviates. Reengaging with healthy family supports, developing a supportive counseling relationship, and meeting age similar recovering others are ideal SUD mediators. However, active SUD students have few healthy family members immediately available, mistrust perceived authority figures (including therapists), and compare rather than identify with recovering students. High scores on this dimension are the norm for college students. Scores of 4 or 5 require active and intense systems intervention.

RAATE Summary

The RAATE has been presented as one approach which offers an efficient, addictions specific, yet comprehensive assessment of the college student with SUD. To broadly apply the RAATE, students scoring less than or equal to 2 across all dimensions are outpatient therapy candidates; students scoring greater than or equal to 4 are potential inpatient referrals. Students falling on midline 3 across all dimensions require most judicious consideration, especially if severities C and E are shaping toward scores of 4 (high severity) rather than 2 (low severity). Whether the RAATE is used or not for the assessment of college students, the concepts of a multivariate model and the corresponding multidimensional assessment of addictions severity is a key approach with this population.

INPATIENT ADDICTIONS TREATMENT

Students with SUD severity profiles matching inpatient care intensity are treatment resistant, medically unstable, emotionally distraught, and isolated from interpersonal supports. General hospital medical/surgical units are ill equipped to offer therapy for the psychosocial dimensions of SUD. Generic psychiatric inpatient programs often have limited knowledge of SUD and are potential liabilities in terms of erroneous information dissemination and mood altering drug prescription (substitution). Reliable high intensity SUD treatment is best received on inpatient units specializing in the therapy of alcohol/drug addiction (ATUs). Most ATUs provide highly structured group oriented programs. Abstinence support, chemical dependence education, living in the present, and taking responsibility for personal growth are basic therapy goals. Quality ATUs are supported by trained staffs experienced in the ongoing cultivation of therapeutic ward atmospheres. Assertive communication, group problem solving, and individual responsibility for behavior is emphasized. In selecting an inpatient program, referral agents should look for adequate staff to patient ratios, 24 hour nursing/medical presence, multidisciplinary treatment planning and a staff mix of recovering and nonrecovering personnel. In addition to group therapy, most ATUs offer individual counseling with the potential for crisis intervention psychotherapy. Family involvement for educational and post-discharge support purposes may be offered. Comprehensive ATUs expose patients to alcohol/drug community self-help recovery groups (Alcoholics Anonymous, Narcotic Anonymous) and accentuate discharge planning. The quintessential property of inpatient ATUs is not what type of treatments are provided, but the intensity with which treatment is applied.

The college student SUD population offers special challenges to treatment providers as a function of psychosocial development. Students are typically working through late adolescent and early adult issues. Relationships with older persons are tenuously negotiated. Requesting emotional support during a time of "independence striving" is contraindicated. Naturally narcissistic and grandiose, processing the need for intrapersonal change is almost unconscionable for 18-22-year-old students. The intense fear of failure and/or losing control exacerbates pathologic SUD denial. Peer group orientation in association with lacking sober/clean supports is a final student recovery disadvantage. These age specific developmental realities underscore the need for high intensity inpatient treatment with seriously addicted undergraduates. A functioning acute ATU will be presented to further demonstrate how inpatient treatment works. Program services and treatment components will be outlined with specific student SUD application.

ADDICTIONS TREATMENT INPATIENT MODEL: NEW DAY CENTER AT FULLER MEMORIAL HOSPITAL

New Day Center at Fuller Memorial Hospital is a 29 bed acute inpatient addictions treatment unit located in Massachusetts. Alcoholism, cocaine addiction, opiate dependence, polydrug abuse and other chemical dependencies are intensively treated with a comprehensive abstinence oriented therapy approach. Patients and significant others are taught that chemical dependency is a biopsychosocial illness affecting every facet of life. All patients are required to attend an intensive group program structure unless medical instability warrants room restricted bed rest. Multidisciplinary patient treatment plans are individually prepared according to specific patient need. Prior to admission inpatient candidates are informed of basic treatment expectations and are required to sign a treatment contract in good faith. If a patient is unable to communicate informed consent on admission (i.e., intoxicated, acute withdrawal) the contract is reviewed the following day. The contract stipulates no alcohol/drug use or possession, no violent acting out, no harm of self or others, mandatory attendance at all scheduled activities, compliance with hospital rules, and willingness to discuss feelings associated with self-harm or acting out. The contingency for contract violation is discharge with the potential for readmission at a later date. The contract serves to inform that SUD treatment is serious and there is patient responsibility for recovery. Following admission, the general course of treatment supports acute detoxification with eventual progression to rehabilitation.

Detoxification

Successful detoxification from drug(s) of choice is a vital first step in the recovery process. Withdrawal can cause a taxing physical and psychological response ranging from slight anxiety to serious medical complications. Treatment of withdrawal requires expert assessment, monitoring, and medical/nursing therapy. While most students will not manifest serious medical problems, physical discomfort may precipitate drug of choice craving and/or generate unfound medical concerns. Craving and health concerns are frequently implicated in student relapse. The continuous educational and medical/nursing support of an acute ATU helps to prevent and/or mediate such relapse triggers. Time limited prescription (72-96 hours) of cross tolerant medication may be necessary if subacute medical instability presents.

The psychological component of withdrawal is underestimated as a cause of treatment noncompliance leading to relapse. Subjective discomfort associated with opiate cessation, post cocaine use depression, and alcohol/benzodiazepine discontinuance, requires intensive support, structure, limits, and reality orientation (Liepman, 1984). During detoxification, the clinical staff approach is supportive with firm reminders that uncomfortable symptoms are a function of excessive drug use. While outpatient detoxification is a potential consideration for selected individuals (Whitfield, 1980), hospitalization is the prudent alternative for students with moderately severe addiction profiles. At New Day, assigned primary workers follow patients from admission through discharge. This enables the supportive relationship born of detoxification crisis to sustain the more confrontive and interpretive rehabilitation counseling approach.

Rehabilitation

Patients enter formal rehabilitation status as soon as acute withdrawal symptoms subside. Following detoxification, patients are better able to cognitively process the here and now life changes required for ongoing recovery. New Day ATU has few structural distinctions separating detox and rehab patients. Rehabilitation is considered a second phase of treatment with five basic client goals:

1. acceptance of SUD,
2. increase self-esteem,
3. learn drug free coping alternatives,
4. increase responsibility for behavior,
5. increase hope for ongoing recovery.

Group and individual therapy relationships are utilized to teach new coping skills, confront past/current irresponsible behavior, and to support personal growth. The Alcoholics Anonymous (AA) and Narcotics Anonymous (NA) program philosophies are reflected in all rehab components. Family and significant other involvement is strongly encouraged and occasionally mandated. The New Day treatment philosophy states that rehabilitation merely provides a foundation for recovery. Transitional care planning is emphasized with the goal of firm post-discharge AA/NA, alumni aftercare, and outpatient therapy involvement. The vital New Day ATU treatment modalities will be reviewed with specific application to college students.

Milieu Therapy

New Day Center functions as a therapeutic community of patients and staff. Nurses and counselors shape the inpatient environment to serve as an active socioemotional education center, where patients can observe, learn, and practice effective interpersonal communication. Morning and evening community meetings evaluate the ward atmosphere and keep patients focused on recovery. Milieu therapy aspires to teach and support drug free assertive communication, problem solving, and conflict resolution skills. Patients are encouraged to directly work through issues with copatients/staff as soon as problems arise. Community members learn that one not only has the right to feelings, but a responsibility to process them appropriately. A "patient government" system is utilized to grant increasing levels of patient freedom contingent on treatment progress. Giving and receiving positive and negative feedback without developing overconfidence or resentment is practiced daily in community meetings and small group therapy.

Milieu therapy works well with college students, most of whom have not been exposed to therapeutic community concepts. Students are frequently returning to difficult group living circumstances. This modality helps students to develop assertive drink/drug refusal skills, increase negotiating confidence, and walk away from high risk relapse situations. Students learn how their behavior affects others and that choices do exist. Negative transference is minimized because recovering copatients are milieu therapy agents and most constructive feedback occurs in the context of supportive groups.

Group Therapy

Group therapy programming is the primary treatment modality of New Day ATU. Participation in 8-10 hours of group therapy per day is mandatory. This group intensity offers a structure by which to reorganize student life. Prior to admission, addicted students routinely miss class and everyday becomes like a bad weekend, unstructured and uninvolved in a meaningful way with others. Isolated interpersonal routines are replaced with extreme structure and interpersonal process. A variety of different groups systematically confronts denial and narcissism, limit sets with projection and drug idealization, and supports guilt reduction and personal growth. The generic goals of ATU group programming are to:

1. facilitate identification with recovering others,
2. promote responsibility for enacting drug free coping behavior,
3. increase self-esteem,
4. improve interpersonal communication.

Addictions Education

Addictions education is a structured group meeting where patient's are taught the consequences of SUD and important recovery strategies. Didactic lectures on medical, social, and emotional sequelae are complemented by forums discussing assertive communication, relapse prevention and the basic principle of AA and NA. Patients discover alcohol/drug addiction is a disease influenced by learned behaviors. Students benefit greatly from this psychoeducational group using intact cognitive skills to reduce ignorance and offset denial.

Small Group Therapy

Small group therapy is a process group experience where feelings are shared and communication skills are refined. Coleaders limit process depth to crisis intervention and reframe issues around chemical dependence and recovery. Care is taken to avoid uncovering and processing long-term therapy issues to keep the focus on here and now problems. Students are initially reticent to share feelings but eventually use the group to work through denial and mediate problems with authority.

Women's and Men's Group

Same sexed process groups meet twice weekly to discuss specific men's or women's recovery issues. Violence, abuse, sex, and relationship problems are confidentially discussed with the opposite gender absent. Students frequently mention concerns related to identity and sexual stereotyping.

Therapeutic Film and Discussion

Dramatic SUD films followed by staff supervised discussions can be powerful treatment motivators. The neutrality of the television monitor and engaging special effects promotes identification and affect stimulation. Quality films serve as an excellent warmup to process family codependence, isolation, denial, guilt, anger, self-esteem, and responsibility issues. Students with negative transference toward staff around authority or dependence are often engaged by this modality. Projective identification techniques during process sessions mediates defensive patient response.

Self-Help Recovery Groups

Self-help recovery group exposure is an essential component of New Day rehabilitation. Alcoholics Anonymous describes itself as a fellowship dedicated to sharing experiences so as to solve common problems and help individuals recover from alcoholism (Alcoholics Anonymous, 1976). Narcotics Anonymous is an analogous program supporting narcotic and other drug addiction recovery. The basic philosophies of both programs support the disease concept and view abstinence as fundamental to recovery (Tournier, 1979). AA and NA are grounded in a program of twelve steps which include but are not limited to:

1. admission of alcoholism/drug addiction.
2. changing isolation to social, personal, and spiritual relatedness.
3. self examination, catharsis, and personal change.
4. helping to support the recoveries of other alcoholics/addicts. (Bean, in press)

At New Day, students are exposed to group meetings and sponsorship, the life blood of AA and NA. There are several types of self-help group meetings. Speaker meetings involve three or four recovering members sharing their life stories in lecture format with a large group. Speakers focus on the consequences of addiction and the value of recovery. Discussion meetings are small groups where recovering individuals share current personal life recovery issues and receive feedback and support. Step meetings are groups which focus on discussing one of the twelve steps of recovery and its personal life application. Group meetings are highly supportive, reducing isolation while providing hope for the future. Students attend onsite and off grounds meetings to prepare for community reentry. All newcomers to the self-help programs are encouraged to select sponsors (recovering individuals with years of abstinence) for additional support and power of example.

Al-Anon and Nar-Anon are twelve step self-help group programs for families of recovering/active alcoholics and addicts. Many students are familiar with Alateen, a self-help group for teenagers with addicted parents. Self-help programs are extremely valuable for students and their families. Students are peer oriented and will require support from a sober/clean peer group for ongoing recovery. Parents are walking a fine line between disengagement and overinvolvement, best negotiated with the help of Al-Anon and/or Nar-Anon.

Individual Counseling and Crisis Intervention

Individual counseling and crisis therapy are important components of SUD rehabilitation. Primary nurses and counselors follow assigned patients from admission through discharge. Primary workers provide comprehensive individual assessment and treatment planning, ongoing individual contact, and crisis intervention if indicated. Initial patient sessions focus on evaluation and engagement in treatment. Severe denial is confronted with a variety of approaches including the Alcohol Troubled Person Model (Willoughby, 1979). Issues concerning guilt, anger, self-esteem and relationships are processed through consistent brief counseling interventions. Milieu therapy and problem solving techniques restrict issues to the here and now context, while giving hands on experience at working through difficult feelings. Patients with acute problems precluding full commitment to SUD treatment receive brief crisis intervention therapy. The goal of such is to facilitate problem resolution to the point where patients can focus on SUD treatment. Interpretive work is generally limited to reframing therapy content so as to relate to current SUD treatment.

The power of the individual counseling relationship with students should not be underestimated. SUD is an illness of isolation and the counselor may represent the first significant adult support since high school. Counselors/therapists must caution against encouraging student pathologic dependence on this relationship. The skilled SUD counselor utilizes the therapeutic alliance to broaden a student's base of support by facilitating healthy dependence on family, AA/NA, and other recovery supports. Long-term issues should be referred to SUD outpatient therapists experienced in pacing therapy according to quality recovery time.

Family Therapy

The addicted student's alcohol/drug use exerts a profound influence on family members and significant others (Liepman, Nirenberg, & White, 1985). Group and individual family treatment is strongly encouraged at New Day and mandated for students living at home full- or part-time. Limited weekday visiting is contingent on family participation in educational group forums. Thrice weekly family groups reduce family isolation, disseminate needed information, and provide support. Group themes center on how chemical dependence has affected family functioning. Family enabling is discussed and more appropriate family support methods are outlined.

Individual assessments on all families identifies those in need of inpatient family crisis intervention and outpatient follow-up. Family evaluations also corroborate patient history and offer additional support to concerned parents or friends. In the best of circumstances, students and parents have difficulty renegotiating boundaries during SUD hospitalization. Students are generally unwilling to relinquish any degree of independence in lieu of parental support. Confused parents may initially respond with intense overinvolvement or complete disengagement. Crisis intervention helps such families to acknowledge the addiction problem together, talk about related feelings, and consider healthier functioning alternatives. Enmeshed families learn to consider more appropriate individuation among members. Disengaged families can begin to develop elementary supportive relationships. Problem families need to be told that the work begun during inpatient treatment must be continued with outpatient follow-up.

Many hospitalized students have one parent who is a recovering or active alcoholic. An actively alcoholic parent can be a liability for the recovering student and signify an extremely dysfunctional family (Liepman, White, & Nirenberg, 1986). In many cases, limited family contact after discharge is the healthiest alternative. Students will require expert help working through feelings resulting from such a reality. Further, practical strategies to defend against high risk involvement with destructive family members should be planned.

In summary, individual family assessment and ongoing family education is vital to student SUD treatment. Family systems must discover how to offer support without taking responsibility for student behavior. Education and occasionally crisis intervention is necessary to achieve such a goal. Families and students need to identify a relapse intervention plan for quick, safe reengagement in treatment should a slip occur.

Outpatient Treatment and Aftercare

While inpatient SUD treatment can provide a strong recovery base, it is outpatient therapy and aftercare support which nurtures ongoing sober/clean personal growth and development. Definitive outpatient and aftercare recovery structures need to be in place long before discharge. Discussion regarding student post-discharge follow-up is initiated during the first multidisciplinary treatment team meeting. Discharge planning requires active student input, and patient informed consent must be secured prior to staff contact with community/college resources. Direct liaison with the college counseling office and appropriate dean is encouraged. It is the role of primary nurses/counselors to educate students about the importance of such contact and to facilitate and supervise inpatient meetings with supportive college representatives. Staff advocacy is essential due to lack of standardization among college/university systems in dealing with impaired students. Some schools have well defined student assistance programs whereby troubled students receive the guidance of a comprehensive net of counseling resources. Many schools do not have such elaborate support programs and staff liaison with campus counseling offices is necessary to search out available recovery supports. Counseling offices are generally aware of on campus student recovery groups as well as on grounds and nearby AA/NA meetings.

Students are to outline a "contract with self" delineating needed outpatient and aftercare appointments which is inclusive of a relapse intervention plan of action. Student contracts can also be effected with appropriate deans and counseling offices if deemed therapeutically beneficial. In cases where halfway house placement or intensive day treatment is the best disposition, students may elect to negotiate a formal leave of absence from college. This is worked out with the appropriate dean and best processed with inpatient staff advocacy. In addition, the college counseling office should be encouraged to work in conjunction with the "Dean of Readmissions" office to maximize student recovery support. At New Day, routine transitional care referrals include twice weekly alumni aftercare support groups, ongoing formal outpatient group or individual therapy, regular contact with AA/NA, and pre-discharge liaison with appropriate college recovery support personnel.

DISCUSSION

Environmental and psychosocial developmental vulnerabilities mark college students as high risk to develop SUD. The potential course of SUD in students can be swift and severe due to a paucity of healthy social supports in tandem with strong peer pressure to use drugs/alcohol. College administrators have recognized SUD as a campus problem and have enacted substance abuse education and prevention programs. While these programs are important first steps, efficiency with students demonstrating major SUD problems has not been established. With the increasing prevalence of SUD among undergraduates and the opportunity to prevent college drop out and further social/physical deterioration, responsible college helping providers can no longer neglect tertiary intervention.

Inpatient ATUs offer comprehensive high intensity SUD treatment away from a student's alcohol/drug use environment. It is the author's bias that inpatient treatment is a viable alternative for students with severe addictions profiles. However, the controversy over effectiveness of inpatient versus outpatient therapy of SUD continues unabated. There are many schools of thought about alcohol/drug addiction in the SUD treatment field. Lack of sophistication and common language regarding SUD in general, and SUD assessment in particular, has further split efforts to achieve common ground. This lack of internal consistency in the SUD treatment field confuses and alienates helping providers, third party reimbursers, and consumers alike. Such confusion exacerbates widespread cultural denial and minimization concerning SUD, from which students and those charged with the maintenance of their well-being are not immune.

In assessing students, conceptualizing a multivariate model of alcohol/drug addiction is important due to the wide variety of SUD student presentations. Such a model views SUD in terms of relative severity with the potential for treatment matching. Assessment instruments and approaches ideally should facilitate comprehensive multidimensional evaluation. The RAATE Assessment and Treatment Evaluator has been presented as one approach offering comprehensive assessment of essential dimensions necessary for students to receive appropriate treatment intervention. The RAATE increases sophistication of language and approach while demystifying the inpatient evaluation process. It also assists in providing a common focus for better communication and teamwork between disciplines interfacing with addicted students.

Inpatient care should be considered for poorly motivated students with SUD exhibiting medical, psychological, and social problems of moderate severity. The intensity of the inpatient setting is required for treatment success with resistant multiproblem students who might otherwise relapse and drop out of school. Continuous ATU group therapies of different persuasions help to diffuse transference response while supporting students with a diverse peer group of recovering others. Inpatient ATUs are engagement mechanisms, supplying via group, individual, and family therapies, the clinical intensity to open the door to SUD recovery. Inpatient transitional care planning should recognize that quality ongoing recovery is only achieved with outpatient self-help and therapy follow-up. On-campus recovery student groups should be utilized for support as soon as feasible, prior to discharge if possible.

College students are among our most precious resources. Students with SUD are young and treatment resistant, making global advocacy efforts for access to costly intensive therapies poorly received. However, current demand for efficient use of health care resources supports a multivariate perspective for SUD assessment leading to cost effective treatment matching. Future theoretical study and treatment outcome research is needed in the area of SUD assessment and treatment matching with the college student population. Such research efforts would further strengthen the ease for what experienced clinicians know to be logically adequate and empirically valid: severely addicted college students need inpatient treatment intensity for recovery.

REFERENCES

Alcoholics Anonymous. *The story of how many thousands of men and women have recovered from alcoholism* (3rd ed.). New York: AA World Services, Inc. 1976.

Bean, M. Alcoholics Anonymous. In C.L. Whitfield and M.R. Liepman (Eds.), *The patient with alcoholism and other drug problems*. Chicago: Year Book Publishers, in press.

Brennan, A.F., Walfish, S. and AuBuchon, P. Alcohol use and abuse in college students. I. A review of individual and personality correlates. *The International Journal of the Addictions*, 1986, 21, 449-474.

Claydon, P. *Setting the right course: Alcohol and drug education on the college campus*. Santa Barbara: University of California, 1984.

Clayton, R. Cocaine use in the United States: In a blizzard or just being snowed? In N. Kozel and E. Adams (Eds.), *Cocaine use in America: Epidemiologic and clinical perspectives*. NIDA Research Monograph Series. DHHS Publication No. (ADM) 85-1414. Washington, D.C.: U.S. Government Printing Office, 1985.

Demonstration Alcohol Education Project. *Summary Report September 1975 to August 1980*, University Health Services, University of Massachusetts, Amherst, Massachusetts, 1980, 1-10.

Friend, K.E., and Koushki, P.A. Student substance use: Stability and change across college years. *The International Journal of the Addictions*, 1984, 19 (5), 571-575.

Hughes, S.P., and Dodder, R.A. Alcohol consumption patterns among American Indian and White college students. *Journal of Studies on Alcohol,* 1984, 45, 433-439.

Humphrey, J.A. and Friedman, J. The onset of drinking and intoxification among university students. *Journal of Studies on Alcohol*, 1986, 47 (6), 455-467.

Humphrey, J.A., Stephans, V. and Allen, D.F. Race, sex, marijuana use and alcohol intoxification in college students. *Journal of Studies on Alcohol*, 1983, 44, 733-738.

Kandel, D.B. Drug and drinking behavior among youth. In A. Inkeles, N.J. Smelser, and R. Turner (Eds.), *Annual Review of Sociology, Vol. 6*. Palo Alto, CA: Annual Reviews, Inc., 1980.

Liepman, M.R., Nirenberg, T.D. and White, W.T. Family oriented treatment of alcoholism. *Rhode Island Medical Journal*, 1985, 68 (3), 123-126.

Liepman, M.R., White, W.T. And Nirenberg, T.D. Children in alcoholic Families. In D.C. Lewis and C.N. Williams (Eds.), *Providing care for children of alcoholics*. Pompano Beach: Health Communications Inc. 1986.

Liepman, M.R. and Whitfield, C. Detoxification. In M. Liepman, R. Anderson, and J. Fisher (Eds.), *Family Medicine Curriculum Guide to Substance Abuse*. Kansas City: Society for Teachers of Family Medicine, 1984.

Mee-Lee, D. The recovery attitude and treatment evaluator (rate) an instrument for patient progress and treatment assignment. *Proceedings of the 34th International Congress on Alcoholism and Drug Dependence*, 1985, 424-426.

Mee-Lee, D. An instrument for treatment progress and matching – the recovery attitude and treatment evaluator (RAATE). Unpublished manuscript 1987.

Nicholi, A. The college student and marijuana: Research findings concerning adverse biological and psychological effects. *Journal of American College Health*, 1983, 32, 73-77.

Nicholi, A. The nontherapeutic use of psychotherapeutic drugs among the college age group: The sedatives and tranquilizers. *Journal of American College Health*, 1984, 33, 87-90.

Pattison, E.M. New directions in alcoholism treatment goals. In B. McGrady, N. Noel and T. Nirenberg (Eds.), *Future directions in alcohol abuse research.* NIAAA Research Monograph-15. DHHS Publication No. (ADM) 85-1322. Washington, DC: U.S. Government Printing Office, 1985.

Perkins, H.W. and Berkowitz, A.D. Perceiving the community norms of alcohol use among students: Some research implications for campus alcohol education programming. *The International Journal of the Addictions*, 1986, 21 (9 & 10), 961-976.

Policy Statement. American college health association statement on college alcohol and drug abuse. *Journal of American College Health*, 1986, 34, 228.

Robins, L.N. and Helzer, J.E. Lifetime prevalence of specific psychiatric disorders in three sites. *Archives of General Psychiatry*, 1984, 41, 949-958.

Temple, M. Trends in collegiate drinking in California, 1979-1984. *Journal of Studies on Alcohol*, 1986, 47 (4), 274-281.
Tournier, R.E. Alcoholics Anonymous as treatment and as ideology. *Journal of Studies on Alcohol*, 1979, 40 (3), 230-239.
Whitfield, C.L. Treatment of alcohol withdrawal without drugs. In J. Masserman (Ed.), *Current Psychiatric Therapies*. Orlando, FL: Grune & Stratton, 1980.
Willoughby, A. *The Alcohol Troubled Person*. Chicago: Nelson Hall Co., 1979.

APPENDIX I: RECOVERY ATTITUDE AND TREATMENT EVALUATOR (RAATE)

RAATE A

A. Degree of Resistance to Treatment

Evaluate patient's awareness and acceptance of addiction problem and commitment to definitive treatment.

A Low Score indicates an open attitude towards recovery with a need for a low level of treatment intensity and few motivating strategies.

A High Score indicates a counter-productive attitude towards recovery with need for a high level of treatment intensity and a variety of motivating strategies.

Score:

1. Admits an alcohol/drug problem; can identify several specific physical, psychological, social and/or occupational impairments; behavior demonstrates openness to, and active involvement with treatment recommendations, with good understanding of addiction: e.g., signs all needed releases of information; participates in therapy with affective involvement; able to give and receive supportive confrontation.

2. Admits an alcohol/drug problem; can identify limited specific physical, psychological, social and/or occupational impairments; behavior demonstrates desire for some treatment, but uneven involvement with treatment recommendations; or lacks understanding of addiction, but keen to learn: e.g., attends therapy, but often remains quiet in group; only occasional affective involvement in therapy; can confront others but has difficulty receiving confrontation.

3. Admits family and/or social/occupational/medical contacts are concerned about an alcohol/drug problem; attributes the alcohol/drug problems and/or reasons for admission to external people, places or things mostly; behavior demonstrates desire for addictions treatment but passive involvement or some struggles with treatment recommendations; lacks understanding of addiction but willing to listen: e.g., "Once I change jobs, there won't be a problem. I'll just stop"; agrees to treatment, but delays making the appointment; takes a "do it to me" stance; "pain" level minimal; intellectualizes; over compliant; distracted by psychological/biomedical problems.

4. A little awareness of alcohol/drug problem; defensive and minimizes any physical, psychological, social and/or occupational impairments; behavior demonstrates desire for addictions treatment, but many struggles with treatment recommendations: e.g., "I don't need alcoholism treatment, I've stopped before for 2 years"; "I don't want you talking to my family"; repeated missed appointments or tardiness and negativity in groups.

5. No awareness of an alcohol/drug problem; behavior indicates inability to seek addictions treatment: e.g., DT's; disoriented to time, place or person; unconscious; psychiatric and/or biomedical problems supercede addiction awareness. "I'm here to get help for my jaundice."

RAATE B

B. Degree of Resistance to Continuing Care

Evaluate patient's commitment to ongoing recovery; awareness that recovery is not a single treatment event; level of self-motivation and personal responsibility for recovery; familiarity with the continuum of recovery programs; and determine how realistic the patient's expectations of him/herself are.

A Low Score indicates a realistic awareness of the personal effort and ongoing vigilance needed for successful recovery. With this recovery attitude, there is a need for low treatment intensity and less education about recovery; fewer motivating strategies.

A High Score indicates a passive "magical" attitude towards recovery with a need for high treatment intensity and structured education about addiction and recovery; active introduction to recovery programs, e.g., AA and NA, and active intervention and motivating strategies.

Score:

1. Believes successful recovery requires active ongoing personal effort and vigilance; behavior demonstrates active participation in recovery treatment planning; overall positive feelings towards need for ongoing recovery: e.g., reaches out to people at AA meetings; initiated appointments for continuing care plans; actively constructing a support system; accepted in a halfway house program.

2. Acknowledges importance of ongoing personal effort and vigilance; behavior demonstrates verbal commitment to an ongoing recovery plan but fluctuating active participation in recovery treatment planning; feels open to need for ongoing recovery: e.g., doesn't call his/her AA sponsor; verbalizes the plans he/she has for recovery, but needs prodding to make concrete plans and contacts; overconfident.

3. Superficially acknowledges need for personal effort and vigilance but more externally-oriented and more focused on changing externals than personal change; behavior demonstrates the commitment to ongoing recovery plan to be only for follow-up appointments to help change people, places and things; expects recovery to result from the current treatment contacts; struggles with need for ongoing recovery: e.g., limited AA attendance; "Once I'm detoxed, I'll be O.K." "I'll change jobs"; "I'll see a counselor to work on the marriage and her nagging me."

4. Passive attitude and involvement in recovery treatment planning; expects recovery to occur spontaneously: e.g., "I'll just stop, I've done it before for two years;" attended AA once before—"didn't get anything out of it; made me want to drink more."

5. No awareness of an alcohol/drug problem; no commitment to an ongoing treatment plan; or sees alcohol/drug related incident as purely coincidental: e.g., "I just happened to be in the wrong place at the wrong time and got arrested for D.W.I."

RAATE C

C. Degree of Acuity of Biomedical Problems

Evaluate patient's biomedical status to determine the acuity and intensity of physical treatment necessary.

A Low Score indicates low acuity of biomedical problems with little or no biomedical treatment necessary.

A High Score indicates high acuity of biomedical problems and the likelihood of greater difficulty for the patient to maintain a focused attitude towards recovery – more structured, intensive biomedical and motivating strategies needed.

Score:

1. No acute biomedical problems needing treatment: e.g., no detoxification problems; no acute or acute-on-chronic physical illnesses accompanying addiction.

2. A few biomedical problems needing only minimal treatment planning: e.g., withdrawal symptoms mild or easily managed by outpatient detoxification; chronic physical illness like hypertension or diabetes well stabilized on current regimen; minor physical symptoms like diarrhea not distracting patient and manageable.

3. Biomedical problems require active treatment planning: e.g., withdrawal symptoms moderate but stabilized by medical detox regimen; chronic back pain requires physical therapy; diabetes needing dietary and medication adjustment occasionally.

4. Significant biomedical problems needing structured biomedical expertise but not 24 hour skilled medical care: e.g., withdrawal symptoms troublesome needing active social and medical treatment; diabetes needing frequent evaluation for dietary and medication adjustment; alcoholic liver disease active with ascites greatly improved but diuresis and jaundice not resolved yet.

5. Many biomedical problems needing acute diagnostic and treatment intensity: e.g., in active withdrawal with seizure potential; impending or actual DTs; unstable diabetes needing daily adjustment; acute pancreatitis; severe liver disease.

RAATE D

D. Degree of Acuity of Psychiatric/Psychological Problems

Evaluate patient's psychiatric/psychological status to determine the acuity and intensity of psychiatric treatment necessary and how easily or hard it will be for the patient to focus on primary addictions treatment.

A Low Score indicates low acuity of psychiatric problems and fewer distractions to allow a more focused attitude towards recovery – little or no non-addictions psychiatric treatment necessary.

A High Score indicates high acuity of psychiatric problems and the likelihood of greater difficulty for the patient to maintain a focused attitude towards recovery – more structured, intensive psychiatric and motivating strategies needed.

Score:

1. No acute psychiatric problems and no psychiatric (non-addictions) issues to distract patient from a focus on recovery: e.g., any anxiety, guilt, depression are all able to be normalized as part of early recovery; no significant stressors aside from addiction-related ones.

2. A few psychiatric problems needing only minimal treatment planning with little distraction from focusing on addiction recovery: e.g., borderline personality features with potential splitting to be monitored; compulsive personality with intellectualization and guilt to be noted and addressed in addiction psychotherapy strategies.

3. Psychiatric problems require active treatment planning with variable distraction from focusing on addiction recovery: e.g., previously diagnosed Bipolar Disorder or Schizophrenic Disorder currently stabilized on medication, but will need continued monitoring for exacerbation of symptoms; significant stressors in addition to addiction losses – child of an alcoholic, unresolved grief.

4. Significant psychiatric problems needing structured psychiatric expertise, but not 24 hour skilled psychiatric care; significant difficulty to keep focused on addiction recovery: e.g., an adolescent with addiction problems and a history of multiple caretakers; recent death in the family; histrionic display of emotions with dependent attempts to have others take responsibility; significant depression but not actively suicidal; overly compliant.

5. Many psychiatric problems needing acute diagnostic and treatment intensity with great difficulty to keep focused on addiction recovery: e.g., Dual diagnosis questions – patient needs diagnostic testing and skilled psychiatric observation; past history of violent or suicidal behavior with previous detoxification; significant learning disability or organicity; mild mental retardation; impending DTs – very anxious and variable orientation.

RAATE E

E. Extent of Social/Family Problems Unsupportive to Recovery

Evaluate the quality and quantity of social supports conducive to recovery; the extent and intensity of systems-intervention necessary to promote recovery.

A Low Score indicates a healthy, variety of social supports; stable work and living situation supportive of recovery with a need to have family, work and friends educated about addiction and recovery, but the systems intervention need only be limited and educational.

A High Score indicates a chaotic and/or isolated poverty of social supports; unstable work and living situation jeopardizing recovery and threatening immediate or early relapse if prematurely returned to that environment; the systems intervention need be active, intense, extensive involving family, employer, legal agents such as probation officers, lawyers and judges.

Score:

1. Many stable social supports to promote recovery; significant others demonstrate good empathy; or anxiety support recovery; few or no legal or work problems: e.g., strong family, friends, work relationships, significant others open to using their own recovery program; resentment resolving.

2. Social supports intact, conducive to recovery; significant others mostly supportive; do not detract from recovery; a few minor legal or work problems: e.g., family members familiar with Al-

Anon or Tough Love but some resistance to attending; concerned persons cooperative with systems treatment, but passive about their own recovery.

3. Social supports mostly intact; significant others demonstrate inconsistent support for recovery; significant legal or work problems: e.g., concerned persons resistant to systems treatment; uneven attendance at systems treatment; job warnings; absenteeism; on probation; drugs available at work.

4. A few social supports intact; significant others indifferent or symbiotically enmeshed; provide some distraction from recovery; numerous legal or work problems: e.g., family barely intact; one or two friends only; family, friend and work relationships impede addiction recovery by constant enabling or unrealistic rejecting limits; pending charges; job threatened/lost; abusive family relationships.

5. Socially isolated; or chaotic, multiple social problems; significant others unavailable, antagonistic or destructive causing active distraction from recovery; chronically unemployed, disabled and/or work record very unstable; or many legal problems presently or in the past: e.g., addicted friends only; destructive family, friend and work relationships if any, indigent or personally unproductive.

Chapter 9

Working with Children of Alcoholics on a College Campus: A Rationale and Strategies for Success

David Landers
Linda Hollingdale

SUMMARY. Collegiate children of alcoholics may make up as much as one-third of our student population. Effective programs have been developed to assist these young people with this issue. The necessity of providing support and intervention for collegiate adult children of alcoholics (ACoAs) is clearly supported by the overwhelming number of people affected by parental alcoholism. The developmental tasks faced by these young people also point out the responsibility college personnel workers have in their role of fostering the growth of their students. The college environment provides an ideal setting for assisting students with ACoA issues. The administration and staff must supply the motivation and commitment towards a pro-active plan of education and recovery for collegiate ACoAs.

As a freshman I was determined to keep my problems from home at home and *never* let anyone enter into my private life to find out the "untold" story of my life.

– *a college senior*

David Landers, PhD, is Director, and Linda Hollingdale, MS, Assistant Director, Student Resource Center, Saint Michael's College, Winooski, VT 05404.

A current membership brochure distributed nationwide from the National Association for Children of Alcoholics based in South Laguna, California (1987) reports the following statistics:

- An estimated 28 million Americans have at least one alcoholic parent;
- Children of alcoholics are at the highest risk of developing alcoholism or marrying someone who becomes alcoholic;
- In up to 90% of child abuse cases, alcohol is a significant factor;
- Children of alcoholics are prone to: learning disabilities, anxiety, eating disorders, stress-related illnesses, and compulsive achieving;
- Children of alcoholics often develop characteristics which can persist throughout adulthood: inability to trust, extreme need to control, excessive sense of responsibility, and denial of feelings.

It would not take much checking with college counseling centers to determine that many of the students being seen by counselors are for issues related to some combination of the above listed characteristics. Learning disabilities are one of the fastest growing minorities on college campuses today. It is impossible to look at college-related professional journals today without finding extensive study being done on eating disorders. Anxiety and stress related illnesses find their way to our college health centers and often end up with referrals to our counseling centers. Compulsive achieving, striving for perfection, control issues, trust issues, overly responsible students, and students who deny or intellectualize their feelings account for a majority of the counseling done on college campuses today. Not all students who present the above issues are adult children of alcoholics (ACoAs) and it could be easy for counselors to miss the ACoA connection if specific questions concerning alcohol and substance abuse in the home are not part of interviewing protocols. The connection between collegiate children of alcoholics and the issues being dealt with in counseling centers is not a coincidence. It is important to point out that while many students will seek assistance from counseling centers for the issues discussed above, few will use the issue of being adult children of alcoholics (ACoAs) as their presenting problem in the counseling center. Since ACoA issues can be treated quite effectively, it is essential that counselors, health service personnel, and campus ministry begin to question students about alcoholism and other chemical abuse in their home as part of regular interviewing protocols.

Berkowitz and Perkins (1987) reported on their research on collegiate children of alcoholics during the 1987 ACPA/NASPA Convention held in Chicago. Their research indicated that one in five students at the collegiate level recognize that at least one parent has an alcohol abuse problem. They further discovered that if you include grandparents who have an alcohol abuse problem, that one in five statistic increases to one in three. Claydon (1986) reports the following from his research at the college level: "Over one quarter (28%) indicated some degree of alcohol problems with one or both parents. Alcoholism in a blood relative (mostly grandfathers and uncles) was identified by 27% of respondents" (p. 15). These statistics indicate that colleges have a significant number of students today who are affected by the disease of alcoholism because of their families.

Growing experience suggests that children raised in an alcoholic home rarely, if ever, are unaffected. ACoAs, very early in their lives, learn the cardinal prohibitions: *"don't talk, don't trust, don't feel"* (Black, 1981). These young people must go through the "normal" developmental phases of college life with the added burden of having been reared in a dysfunctional home. That experience teaches them not to do the things we expect college students to do such as: develop positive identities, develop intimate relationships, talk, trust, and feel. Students raised in an alcoholic home who may have experienced abuse in many forms (verbal, physical and sexual) find it hard to know what is normal and what is abnormal. Accepting bizarre behaviors such as parents passed out on the floor, fights, inconsistency, and broken promises as normal distorts a person's sense of normality. In addition, ACoAs leave a dysfunctional home where alcohol was abused and often enter a college or university residential life environment where alcohol use and/or abuse surrounds them.

DEVELOPMENTAL ISSUES

> I never seemed to fit into the dorm life. They were all worried about clothes and dates and that stuff. I just never seemed to fit. They couldn't understand what I was dealing with. I moved off campus my sophomore year.
>
> *–a college junior*

Developmental issues surrounding college students and in particular collegiate children of alcoholics present an interesting framework in which to understand the issue of ACoAs at the college level.

Erikson's eight stages of development and the outcomes at each stage provide us with a picture of the adult child of an alcoholic (1950). If we look at the first six stages, which bring us up to young adulthood, and look at the conflicts within those stages we have a fairly accurate description of the struggles of the ACoA.

Stage one – infancy	trust vs mistrust
Stage two – early childhood	autonomy vs shame, doubt
Stage three – play age	initiative vs guilt
Stage four – school age	industry vs inferiority
Stage five – adolescence	identity vs identity confusion
Stage six – young adulthood	intimacy vs isolation

Erikson theorized that people must grapple with the conflicts of one stage before they can move on to a higher one. Many of these conflicts are in fact resolved by collegiate children of alcoholics however they resolve them in the negative and then move on to the next stage. ACoAs learn not to trust, they carry shame and doubt over parents' behaviors, feel guilty because of an inability to change or prevent parents' behaviors, often feel inferior due to a diminished self-concept and are terribly confused over who they are. Thus they end up in college isolating themselves from others because they are afraid that no one would understand or listen to them anyway.

The developmental stages which college students go through are also identified and explained by the work of Chickering (1969). His seven vectors of development are: competence, emotions, autonomy, interpersonal relationships, purpose, identity, and integrity.

This paper will deal with those vectors which would be most impacted by being raised in an alcoholic home.

Competence is defined by Chickering as the confidence one has in his/her ability to cope with what comes and to achieve successfully what he/she sets out to do. Intellectual, physical, social, and interpersonal competencies are difficult for the ACoA to grasp due to the inconsistent life in a dysfunctional home. One student related that he never could succeed as a child – no matter how good he was in school or in sports, no matter how much he tried he could not be successful (competent) because in his eyes success was measured by his parent's drinking behaviors. He was unable to get them to stop drinking and fighting and their alcoholism wasn't accepted by them nor understood by him. Competence and its impact on self-concept has implications for the student entering college who is expected to perform well intellectually as well as physically and interpersonally.

Emotions are explained by Chickering (1969) in this manner.

> . . . the student's first task is to become aware of feelings and to trust them more, to recognize that they provide information relevant to contemplated behavior or to decisions about future plans. Before emotional control can become effective, emotions have to be experienced, to be felt and perceived for what they are. (p. 10)

The following excerpt from Black (1981) points out the conflict confronting students who were raised in an alcoholic home.

> Children learn not to share their feelings and inevitably, learn to deny feelings because they don't trust these feelings will be validated by family members, other relatives, or friends. They don't trust their feelings will receive the necessary nurturing. Being isolated with feelings of fear, worry, embarrassment, guilt, anger, loneliness, etc., leads to a state of desperation, of being overwhelmed. Such a state does not lend itself to survival, so the children learn other ways to cope. They learn how to discount and repress feelings, and some learn simply not to feel. (p. 46)

College and university life provides students with the opportunity to spend quality time with others free from the constraints of family. This is the time when people take risks, learn to manage and trust emotions and learn to integrate those emotions into a maturing self-concept. Being raised in an alcoholic home, which teaches you by harsh experience that you cannot trust your feelings, leaves you vulnerable to becoming isolated, distrustful, and alone. The rule of not talking about the alcoholic home also results in ACoAs not being able to share their isolation, distrust, and loneliness with others including roommates, residence hall staff, faculty, or counselors.

Chickering (1969) talks about *autonomy* and its development in detail.

> Change occurs along three major vectors, emotional independence, instrumental independence, and recognition and acceptance of interdependencies. Development of emotional independence begins with disengagement from the parents, and rebelliousness in relation to them, to other adult authorities, and to established institutions. During this period, relationships with peers and sympathetic adults provide transitory emotional support. (p. 77)

In light of the above definition, collegiate children of alcoholics do not have much chance to develop autonomy. It is difficult to disengage from parents when there are issues of alcohol involved. For many college students there are siblings at home who are still going through the difficulties of a dysfunctional home. We find that many of the students we work with are preoccupied with worries about siblings. This worry is very real for them for they can remember what they went through and they have a genuine fear for their younger brothers and sisters. In addition, there is also the fear that something will happen to parents because of their drinking and the responsible student is torn between the emotions of guilt and fear and an intellectual awareness that they need to be away from that home environment. It is difficult to concentrate on academics when your mind is preoccupied with realistic concerns about home. Instrumental independence may be more easily developed than the others because students raised in an alcoholic home learn to trust and rely on themselves.

Developing purpose requires formulating plans of action to integrate avocational, vocational, and life style issues (Chickering, 1969). Adult children of alcoholics often have a difficult time in identifying avocational and recreational interests. We find that ACoAs don't know how to have fun. They often are so busy being the twelve-year-old-going-on-thirty-five that they don't take the time to play. A second element is vocational plans and aspirations (Chickering, 1969, p. 109)—many children of alcoholics end up in the helping professions. Adult children of alcoholics carry lessons learned in childhood into a work environment and this may result in dysfunctional work environments. The process of career development depends on self-awareness activities which enable the student to identify strengths and weaknesses as well as interests. This step, vital to the process of career development can be very threatening to collegiate children of an alcoholic. This factor certainly has relevance for college career development personnel. The third element is life style (Chickering, 1969. p. 120)—the development of intimate relationships can be very threatening to collegiate children of alcoholics because the combination of "don't talk, don't trust and don't feel" results in barriers to every relationship. It is also difficult for those around collegiate children of alcoholics to understand why the person is so reluctant to develop the intimacy that results in a positive life style. In fact, some ACoAs perhaps don't even know that intimacy is a positive, rather than a negative experience.

Developing integrity is closely tied to the other vectors mentioned in this article. Integrity comes about as a result of an individualized set of values which have been tried and tested by each person. Internal consistency helps each person to become committed to these values. Internal consistency is one thing ACoAs do have, but they have a difficult time in believing their values because they are not validated by others. This lack of validation comes about through an unwillingness on the part of the student to share these ideas with others.

Developmental issues which face all of us as we grow and mature are difficult and often painful. For collegiate children of alcoholics it becomes more painful because of the lessons learned in a dysfunctional home.

It is not enough for college counselors alone to be aware of the issues surrounding adult children of alcoholics. It takes a commitment on the part of the entire college or university to effectively provide an atmosphere where the issues can be dealt with constructively. The faculty, Health Services, residential life staff–including resident assistants, resident directors and resident coordinators, Student Activities, Campus Ministry, and administration working together can make a difference. It is not always easy to educate these populations so that they can make that difference. Claydon (1986) comments that: "Denial, rationalization and minimalization of substance abuse problems are as common to institutions of higher education as they are elsewhere" (p. 15). In addition, it is not always easy to educate a campus population that services are available in this area. Many college students faced with this issue feel that they are the only ones dealing with this issue. They feel that way due to the fact that, unlike other developmental issues facing college students, this issue is not one which is openly discussed in floor meetings, during late night discussions, nor is it an issue which is usually talked about at all. We have seen cases where best friends for four years, roommates living in townhouse situations, never discussed with each other that they were both children of alcoholics. Attempting to deal with these issues alone, in isolation, takes a great deal of energy, energy which could be put to better use in constructive recovery.

WHY AND HOW ACoA GROUPS DEVELOPED AT SAINT MICHAEL'S COLLEGE

The study of the issues of ACoAs is only ten years old. Prior to five years ago seldom, if ever, was this area of counseling mentioned during graduate training courses. Claudia Black is a pioneer in this field and while many professionals were busy dealing with the alcoholic, she began recognizing the issues surrounding the family of the alcoholic. Her first book, *My Dad Loves Me, My Dad Has A Disease* (1979), came about as a result of her work with children whose parent(s) were in treatment. One of the authors had worked with her in Michigan prior to his moving to Saint Michael's College and he had seen the tremendous impact that her work had on adult children. Claudia Black was invited to speak at the college. That was five years ago. Her speech and her presentation to student service personnel on campus opened the eyes of many to the need for dealing with this issue in a pro-active manner. Groups were formed as a result of individual counseling being done with students. In addition, referrals from Health Services and Campus Ministry helped many students come forward to address this subject. Campus Ministry personnel agreed to deliver a homily on this topic. One Sunday evening over eight hundred students at Mass heard a priest give them permission to deal with this issue. After working closely with the college counselors in the development of the homily, the priest told students that their parents' alcoholism was not their fault, that they could not help but be affected by this issue and that there were many resources on campus to help them deal with this. The expectation was not that dozens of students would come rushing into counseling, the expectation was that students would do a great deal of thinking and perhaps talking about this issue. Giving people permission to deal with issues which have been kept silent all of their lives made a difference and over the next several months many students did indeed seek out help. Several faculty members also heard the sermon and the presentation by Claudia Black and they became more sensitized to this issue. We contacted the campus newspaper asking them to cover this topic and articles started to appear discussing this subject. Claudia Black's presentation was covered by the alumni newsletter which is also sent to parents of current students. This vehicle alone resulted in several referrals from parents who were surprised and grateful that the college was dealing with this issue in a proactive manner. Parents also began to refer their sons and daughters for counseling. In addition, the training program for our residential life staff was set up to include a discussion which promotes understanding of this issue and awareness of the resources available on campus. We began to offer seven-week group sessions each semester for our students to assist them in dealing constructively with their own recovery as ACoAs.

ACoA GROUP FORMAT

College life requires students to learn how to function and thrive academically, personally, interpersonally, and socially. With this juggling act in progress, student personnel workers have many arenas in which to interact with students. In our interaction with ACoAs we see five basic responsibilities:

1. to disseminate information about alcoholism and adult children of alcoholics;
2. to have active outreach networks to assist with identifying and connecting with ACoAs;
3. to provide individual counseling for ACoAs;
4. to conduct ACoA groups specifically designed for the college population;
5. to establish an ongoing support network for ACoAs.

Although each area of responsibility is important, this article will report specifically on the ACoA group work conducted by the authors.

Working with college students provides unique challenges and benefits. Generally, the challenges include: a high rate of alcohol abuse, peer pressure and acceptance, a shaky self-esteem and self-awareness, and students' desire to stretch or break family ties. The benefits are: a targeted population, teachable young people who are naturally seeking self-awareness, acceptance, and autonomy, the opportunity to see people in many facets of their lives, and a specified time frame in which to work.

With these factors in mind our goal is to aim for an effective balance of structure and flexibility in our groups. Supplying direction in an atmosphere of freedom and acceptance has been most successful. For most students this is a first encounter with the fact that they were raised in an alcoholic home, therefore their readiness to be involved varies greatly. To be able to meet each student where he or she is and to work from there is crucial.

Our groups run for seven weeks meeting once a week for two hours. Students are either invited by a counselor as a result of individual counseling, are referred by another staff member, or respond to advertisements in the student newspaper. Each student is interviewed by one of the counselors in order to be accepted into a group. Six to nine people has been the optimum number of participants. Students are asked for a firm commitment to attend each session, and once the second session begins no new students are accepted. Confidentiality is a major issue.

Certainly each student enters into the group experience with his or her personal expectations. As group leaders, our expectations are well reflected in the following excerpt:

> A group gives members the opportunity to create a community based on trust, honesty, intimacy, and acceptance. This community helps members build relationships with each other, challenge members to reveal themselves and their learned defensive patterns, and gives members the opportunity to experience and share feelings freely and unconditionally. It gives members a chance to be accepted by others more than they can presently accept themselves. (Curtin, 1985, p. 5)

In planning the structure of the sessions, it's important to remember three things:

1. students are afraid of information leaking out to friends and professors;
2. students are used to being lectured to and are frequently willing to let an authority figure take charge and be the expert;
3. ACoAs are very skilled at rationalizing and discussing feelings, it is therefore necessary to combine experiential work with group discussion.

In light of these points, the importance of confidentiality must be discussed often. However, since learning how to share with and trust other people is a major goal for our students, it is necessary to help them understand the difference between appropriate personal disclosure and harmful gossip. Secondly, the group leader must not overdo the information giving part of the process. Reading assignments and homework are good ways to provide necessary information without using group time for lecturing. Finally, the group leader (especially if he or she is an ACoA) must be willing to challenge personal fears about the expression of feelings and use non-discussion techniques such as: guided imagery, family sculptures, Black's *The Stamp Game* (1984), letter writing, and other creative outlets. It is important that the group leader(s) be experienced and trained in any techniques used since powerful emotional expression is often triggered by these experiences.

Because students work through many of their thoughts, feelings, and insights away from the group, a notebook for journal writing is provided for each of them. Any exercises conducted during sessions are also done within this notebook. Before the group meetings begin each student is asked to read Black's *It Will Never Happen To Me* (1981).

The students' needs, interactions, and personalities guide the course of the group process. It would be irresponsible to suggest a "recipe" approach to group work. Therefore, what follows here is simply a brief summary of what has worked for our groups.

Session One

The first meeting is introductory in nature. All members introduce themselves, give a brief family background, and explain what brought them to the group. Specific details and ground rules regarding the group meetings are established. The group leader then spends some time discussing basic information on topics such as: alcoholism, defense mechanisms, survival, emotions, control and risk issues. Confidentiality is highly stressed and agreed upon. Finally, a videotape, *Children of Denial*, by Claudia Black (1982) is shown and discussed.

During the first meeting the students are generally anxious and tentative, however most usually report a sense of excitement and anticipation about the coming weeks. Although dialogue is minimal at this point, it is important to ask each participant to report on how they are feeling about the first session. This begins the process of sharing and validation. Individual counseling sessions are offered in conjunction with the group meetings for students who are in need of additional support.

Session Two

Begin with brief reintroductions. The group leader spends a few moments commenting on the goals and possibilities of the group experience, validating the students' willingness to participate, and encouraging each person to accept the responsibility of creating the type of experience he or she would like to have during the coming weeks.

The incomplete sentence exercise (Black, 1985, p. 16) is used to help generate discussion. In dyads or triads the students are asked to take turns completing several incomplete statements. They face their partner(s) and respond out loud to the statement called out by the group leader. Statements such as: "When I feel sad I ______," "When I was growing up, alcohol ______," "I don't trust people ______," "What I like best about myself is ______" provide a helpful starting point for self-exploration. Each student is instructed to respond to the same statement five consecutive times with five different responses. Black theorizes that we become more truthful with each subsequent response.

During the exercise the group leader creates the incomplete statements, circulates and observes the group members, assesses the comfort level, and decides the amount of time needed for the exercise. It is not necessary for the group leader to hear all the responses given by the students. By the end of the exercise the students are more relaxed and have experienced personal disclosure.

Following a brief discussion about the exercise, the group leader introduces the concept of Dr. J. L. Moreno's action sociogram in the form of a family structure (Blatner, 1973, p. 46). This exercise allows a student to introduce his or her family to the group by means of creating a sculpture, or a three-dimensional painting, of the relationships among family members. The student uses other students in the group to portray his or her family members. With the help of the group leader the student uses posture, position, proximity, height, touch, isolation, and facial expression to show the dynamics within the family. A towel is thrown over the heads of all alcoholics in the family to represent the masking effect of alcohol. The student places him or herself into the sculpture to make it complete.

The group leader then questions the "members" of the family about how they feel in their particular positions. This often proves enlightening to the student who may never have considered how other family members might feel in their situations. The group leader may also ask the student to make changes in the sculpture to show how the family has changed over time. The fluidity of the exercise gives it added effectiveness. After questions and comments from the group members are heard it is important to allow the student sculptor to comment on how the exercise affected him or her.

With approximately ten to fifteen minutes allowed for each student, all students have the opportunity to introduce their families in this manner. It is important to have time available for group discussion when the exercise has been completed. At this time students may report on what they learned from their own sculpture and other students' sculptures, and how it felt to play other students' family members. This is a good time to encourage discussion of feelings and relationships. Finally, encourage the students to use their journals to report further reactions to the day's events.

Session Three

The goal of this session is to encourage awareness and expression of past and present feelings. In order to avoid total rationalization of feelings, *The Stamp Game* by Claudia Black (1984) is used. In this game students use colorful stamps to represent emotions they've experienced such as guilt, confusion, anger, and happiness. By selecting differing amounts of stamps to represent the intensity of each emotion, and by arranging the piles of stamps in a certain order, it is possible to see what the students' experiences have been. The students then discuss with the group the source and consequences of each feeling. Questions are allowed by other group members, however no opinions or analyses are allowed at this time.

Each student does two sets of feelings, one to represent a time in his/her childhood and one to represent the present time. Comparisons are made between the two sets in order to see changes the student has experienced. To save time this exercise is conducted in dyads and triads. The group comes together for discussion when each student has shared his or her feelings within the small group. At this time the students discuss what was difficult for them, what they were glad to share, and what they learned about themselves during the game.

The Stamp Game comes with directions that describe several variations of the game. The group leader may design the type of exercise that best suits the needs and personalities of the group.

Session Four

By this session each person has had the opportunity to explore the past, experience old and new feelings, and share with the other group members. In general the students are more comfortable with one another, are able to take more risks, and therefore are interacting with one another to a greater extent. Bonds are often being formed beyond the group environment.

The goal of this session is to allow more discussion time for students to share what they have learned and felt. To assist the students with the integration of past and present, a guided fantasy, *The Inner Child* by Sharon Wegscheider-Cruse (1987), is used. During this journey the student is guided from the present slowly back through the past to the childhood home. After visualizing childhood memories, talking with one's self as a "child," and making peace with painful childhood emotions, the student is gradually brought back to the present. Personal strengths, positive qualities, and realistic views are emphasized throughout this guided fantasy. The student has the opportunity to understand his or her "child" with the help of adult knowledge and awareness.

If the group leader has not conducted many guided fantasies, it is important to have a complete script to read from with the appropriate pauses marked. The guidelines should be clear and allow plenty of room for each student's personal fantasy. There is a great possibility for powerful emotional reactions to this exercise, therefore the remainder of the session is used for processing and discussion. Throughout the discussion encourage students to focus not only on the painful memories but also on the strengths each developed as a result of his/her childhood experiences and perceptions. This exercise is a vital component in the development of each student's self-esteem and sense of autonomy.

Session Five

The exercise used during the fifth session is Claudia Black's "letter to a parent." The students are asked to compose a letter to either parent – the alcoholic, the non-alcoholic, a living or deceased parent. In relation to that parent the letter should include: a message of thanks or appreciation, comments on harmful, hurtful things that happened, and a statement by the student about what he or she plans to do for him or herself at the present time. The exercise takes about one half hour.

Each student then reads his or her letter aloud to the group. Since they are unaware of this part of the exercise while they are writing, most letters are honest and powerful. This part of the exercise is very difficult for most students, the group support and empathy often peaks at this time. Group discussion can be difficult but flows naturally from this exercise. The vulnerability level is usually high, therefore sensitivity and clarification of any ambiguities is important. Most students leave this session feeling very exposed and afraid. Leave enough time to carefully check-in with each student before they leave.

Session Six

Give time for the students to discuss any feelings and thoughts regarding the previous week's exercise. Then ask the students to write about how the group experience and what they've learned have impacted their lives at college. If they haven't begun to tie the many facets of their life experiences together, this will assist them with the integration process.

Group discussion follows with emphasis on their relationships and behaviors at school. How do they present themselves, how do they interact with friends, what is positive about their behaviors, what is unhealthy, how do they sabotage their own success, how have they grown in the past weeks? It is interesting to ask them what they expect for themselves beyond college. What type of adults will they be? This forward thinking is a good way to measure their self-concept, confidence, and hope levels. It also helps them see that many options are ahead of them with choice and responsibility in their power.

Session Seven

During the earlier sessions the students were given a long-term assignment. They were asked to create something to share with the rest of the group that represented anything they gained from the group. It could be a gift of art work, music, words, a collage, or any personal expression of thoughts and feelings. The last session opens with sharing these projects.

The videotape, *The Process of Recovery* by Claudia Black (1987), is shown. This tape gives a hopeful and realistic message about the work they've begun, what lies ahead, and the fact that they're not alone.

The session closes with each student giving a brief, personal, spoken message to every other person in the group. The group leader also joins in this exercise. The leader may in fact want to start the exercise in order to set a genuine and serious tone. This interaction helps each student understand how the others have seen him or her. It also validates the necessary process of give and take between people.

With the formal sessions completed, students are reminded that this has been the first step in their recovery process. They are encouraged to continue their own recovery and we let them know that support continues to be available through individual counseling and through a campus wide ACoA support network. Faculty, staff, and students meet voluntarily throughout the school year to share information and encouragement.

CONCLUSION

The necessity of providing support and intervention for collegiate ACoAs is clearly supported by the overwhelming number of people affected by parental alcoholism. The developmental tasks faced by these young people also point out the responsibility college personnel workers have in their role of fostering the growth of their students. The college environment provides an ideal setting for assisting students with ACoA issues. The administration and staff must supply the motivation and commitment towards a pro-active plan of education and recovery for ACoAs.

REFERENCES

Berkowitz, A. D., & Perkins, W. H. (1987, March). Research on Collegiate Children of Alcoholics: Implications for Counseling and Program Activities. Report presented at the joint meeting of the American College Personnel Association and the National Association of Student Personnel Administrators, Chicago, IL.

Black, C. (1979). *My dad loves me, my dad has a disease*. Denver: MAC, Printing and Publishing Division, 1850 High Street.

Black, C. (1981). *It will never happen to me*. Denver: MAC.

Black, C. (1982). *Children of denial.* [Videotape, No. 1]. Denver: MAC.
Black, C. (1984). *The stamp game*. Denver: MAC.
Black, C. (1985). *Repeat after me*. Denver: MAC.
Black, C. (1987). *The process of recovery*. [Videotape, No. 3]. Denver: MAC.
Blatner, H. A. (1973). *Acting-in practical applications of psychodramatic methods*. New York: Springer Publishing Company.
Chickering, A. W. (1969). *Education and identity*. San Francisco: Jossey-Bass.
Claydon, P. (1986, September-October). Off to college, the first home away from home for acoas. *Changes*, p. 15.
Curtin, P. J. (1985). *Tumbleweeds; a therapists guide to treatment of acoas*. Stroudsburg, PA: Quotidian.
Erikson, E. H. (1950). *Childhood and society*. New York: W.W. Norton & Company, Inc.
National Association for Children of Alcoholics. (1987). Membership brochure. South Laguna, CA: NACOA.
Wegsheider-Cruse, S. (1987, February). Presentation delivered at the National Conference on Addictions, Clearwater, FL.

Chapter 10

Alcohol and Other Drug Issues at Brown University: Two Administrative Perspectives on a Common Problem

Bruce Donovan
Toby Simon

SUMMARY. For over a decade Brown University has been concerned with issues of chemical dependency. From the establishment of a position of Associate Dean for Chemical Dependency in 1977 to the opening of the Office of Health Education in 1981, the university's commitment to programmatic concerns with chemical dependency has been quite apparent and highly visible. Brown's approach has centered on the design and continual development of a loosely, but well connected network of services. The Brown network has been characterized by the breadth of its approach and a refusal to deal with only one aspect of this vast problem or only one segment of the campus community. This paper highlights the efforts of two administrators at Brown over the past ten years with a glimpse at the decade to come. The administrative perspectives are those of the Associate Dean for Chemical Dependency and the Director of Health Education.

The creation by Brown's president in 1977 of the position of As-

Bruce Donovan, PhD, is Dean of Freshman and Sophomores, Professor of Classics, Associate Dean/Chemical Dependency, and Toby Simon, MEd, is Assistant Dean of Student Life, Director of Health Education, Brown University, Providence, RI.

Address reprint requests to: Box 1865, Brown University, Providence, RI 02912.

sociate Dean with Special Responsibilities in the Area of Chemical Dependency stressed that chemical dependency was a significant issue for the institution and initiated the University's current concern with questions of alcohol and other drug use. Part I of this article, by Bruce Donovan, concerns itself with the role and responsibilities of the Associate Dean and the evolution of that office.

Part II of this article, by Toby Simon, describes the development of the Office of Health Education on the Brown campus and highlights the activities of that Office over the past six years. Health Education permeates various aspects of campus life and the integration of it into the daily lives of college students is discussed in this section.

PART I

For over a decade, programmatic concern with chemical dependency at Brown University has centered on the design and continual development of a loosely, but surely connected network of services.[1] The "network," which involves the University's major constituencies and which addresses issues of prevention and education and treatment, has been characterized by one observer as a "collection of opportunities" rather than a formal, tightly constructed program. This seems a fair observation. Particularly in its early stages, but even today, the Brown network has been characterized by the breadth of its approach and a refusal to deal with only one aspect of this vast problem or only one segment of the campus community. As a result, services are now in place for all members of the community and have been designed to address all aspects of substance abuse.

The creation by Brown's president in 1977 of the position of Associate Dean with Special Responsibilities in the Area of Chemical Dependency, served notice that chemical dependency was a significant issue for the institution and initiated the University's current concern with questions of alcohol and other drug use. The title itself makes clear several points. The new dean was to be concerned with a variety of issues, but the role was cooperative, not intended to assume total or exclusive responsibility. For example, the incum-

[1] The network concept is also familiar at Brown in arrangements for academic advising. Both adaptations of the network principle reflect ideas originally advanced by F. Jones and G. Najera (1976).

bent would not offer formal classroom instruction nor attempt to offer medical treatment. Again, the concern of the dean was not limited to alcohol only, but would include questions of drug use generally.

This appointment was significant in various ways. Top-level support for addressing issues of substance abuse was manifest. The direct concern with dependency made clear that issues of pathology and general health were of interest, as well as communal aspects of drug use such as party planning and social regulation. This title also embraced attention to alcoholism when other programs generally concerned themselves with the less severe aspects of alcohol and other drug use, aspects that were also part of the Brown model. Appointment to the new position of a recovering alcoholic humanist on the Brown faculty, not a professional in the fledgling field of substance abuse, and most especially, someone without direct affiliation with the Brown Program in Medicine, demonstrated an openness to innovation: a recovering person familiar with drug issues and with a degree of training would in the University setting cooperate with professionals with more traditional, formal education in the field. Appointment of a member of the Brown faculty, who had long association with the institution, further demonstrated the appropriateness of every campus's addressing a common difficulty in its own way, with each institution honoring its particular available resources. Of importance, too, was the position's initial focus on faculty at a time when most campuses concentrated on student aspects of chemical dependency. Significant, too, was the housing of the new administrator in the academic deanery, a decision which wedded the position to the central purposes of the institution. This affiliation also gave the position an unmistakable identification with wellness, achievement and healthy productivity and less ready identification with issues of misbehavior and psychological or medical maladjustment. Finally, the new deanship was designed to be highly effective and visible, yet modestly funded. Each of these details would have provided the wise observer, in the late seventies, signals to the development of a program that is in its essence, uniquely Brunonian and yet highly adaptable to other settings.[2]

---

[2] For a fuller description of the ideas behind the formation of the Brown "program," see Donovan (1981).

The President, in making this appointment, responded to a small faculty group which had devised for the University a policy addressing chemical dependency among its faculty. The Associate Dean was to advertise this policy and assist with its implementation for individual members of the faculty in their own right and for chairpersons as supervisors. Additionally, the Dean was charged with development of similar procedures for members of the staff and administration. And not least of his responsibilities was developing for students, graduate but particularly undergraduate, a program which would increase awareness of issues of chemical dependency and provide support for those experiencing difficulty.

This overarching focus on the whole community received a major thrust forward in the President's early signing during the academic year 1977-78 of a simple statement requiring that non-alcoholic beverages be available at events where alcohol was served, no matter for whom or at what level. This policy guaranteed a new *modus operandi* for social events. Of equal importance was the implicit empowering of all members of the University community in the establishment of new norms for social life: anyone displeased at a campus event where alcohol was served could request change on the basis of the new policy.

A similarly straightforward community-wide and low-cost initiative established meetings on-campus of both Alcoholics Anonymous and Al-Anon. (Meetings of both Narcotics Anonymous and Nar-Anon, and meetings for Adult Children of Alcoholics, are now easily accessible to campus populations.) Concomitant notice of these meetings in campus newspapers (and in special mailings at reunion time) made clear that issues of chemical dependency would henceforth be taken very seriously at Brown, that they were problems that affect all members of the University community, and that they were appropriate matters of concern and conversation. (It is important to note that in the late 1970s, such meetings, open to all members of the University community and not restricted to either staff or faculty or students, were a topic for debate at national conferences on campus drug problems.)

Let me add that self-help groups such as Alcoholics or Narcotics Anonymous and Al-Anon or Nar-Anon are committed to the principle of increasing their membership by attraction, as potential members observe the success of these several programs in the lives of others, and not by promotional activity. This procedure has been followed in the expansion of these meetings on the Brown campus. Some new members have affiliated after having read the notice of meetings carried in the bi-weekly published Brown community newspaper. Others come on referral from the various offices on campus who see those troubled by addiction. Others know members of these fellowships and are attracted by the promise which they see realized in the lives of friends and colleagues. In several academic departments and certain living units, one member has had a significant impact on a number of peers.

There are no particular tricks in the advertising of these meetings to campus populations. One pitfall to be avoided is over-explaining, e.g., clarification in excessive detail that these are not religious groups or insistence that their lay, non-professional and non-trained approaches are worthy, after all, of attention. Students, faculty members and staff seem to respond best when they are initially accompanied by a sympathetic member. The precise reason why individuals find these meetings to their taste vary from individual to individual; and those reasons why University personnel avoid meetings quite often have little to do with what might be perceived as "obvious" reasons for disaffection.

This abiding concern with the community-wide dimensions of substance abuse, of which establishment of Anonymous meetings is emblematic, has continually informed the development of Brown's program over the last decade. Another example is the Brown Group on Alcohol which in the late seventies met weekly for hour-long "brown bag" lunches; members of the local and University communities briefly addressed a drug-related topic and then led informal discussion.[3] More recently, a group hosted by the Associate Dean for Chemical Dependency, known as "the Lunch Bunch," dines together five or six times a year – for lunch, dinner, barbecues, pot-lucks – and unites all those on campus who have addictive histories and who are living drug-free, whatever their primary form of support may be.

On the other hand, in addition to policies and services that apply to the whole community, different populations have called forth specially targeted programming. For example, a colloquium on al-

---

[3] For more on the Brown Group on Alcohol, see Donovan (1979).

cohol and creativity was designed especially for faculty, a number of whom had wondered about their scholarly productivity and its relationships to alcohol or other drug use: a pair of recovering, productive addicts exploded the myths and advertised the realities of this issue.

The staff of the Personnel Office profited from a session led by the director of the Employee Assistance Program for the Kemper Insurance Company. Additionally, in-service training was provided to a variety of service departments, and a referral list containing the names of individuals on campus prepared to provide confidential information on alcohol and other drugs was mailed to departmental chairmen and supervisors.

Special groups of students also received particular attention. Materials that had special relevance for Black, Asian and Latino students were distributed to the Third World Center. The Women's Center was provided with a selection of pamphlets, as were gay and Lesbian students. Residential Counselors in freshman dormitories were offered a full training program that was open to the community at large. Other peer counseling groups reviewed case studies and were instructed in the principles and skills of intervention.

Clearly, one associate dean could not effect all the changes that have been made in the Brown environment. Cooperation from many other individuals has been of crucial importance. A professor of anthropology annually has offered a course on alcohol, health and culture. The Medical Program has introduced drug-related material across the medical curriculum, and houses a Center for Alcohol and Addiction Studies of which one subgroup has special interest in campus projects in education, evaluation and prevention. In 1981 the Office of Health Education opened and undertook outreach and publicity that had previously been the purview of the Associate Dean.[4]

Over time individuals in a variety of offices have come to exercise firmer and more informed control over those aspects of drug use which are their particular responsibility. This change is clear in an apocryphal tale from the late '70s of a certain dean of students who doubted whether the University could *seriously* contemplate

[4] The Office of Health Education is discussed more fully in Part II of this article.

punishing students whose misbehavior might be attributed to drunkenness. (The answer, of course, was a clear and resounding "yes.") Such an attitude is now foreign to most administrators at Brown. Indeed, those students who are involved with Police and Security Services for alcohol- and other drug-related behavior are now routinely discussed by the deans of students, and penalties for offenses are arranged by that group. All such students are also automatically required to attend a drug education seminar to learn more about drugs and their use thereof, quite apart from any penalty levied for the social offense. (These referrals to the Office of Health Education apply both to miscreant students and also to students who require emergency medical assistance for over-indulgence.) These particular changes reflect increased understanding on the part of deans and also more careful and full training for security officers.

A similar change in attitude (and consequent penalties levied) has been evident in Brown's judicial board, the Undergraduate Council on Student Affairs, who insightfully propose a range of recommendations for those who come before them for drug-related offenses.

Again, that dean responsible for leaves and withdrawals, who has always been open to learning more about drug issues, as an extension of the University's sense of responsibility to and concern for its students, now releases on voluntary (and occasionally involuntary) medical leave those whose drinking behavior serially poses problems to self or to the campus community.

The Division of Athletics has also been increasingly active. Coaches have received in-service training by members of the University staff. Outside speakers have worked with student athletes and the Division's coaching and administrative staff. This activity, again, reflects the University's desire to address the drug-related issues wherever they may appear.

It is ironic that on University campuses, and at Brown as well, the narrow academic sphere is, perhaps, least ready to address directly problems of substance abuse. Faculty members often feel poorly equipped to approach students and see such personal issues as beyond their professional competence and responsibility. Effort must be made to help faculty understand that drug use which affects student performance – attendance, note-taking, attention to lectures, writing – is very much their proper concern, not for treatment, surely, but for identification and referral.

Current concern in the academic area at Brown focuses on recovering students and their inability to do their work with ease and comfort. A most common characteristic of these students is diminished self-esteem which inhibits their approaches to faculty. In many instances slothful habits, outright lies and dereliction of duty related to alcohol or other drug use provide copious grounds for guilt and a feeling that no accommodations are appropriate, including those that are available to all students, e.g., extensions and permission for completing work beyond the end of a semester. Students must be encouraged to realize that their past is past, that they are worthy, and that faculty who are given appropriate evidence will generally sympathize with the demands and uncertainties of recovery.

Examples of specific academic difficulties are easy to cite. Many addicted students have avoided faculty for so long that they need reminding of what office hours are, what making an appointment may involve and even how to phrase an approach to a faculty member. Tutoring opportunities and the most basic aspects of study—time management, notetaking, examsmanship—also need review. And through all of this counseling and advising, attention must be paid to the basic mechanics of recovery itself, a constant focus maintained on the importance of not drinking nor drugging.

At Brown, effort is made to address these academic aspects of the drug issue, though much needs to be done to increase faculty awareness and receptivity to the idea of intervention.

The assumption of responsibility by different offices and groups for different aspects of the drug issue—deans of students, athletics, academic deans are the examples cited here—is the primary way in which full use is made of existing personnel, and the need for new budget and new personnel kept low.

A meeting of senior administrators, deans, counselors, coaches and other University officers concerned with matters of substance abuse was held just before the opening of college in Fall 1986. This meeting, which culminated efforts of prior years to bring together for occasional conversation individuals charged with responsibility for drug issues, led ultimately to the formation during the academic year 1986-1987 of a group of eighteen administrators who had "hands-on" responsibility for some aspect of the drug issue. This group met monthly through the academic year to strengthen drug-related services, to review policy and protocols of different offices and to discuss in candor what actually goes on and how things might be improved. This new arena for informed conversation and frank debate has proved to be very helpful.

An initial concern was the reconsideration of the University's already fairly complete policy on alcohol and the various published recommendations and prohibitions related to campus use of other drugs. A decision was made to fold all of these concerns and stipulations into one document, which would cover both the legal and health-related aspects of all manner of drug use, from cocaine to caffeine, for faculty, staff and students. In consideration of this policy, the complex issue of how to address legal sanctions on drug use resulted in dual acknowledgements of the fact that drug use is well nigh inevitable on a college campus such as Brown's and that local and federal law must be respected and the University not allowed to become a sanctuary for illegal drug activity. Deliberation was lively and served to educate contributing discussants regarding the problems and priorities of other offices on campus. Discussion of the new drug policy continued through the year and was capped late in Semester II by revision of the policy in response to student experience and recommendation. In particular, students voiced appropriate concern about the degree of specificity with which levels of drug-involvement were defined in the policy.

A particular concern that has surfaced in the deliberations of this group involves those students whose drug-related behavior is not so advanced and troublesome that it becomes the direct topic of a police or security report, or decanal intervention, but which is sufficiently worrisome to concern friends or an occasional administrator. A new sub-group including health educators, medical staff, and academic and social deans meets bi-weekly to discuss such individuals, and procedures whereby they may receive continuing and preventive attention.

Development of such broad awareness and responsibility has created an environment in which troubled students are likely to be confronted and receive help from a variety of quarters. A student who has recently entered into recovery from alcoholism was amazed to learn the scope and variety of services available, and a new member of the University staff, a recovering alcoholic, found early that the atmosphere on campus, because of the breadth of concern, is congenial to recovery and even to disclosure of one's drug history. Such comments should perhaps not surprise: from the beginning the University has provided special supports for those with drug problems, and stressed education of the general community. These comments, however, must not obscure the continuing need to educate the campus community at large and the difficult task faced by health educators and program planners as they seek to change community norms without wholly tarnishing the luster of "bright college days."

Brown now boasts a sophisticated set of referral opportunities, both within and beyond its walls. A trouble student – or other individual – may choose direct use of agencies and therapists in the Providence area. Folk wisdom attributes this procedure to those troubled most particularly by illicit drugs who may choose this option to avoid possible detection by University authorities; such a conjecture cannot be well documented except by anecdotal evidence. Others may participate directly in meetings of the Anonymous programs. Others will apply to the Associate Dean for Chemical Dependency, the Office of Health Education or the various groups sponsored by this Office, University Health Services, the Psychological Counseling Office, Chaplains, Deans, or any number of other individuals and offices, including a number of student peer counseling groups. Faculty and staff may apply directly to the Faculty and Staff Assistance Program which operates on a contractual basis through a counseling center close by the campus. (All of these resources also accept third person referrals.) And, as mentioned above, effort is made to bring together all those troubled with addiction to create a broad, informal network of support on campus.

Questions have occasionally been raised about drug testing. Brown has not embraced testing as a useful way to identify users, nor is it a strategy used generally on any campus, aside from compliance with the National Collegiate Athletic Association. Testing does not seem a wise path to follow, chiefly because testing is more concerned with the substance than the user. Although tests improve, a basic test still cannot distinguish among the simple presence of a drug, the presence of continuing use which may be problematic, or the presence of addiction. Better to the extent possible, and especially in an institution where trust is essential, to start with the user or the suspected user, observing changes in lifestyle or personality and character, the social involvements, and the various obligations which any student incurs. When things change markedly, and where various segments of the community, as has been mentioned, are prepared to face drug issues, counseling and intervention seem more appropriate forms of discovery of drug problems and of initiating the process of recovery.

Testing, however, does seem appropriate in some special instances. In instances of addiction to cocaine, for example, where the attraction is strong, the tendency to relapse is compelling and the manipulativeness of the user so effective, testing may be the necessary instrument to identify renewed use and to help individuals to help themselves.

What is envisioned for the second decade of this "collection of opportunities" known as the Brown Program in Chemical Dependency? Surely an active interest in new ideas and trends will continue, as will the effort to inform all parts of the community of their role in maintaining a sane environment regarding issues of drug use. Committed to the notion that the problems of substance-abuse are community-wide and therefore demand community-wide responses, the University will continue a pragmatic approach which also prides itself on its spirit of innovation. Collegiality, creative use of professional and lay experience, and use of personnel already on campus, in lieu of infusion of funds or the arrival of "experts," will continue to assure vital response to problems which will not soon disappear, on this campus or any other.

PART II

Health Education has become an integral part of health services on many college campuses. The introduction or enhancement of health education in this setting is related to a change in the philosophy upon which college health services are founded. The old philosophy focused on sickness, and logically led to a cure-oriented organization of staff and facilities, like the college infirmary. The new philosophy recognizes that students of college age are primarily well, but have reached a critical stage in the formation of health habits. Although the new philosophy does not deny the importance of curative resources, it tends to emphasize the use of staff and facilities for "wellness promotion" (Mezey & Chiamulera, 1980; Hettler, 1980) or "risk reduction" (McEvoy, 1983; Nagelberg, 1981). The new philosophy also recognizes that health education is an integral part of student life.

It is important that health education permeate varied aspects of college life (Council of the American College Health Association, 1977). Health Education is likely to be most effective when it ventures from the "Health Center" into the life of college dormitories, fraternities, and other residences and makes an impact on the daily concerns of students, as they make real life decisions. Brown University made a major commitment to wellness promotion in 1983 when it established the Office of Health Education. The office concerns itself chiefly with issues of sexuality, eating disorders, and alcohol/drug use and abuse. Although the office is physically located in the Health Services building on campus, the health educators are part of the staff of the Office of Student Life at Brown. As a result the office has daily interactions with various other offices on campus, i.e., Residential Life, Psychological Services, Police and Security, Chaplains, and Deans of Students. The health educators are neither isolated nor removed from the mainstream of campus life. Attempts at other universities to "bring" health education to the campus have not always been successful because the health educators were operating in a vacuum. Often these health educators are not fully integrated into the office of Student Life or the equivalent. Issues of sexuality, eating concerns, drug use and abuse affect many offices in a university. The philosophy, teachings, and health promotion strategies of the health educators have to be integrated into the daily routine of the campus. The model at Brown in which the Office of Health Education is connected to the Student Life office has worked successfully over the past six years.

As stated earlier by Dean Donovan, much work had previously been done in the alcohol and drug field prior to the establishment of the Health Education Office in 1981. Therefore, the integration of this new office into the established campus routine was a relatively easy one. One of the goals of the Health Education office at Brown is to promote informed and responsible alcohol use among students through a network of complementary alcohol education programs. The network is coordinated by a group of students, faculty, and administrators with the goal of creating a *continuous* environment of alcohol awareness on the college campus. Educational programs are targeted at groups, rather than individuals, in an attempt to structure *community norms* about the use of alcohol. Individual students however do receive counseling and referral. (This will be addressed in detail at another point in this article.) Interspersed among ongoing educational programs are special events designed to complement unique or periodic campus activities in which heavy drinking has been the norm in the past.

Alcohol and Drug Education at Brown

With the establishment of the office in 1981, alcohol and other drugs were immediately identified as an important and significant health issue. A second health educator was hired who would devote half time to alcohol and drug education. Brown, like many of the other Ivy League schools, has had a long tradition of drinking, complete with various songs and major events which often centered around alcohol. Talking openly and honestly about alcohol use and abuse goes against the grain of tradition. The task of creating an environment of alcohol awareness was not an easy one and is made more difficult by some ambivalence on the part of university administrators. Prior to this office's existence, Dean Donovan had assumed the difficult responsibility of introducing the concept of alcohol awareness on campus. In the early '80s, alcohol education was somewhat of an unpopular subject although there is some recent evidence that this attitude is changing. Clearly in 1981, the unpopularity of the subject was apparent. A needs assessment for first year students was conducted on campus in the fall of that year, and very few students were interested in learning more about alcohol. Furthermore, during Freshmen Orientation week, only a handful of students attended the forum on "Drinking at Brown."

Bearing this in mind, the Office set out to raise awareness about alcohol and other drugs. The notion of "responsible drinking" is not new at Brown or any other campus. The Task Force on Campus

Activities lists responsible drinking as the core of the alcohol education on campus. Specifically we promote: (1) using alcohol as an adjunct to an activity rather than the primary focus, (2) setting a limit on how many drinks one consumes when one is going to drink, (3) knowing one's limit and sticking to it, (4) always serving food with alcohol, (5) showing displeasure to someone who has had too much to drink, (6) always providing alternative non-alcoholic drinks at parties, (7) not being insistent about refilling drinks, (8) respecting a person who chooses not to drink, (9) supporting students who are wishing to remain abstinent, and (10) seeking help if one has a drinking problem.

One of Brown's earliest strategies was to form a student group on campus who would promote alcohol awareness. This group was known as "Rhapsody in Booze" and used a multi-media educational approach. The group was fairly successful in informing the Brown community of their existence (Dohm, 1987). They developed brochures, posters, and bookmarks, ran ads in the student newspaper, and sponsored lectures and workshops on campus.

Several points need to be mentioned when examining the office's early years. From its inception our model was based on four concepts: (1) saturation approach, (2) a changing of community norms, (3) surveillance of alcohol use and abuse, and (4) consciousness raising. The saturation approach is based on a primary concept of learning, namely repetition. Rhapsody in Booze and the Health Education office provided continuous information and health promotion around alcohol and drug issues. Every opportunity via student publications and campus events was seized upon to promote alcohol behavior conducive to health. Changing community norms has taken place slowly as a result of involving many different offices on campus in addressing the issues around alcohol and other drugs. As early as 1982, a group of administrators, deans, and health educators at Brown began meeting regularly to discuss the formation of an alcohol policy, party registration and party planning, and disciplinary cases. Surveillance of alcohol use and abuse takes place on a weekly basis at Brown with a group of administrators and deans meeting every Monday morning to review the weekend. Data is collected on the types of alcohol incidents which take place as well as the increase or decrease in the number of incidents according to major events happening on campus. For example, the Monday morning following Spring Weekend is abysmal, replete with an extensive list of alcohol related injuries, accidents, and mishaps. The Monday morning following Parent's Weekend is a breeze: there are very few overdoses or incidences of careless alcohol behavior. Students who get in trouble at Brown where alcohol has been a factor have to go through the University's disciplinary system. Part of Brown's judicial system states clearly that alcohol is not an excuse for inappropriate or obnoxious behavior but rather will be considered an exacerbating factor. Stricter penalties are often placed on a student where alcohol has been involved. Often these cases are automatically referred to either the Associate Dean for Chemical Dependency or the Health Education office for assessment and referral. Raising consciousness about alcohol and other drugs continues to be a challenge but there is growing evidence on our campus that students are less willing to accept outrageous drunken behaviour than in previous years (Dohm, 1987). Members of the administration have demonstrated an increased sensitivity to alcohol issues, i.e., discussion about the availability of alcohol at certain events, changes in the party registration form, and the formation of an Alcohol/Drug policy. One of the most successful parties given on campus several years ago was organized by an undergraduate who then repeated these parties for several years. There was no alcohol served and attendance ran over 1200 students at each party. In addition there were a minimal number of reported alcohol intoxications, confiscations, or injuries.

As early as 1983 students approached the Health Education Office with the idea of providing peer education for freshmen. This approach was successful in reaching students for the next few semesters but the student initiative waned and the program was dropped for a brief period of time. Redefinition and restructuring of the alcohol education program took place in 1986 with the arrival of a new health educator. In addition to implementing an effective drug education program to promote responsible, legal, and safe drinking on campus and to discourage illicit drugs, the following job responsibilities were added: (1) providing short-term counseling and follow-up for students who are troubled by their own or someone else's use of drugs by assessing the problem and making appropriate referrals in the community, (2) providing ongoing support services for troubled students, (3) consulting with administrators, faculty, and other staff regarding appropriate policy and procedure for preventing student alcohol and other drug abuse, and (4) identifying, intervening with, and following-up on troubled students.

The use of students as alcohol peer educators resurfaced in 1986 and the training and supervision of these students was part of the responsibility of the Office. Part of our ongoing educational activity includes a monthly, mandatory alcohol/drug education session for those students who are mentioned on a Police and Security Report for violation of the Drug Policy, intoxication, medical assist or any inappropriate behavior associated with the use of alcohol or other drugs. Education is also available for those students who are referred by the medical staff for having been treated for intoxication or an alcohol/drug injury.

The counseling component of the alcohol program has been enhanced to include more individual sessions with students. Individuals who are concerned about their own or someone else's use of alcohol or other drugs are encouraged to seek counseling at the office where their problems can be assessed and referrals made to the appropriate on or off campus resources. Counseling is also available for students upon the request of a Dean who may feel a student needs to be evaluated for an alcohol or other drug problem. Of the students seeking help from the Office, the majority of students presented with concerns about their alcohol use or alcohol in combination with some other drug or drugs. Many students seek advice and counsel from the office because of their concerns about friends' drinking or for current adjustment problems relating to having a parent(s) who is alcoholic.

For the first time since the Office was established, an abstinence support group was available to students. This group meets weekly and is a confidential support group for students who have a problem with alcohol or other drug use and who want to support each other to remain chemical-free. This group has met weekly for the entire academic year and new students may join at any time upon the recommendation of the Drug specialist. Deans may make mandatory referrals to this group as long as the student agrees to comply with group guidelines and does not disrupt the group. Upon the student's agreement, the facilitator will validate his/her attendance with the Dean. It is interesting to note that attendance at this weekly meeting is excellent and unlike other year long support groups students' attendance didn't wane throughout the year. Most of the students in this group attend Alcoholics Anonymous meetings as well.

The Health Education office also offers an Adult Children of Alcoholics Self-Esteem Group for students who are children of alcoholics/addicts and want to acquire skills in improving self-esteem. This group has been offered at Brown for the past three years and continues to be well received by the students.

The Office is able to serve in a consultative capacity by participating as staff members of the Center for Alcohol and Addiction Studies. In addition, there is health education input in the monthly meeting of administrators concerned with alcohol and other drugs. The weekly Monday morning review meetings are attended by a member of the Health Education office in order to provide ongoing surveillance of alcohol related incidents on campus.

The expanded role of the alcohol/drug educator within the Office of Health Education demonstrated the need for specific programs and counseling capabilities for the Brown campus. The need was also established by the amount and nature of the individual requests for information, education, counseling and support, by students, by administrators, and by medical personnel. Brown prides itself on having a particularly large safety net for students, that students on our campus don't get "lost in the cracks." Because of the manner in which health education and specifically alcohol/drug education is integrated into the operation of the university, the safety net appears to work most of the time.

Brown's response to the rise in drinking age was to formulate an alcohol policy in 1985. In the fall of 1986, the policy was revised to become an alcohol/drug policy which dealt not only with alcohol but addressed issues of dealing, providing, and using drugs. This policy was a joint effort of many administrators and deans including the Director of Police and Security, the Dean of Students, the Associate Dean for Chemical Dependency, and Health Education staff. The 1985 version stresses the following points: (1) to observe the laws of the state; (2) to stress moderation, safety and individual accountability for those who choose to drink; (3) to provide a college atmosphere free of coercion for those who choose not to drink; (4) to maintain a community where the effects of alcohol abuse are minimal and where problem behavior is reduced; (5) to provide information and education for all students; and (6) to provide confidential counseling for those with special needs related to alcohol/drug use, alcoholism and drug addiction.

Increasingly, over the past several years, attempts have been made to ensure that alcohol is not the focus at social events. This is evidenced by changes in alcohol service at Parents' Weekend, University wide events, concerts, and Spring Weekend. In addition University funds may not be used to purchase alcohol to serve to undergraduates by faculty or others. The university (and not only the Office of Health Education) tries to influence groups and individuals either to exclude alcohol or focus away from alcoholic activities.

The university's strategy in its approach to alcohol and other drugs is long-term. As generations of students move through the Brown experience, we hope that each entering class will be more conscious, aware and respectful of their own mortality. Ultimately, we want students on our campus to see alcohol and other drugs as less of a focus for their social and sexual interactions. This is a gradual process, the tactics we employ are subtle, and results are not always immediately visible.

Finally, it is interesting to look at a recent evaluation of drinking and drug use at Brown. With the risk of sounding overly confident, it appears that on some levels the Brown approach – both the safety net and the integration of alcohol/drug education on campus – is working. The evaluation revealed that the University has accomplished much with respect to dealing with its substance abuse problems. Overall, Brown's program (including its treatment and referral services, prevention and education programs and courses, legislative policies, public relations and mass media operations, enforcement and judicial projects and procedures) has been found to exceed most colleges and universities in the U.S. in terms of both its scope and comprehensiveness (Bloch & Ungerleider, 1987).

CONCLUSION

Brown University in 1977 appointed an Associate Dean with Special Responsibilities in the Area of Chemical Dependency. With this appointment the University signaled its interest in issues of substance abuse. From this point the University has taken strides that have been recognized nationally as creative and pioneering.

Brown realized at the beginning the importance of forging innovative responses to traditional issues, responses which occasionally rubbed against the grain of common belief. The Program in Chemical Dependency, for example, had an early focus on addiction and alcoholism, while other campuses occupied themselves with matters of prevention, matters of importance at Brown but matters which did not achieve primary attention. Reasoning suggested that if one paid heed to students in serious difficulty, and created an environment that was welcoming for them, prevention would surely follow. Such has been the case. In fact, the University has now developed a comprehensive campus-wide program which is similar to those on other campuses where first efforts focused on prevention and branched out later to issues of treatment and recovery. Equally novel in those early days was an insistence on developing resources for all University constituencies, not students only. This decision "to go it alone" has been characteristic of the program in other respects.

The prime mover for issues of chemical dependency—matters of policy, matters of counseling and treatment, coordination of services—is still the Associate Dean who is housed, again quite atypically, in the Academic Deanery. Over time the Associate Dean has been joined by specially trained colleagues in Health Education which is housed in the University Health Services. Equally important, individuals in a variety of other roles—Dean of Undergraduate Counseling, staff psychologists, Deans of Students, Residential Life Officers—have assumed ever-increasing responsibilities with reference to alcohol and other drugs. As a result, the program, building on existing personnel, has been low in cost and diversified in its approach.

Relying on a cooperative venture involving various colleagues has required an emphasis on flexibility. Flexibility has also characterized the ebb and flow of programs. Health Education has supported a vital and ever-changing program for undergraduates interested in issues of alcohol and drug prevention; the group's name and focus has changed every two or three years. Similarly, as programs in other areas have outworn their usefulness, they have fallen by the wayside and been replaced by other ventures. The Brown

Group on Alcohol provides one example, as does "The Pressure Point," a group which helped students deal with matters of stress in the early '80s, a group which highlighted procedures that sought to reduce anxiety through means other than use of chemicals.

In the early days, because of limited funds, research was not a primary focus. Recently, the Center for Alcohol and Addiction Studies at Brown has formed a group concerned with activity on campus, including research and evaluation of that activity. The environment is well-suited for research, given its focus on the novel and its continuing determination to try new approaches.

This article has given a summation both of the decade-long and evolving experience of Brown University overall and the continuing history of Health Education in particular.

REFERENCES

Bloch, S., Ungerleider, S. (1986). *Brown University Chemical Dependency Project*, Final Report, Executive Summary, 6-9.

Council of the American College Health Association (1977). Recommended standards and practices for a college health program. *JACH*, 25, 1-35.

Dohm, W. *Brown Daily Herald*, Student Newspaper, February 2, 1987, 5.

Donovan, B. E. (1979). The Brown group on alcohol: Development of an on-campus education/prevention/treatment forum. *Journal of Alcohol and Drug Education*, 24(3), 56-65.

Donovan, B. E. (1981). Establishing a university alcohol education/prevention program and some principles. *Journal of Alcohol and Drug Education*, 27(1), 62-77.

Hettler, B. (1980). Wellness promotion on a university campus. *Family and Community Health*, 3, 77-92.

Jones, F., & Najera, G. (1976). The helping network: Reactions and actions stimulated by students' acute mental illness in a university community. *The Journal of the American College Health Association*, 24(4), 198-202.

McEvoy, M. D. (1983). The development and implementation of a nursing clinic on a college campus. *JACH*, 31, 168-169.

Mezey, M., Chiamulera, D. N. (1980). Implementation of a campus nursing and health information center in the baccalaureate curriculum. *Journal of Nursing Education*, 19, 7-10.

Nagelberg, D. B. (1981). Evaluating a health risk reduction program. *JACH*, 29, 269-271.

Afterword

Joseph A. Califano, Jr.

Here are four questions:

- What is the major culprit in suicides among college students?
- What creates the greatest number of discipline problems on college campuses?
- What most inhibits the social, intellectual and emotional maturation of men and women in their later adolescent years and early twenties?
- What most seriously interferes with the ability of students to learn while they attend our best universities?

If you answered alcohol and substance abuse to each of the four questions, you scored 100%.

This volume confronts the grim presence on our best and brightest campuses of alcohol and drug abuse – from beer and pills to marijuana, cocaine and whatever else our curious collegiates can find. The problem is serious: from the dramatic increase in alcohol and drug use among freshmen students to the alcohol- and drug-related accidents at graduation events that have crippled and even killed matriculating seniors. The toll of alcohol and drug abuse on our college campuses is color-blind and sex-neutral; it honors no economic, ethnic, religious or social boundaries.

This volume represents the most comprehensive effort to date not only to face the facts, but to describe what is being and can be done

---

Mr. Califano was Secretary of Health, Education and Welfare from 1977 to 1979. He has authored numerous articles on health care and substance abuse matters. His most recent book, *America's Health Care Revolution – Who Lives? Who Dies? Who Pays?*, was published by Random House in 1986.

about alcohol and drug abuse at the university. It records the history of Brown's ten-year experience with an Associate Dean for Chemical Dependency and its five-year experience with an Office of Health Education. The essays describe experiences and offer judgments about programs focused on alcohol and drug abuse on campuses and among students from across the country. And the following pages are amply filled with suggestions – concrete, specific, workable – about what to do.

I have long believed that addiction and substance abuse sits at the top of our nation's health and criminal justice problems.

Addiction is America's number-one health problem. The deaths, disabilities, and diseases from alcohol, cigarettes, heroin and other opiates, cocaine, marijuana, angel dust, Valium and other tranquilizers, sedatives, and barbiturates far exceed the mortality and morbidity toll of any other illness, indeed of most other illnesses combined.

Addiction sends thousands of Americans to hospitals each day and thousands more to emergency rooms. It destroys young lives and shatters the hopes and aspirations of parent and grandparents.

In a sense, addiction is also our most wanted criminal. It fills our jails not only with those who are imprisoned for crimes of selling and possessing illegal drugs, but also for offenses like robbery, burglary, larceny, murder and assault, prompted by addiction or misuse of alcohol or a drug. The crime that addiction spawns terrorizes our citizens, destroys neighborhoods, and renders many of our inner cities' streets unsafe to walk on. Alcohol is implicated in more than half the nation's incidents of rape and child molesting, and up to two-thirds of its homicides.

Addiction may also be America's biggest business. Alcohol, nicotine, narcotics, pills, and other addictive drugs are certainly one of America's biggest consumer businesses: 1987 sales just for alcohol and cigarettes topped $100 billion. Add in the cost of amphetamines, heroin, cocaine, marijuana, and all the rest, and the total approaches twice the amount.

Consider the number of people involved: fifty million Americans are hooked on cigarettes; thirteen million are addicted to alcohol or abuse it; half a million are addicted to heroin. At least a million abuse barbiturates and other sedatives-hypnotic drugs; fifty-three million have used marijuana at least once, fourteen to seventeen million have tried cocaine at least once; no one knows how many millions of them are dependent, in one way or another, on those drugs. Even considering that many individuals abuse a variety of substances, and therefore show up in more than one category, the number of Americans in servitude to drugs is frightening.

The economic cost of addiction – health care, days away from work, lost productivity – is coming up on $200 billion a year. The human costs can't be calculated: there's no price tag on sorrow and family tragedy, or on life itself. Only the most massive commitment to research and health promotion, education and prevention holds hope of successfully attacking this problem.

So it's not surprising that this volume reveals the widespread impact of alcohol and drug abuse on our campuses – to the point where such abuse threatens to curdle the cream of our youth and scramble their brains and spirits. University campuses can't exist in a vacuum free of the American society in the 1980s any more than elementary and secondary schools were able to desegregate in a societal vacuum in the 1960s.

What comes through in these pages is not just the need to act, but the need to act comprehensively – to engage the entire university community in the effort to educate our young about the dangers of alcohol and drug abuse, to teach and imbue students with the importance of a sound mind and body, to set standards, to wage war against drug and alcohol abuse, and in those cases where students become victims of substance abuse, alcoholism or addiction, to provide the personal attention and support systems – from Alcoholics Anonymous to individual psychiatric care and group therapy – with compassion and openness. Professors – and fellow students – should be well enough informed to know about particular susceptibilities, such as those of children of alcoholics, so that they can be more helpful. Sufficient education for early detection is also important because the sooner an abuser is identified, the more likely the abuse can be arrested.

If there is anything I would add to the essays in this volume, it would be to recognize the importance of religion – Jewish, Catholic, Protestant, Eastern – the significance of a man's and woman's relationship with God, as a factor in prevention and reform. That's as true of alcoholics and narcotics anonymous as it is of individual therapies.

Finally, we must remember that there is only one invariably successful treatment for alcohol and substance abuse: prevention. Those who work in this field know how difficult it is to reform an alcoholic or drug addict, that the best cure still is, as grandmother taught, prevention.

If the solution is simple – don't abuse alcohol or the chemical substances – the problem is as complex as peer pressure, chemistry, the human body, mind and soul, and original sin. Considering that complexity, there isn't a campus in America that won't benefit from this collection. And so will our nation – and most importantly, the precious young men and women who can be spared the ravages of abusing alcohol, marijuana, cocaine, quaaludes, tranquilizers, barbiturates and other substances, from cigarettes to heroin.

Index